THE CLAIM OF SCOTLAND

BY H. J. PATON

Kant's Metaphysic of Experience
The Modern Predicament
The Categorical Imperative
The Moral Law
In Defence of Reason
The Good Will

THE CLAIM
OF SCOTLAND

BY

H. J. PATON
Fellow of the British Academy

London

GEORGE ALLEN & UNWIN LTD
RUSKIN HOUSE   MUSEUM STREET

PRINTED IN GREAT BRITAIN
in 11 point Baskerville type
BY THE UNIVERSITY PRESS
ABERDEEN

There has been in England a gradual and progressive system of assuming the management of affairs entirely and exclusively proper to Scotland, as if we were totally unworthy of having the management of our own concerns.

SIR WALTER SCOTT

FOREWORD

This is a book that had to be written. I only wish it had been written by some one else. What was intended to be a brief relaxation from more serious labours became a heavy and absorbing task.

The claim of Scotland to govern herself is not new, but it has become more pressing in recent years. Nothing else could be expected when, for administrative convenience, a centralising Government seeks, however unconsciously, to blot out 'regional' and other differences: almost absent-mindedly it destroys by stages everything which is distinctive of Scotland and has been the source of her greatness. Even since I began to write, this practice has increasingly provoked Scottish national feeling. To-day the cause of Scotland seems to have captured the imagination of the young, and this has begun to show itself at the polls – the one argument which politicians cannot afford to overlook. No time could be more propitious for a review of the situation as a whole.

The problems I discuss are, at least in isolation, not unfamiliar in Scotland: south of the Border they are almost unknown. What is needed is that they should be brought together in a readable form, and this is what I have attempted to do. A general review is necessary if Scotsmen are to understand what is happening to their native country. It may, I trust, be useful also to friendly Englishmen who are concerned about the fate of their Northern partner and would wish to avoid the political blindness that lost Ireland and, at an earlier stage, the American Colonies. It is my wistful hope to offer them some enlightenment.

In this overbold endeavour I have sought to aim at clarity rather than emotion, at argument rather than rhetoric. I have tried, even under provocation, to refrain from the abuse, and the imputation of unworthy motives, which so many politicians appear to find an agreeable substitute for serious discussion. On occasion I may have fallen short of this standard and may have lapsed into satire and even into frivolity. I trust that such

9

departures from the norm will not make my pleas less likely to be heard.

By an odd chance I became involved, as early as 1919, in similar European problems, especially in connexion with the frontiers of Poland; and my account of some of these may be found in Volume VI of *A History of the Peace Conference of Paris*. I hope this may have helped me to take a more objective view of topics where I am bound to be less detached. It has at least enabled me to see through specious arguments which in that earlier period were sufficiently refuted by events.

As to British politics in general, I have sought to be neutral as between the Conservative and Labour parties; but I am bound to be specially critical of whatever Government happens to be in power. Politicians concerned with Scotland are almost nationalistic when they are out of office: when they form a government they become obstinately and even blindly unionist.

Words like 'nationalistic' and 'nationalist' I tend in general to avoid because of their modern ambiguity, but I do not accept the barbarous usages recently imported from Germany and Italy. It is ludicrous, if not dishonest, to say that even the Scottish National Party is 'nationalistic' in the sense applied to Hitler and Mussolini: no serious political parties in Britain are either Nazi or Fascist. If 'nationalistic' means 'opposed to alien domination', this is in the main a good quality; if it means 'seeking to dominate other nations', we must look for examples elsewhere than in Scotland (or Wales).

So too if I speak of 'race', I do not accept the absurd fiction of a so-called 'pure race'. In this country, as elsewhere, we are all mongrels; but mongrels may be more or less distinguishable as products of different kinds of mixture.

In writing a book of so wide a range it would be desirable to have an army of helpers in close touch with a great library. Without this advantage I have had to depend on secondary sources (including newspapers). Rather than give a misleading, and perhaps intimidating, appearance of exact scholarship, I have avoided references and footnotes. Since I have no quarrel with individuals, but only with their published views, I have also refrained, as a rule, from name-dropping – perhaps rather too much. Since the situation is continually changing, some mistakes are inevitable; and in matters so complicated it is often necessary to over-simplify. I hope some one some day will write a more elaborate work full of footnotes and references and appendices and graphs and statistical tables. But I still think my simpler methods more suitable for an introduction to the subject. I believe the general picture to be accurate, and the whole argument to be sound, even if some of the details may be wrong.

Chapters I–III may be taken as a sketch of the background. In Chapters IV–X I deal with more directly practical affairs – political, administrative, legal, and economic. In Chapters XI–XV I turn to what I may call the invasion of the mind in broadcasting and education. In the final Chapter I try to gather together some of the loose ends. By the variety of fields surveyed I hope to have avoided the dangers of monotony.

Although I have consulted neither party organisations nor party leaders, I have to thank Dr. Douglas Young for some trenchant criticisms at an early stage of my first draft. I have also to thank for valuable comments Mr. C. B. H. Barford, the first Englishman – I hope not the last – to read my book with forbearance and sympathy. I am indebted to Mrs. M. J. Gregor, Mrs. Muriel Mitchell and Miss Kerstin Dow for help with my newspaper cuttings and in many other ways; and I am grateful to Mrs. T. Hawthorn for typing my manuscript with her customary care and skill. To Lady Taylor I am particularly beholden for permission to quote from a private letter of her late husband, Sir Thomas Taylor, whose death was so great a loss to Scotland as well as to all his friends.

I owe very special thanks to Sir Malcolm Knox and Dr. Douglas Young for reading my proofs in a race against time: the former has also shown me the very great kindness of taking the index entirely off my hands.

If, as I hope, my book gives rise to controversy, I must beg to be excused from taking part. Corrections of fact I will note for any possible future edition; but I shall not be able to answer letters of approval or disapproval either privately or in the press.

I have made my contribution to a cause which is widely ignored or misunderstood, and I must leave its defence to younger men.

H. J. PATON

September, 1967

CONTENTS

CONTENTS

CONTENTS

CHAPTER I

TO OUR ENGLISH BROTHER

We've drunk to our English brother
(But he does not understand)
Rudyard Kipling

1. *To our English brother*

During the Second World War – in a section of the Foreign
Office set up for a time in Oxford – a distinguished scholar and
political thinker, beaming benevolently through his spectacles,
suddenly remarked to me, 'It must be a wonderful thing to be a
Scotsman'. This I had never doubted; but I asked him politely
why he should think so. 'Because', he replied, 'you have a
double loyalty'. I was a trifle taken aback; and since my friend,
although English of the English in outlook and education,
happened to have an obviously un-British name, I found my
mind wandering down forbidden paths.

When it returned, he was still explaining, with unnecessary
elaboration, that Scotsmen were loyal to Scotland and also to
the United Kingdom. Only then did the horrid implications of
his doctrine begin to dawn on me. In my innocence I had
imagined that all the nations constituting the United Kingdom
of Great Britain and Northern Ireland had a double loyalty –
that the English too were loyal both to England and to the
United Kingdom, perhaps even to the British Commonwealth
of Nations as well. Now I saw only too clearly what he meant:
an Englishman was loyal only to England and for him there
was no distinction between England and Britain – it was all
just England.

This was put more crudely by a poet in *Punch*, who was
complaining about the way in which modern countries kept
changing their names. He ended:

'Under Mr. de Valera
Ireland changed its name to Eire.
Britain strictly keeps its name,
It's called England just the same.'

It may seem frivolous to begin a plea for Scotland with a
trivial quirk of language, but such quirks may have a deeper
psychological import. The attitude of the English to Scotland is
no doubt complicated. For the most part they do not think
about Scotland at all. When they do think about it, they
regard it sometimes as a place utterly remote, where strange
things may happen which have no bearing on their own lives.
At other times they think of everything that happens there as
barely distinguishable from what is familiar to them in England.
But when it comes to action, they tend to assume that whatever
may suit England must be well adapted to the needs of Scotland.
Pleas to the contrary are apt to be regarded at first as funny,
and then as irritating, and finally, if persisted in, as the product
of some provincial irrationalism, not to say madness: they are
attributed to what is politely called the lunatic tartan fringe.

Such an attitude is hardly generous or even just, nor does it
seem worthy of a partnership which has stood for so long. Yet,
broadly speaking, it is actions based on this attitude which have
produced the feeling of frustration so wide-spread in Scotland
at the present time. You may think that this feeling is perverse,
and you may put it down to original sin or some other occult
cause, but no reasonable man can deny that it exists, unless he
has cultivated the wilful blindness of the professional politician.

The whole body cannot be healthy if one part of it is sick, and
this is true also of the body politic. Hence the malady of Scotland
should be of concern to all of us – to the English, the Welsh,
and the Northern Irish as well as to the Scots. Indeed should it
not be of special concern to the English? It is they who, by their
very numbers, have the final say in every question affecting any
part of the United Kingdom. Even without regard to the claims
of justice and the ties of friendship should they not out of
enlightened self-interest consider seriously the claim put
forward by any considerable part of our common country?

It is hard for a Scotsman, especially for one who is very much at home in England, to accept the view that such a hope can have no chance of being fulfilled.

Hence I write this plea for Scotland even at the risk of losing whatever reputation for sanity I may have acquired in the course of a life spent almost equally in Scotland and in England. It is written for men of good will who seek to establish justice and promote freedom. I hope it may be read by our English brothers and by Scotsmen who acquiesce too readily in a purely English point of view. Even if I fail to make any impression on deep-rooted prejudice, I hope that I may be able in some degree to express the often inarticulate feelings of the mass of the Scottish people.

2. *Difficulties*

The difficulties of the task I have undertaken are formidable.

A man with a grievance may easily become a bore, and this may be true of a nation with a grievance – or with a series of grievances. A discussion of these may become a catalogue of complaints, many of which may seem trifling in themselves; and the problem may become obscured in a mass of details. It is not merely the details that are wrong, but the whole system by which these have been produced. If an appearance of nagging is to be avoided – and this is not easy – the details must be restricted to typical examples which can do no more than illustrate the unsatisfactory working of a system unsatisfactory in itself.

Again, it is impossible to complain of the present relation between Scotland and England without criticising those who are primarily responsible for it. Men do not like to be criticised, and the English are no exception. Personal resentment is apt to be fortified by national pride. Yet it is English complacency about the treatment of Scotland which requires to be disturbed, if this is possible; and why should it not be? This can hardly be done without some harsh words which may arouse resentment. On the other side it is difficult for Scotsmen who feel strongly about the way in which Scotland is treated not to become bitter;

and this may cause their complaints to be dismissed as unreasonable, no matter how reasonable they may be in themselves.

All of this calls for an attempt at better understanding, which ought not to be too difficult in view of all the circumstances. I want to make it clear at the outset that if I say some hard things about 'the English', I mean 'the English in their attitude to Scotland' – or more precisely 'the English attitude to Scotland', though it would be intolerable to use such abstract language throughout. For the English as such I have the utmost admiration and affection. The stirring up of national animosities is deplorable, but this is only one more reason why the source of these animosities should be investigated and, where possible, removed.

Even the phrase 'the English in their attitude to Scotland' is not meant to cover all Englishmen. There are some, I hope many, who are ready to be sympathetic to the troubles of their northern partner if only they can be made to understand what these troubles are.

Another point that should be made clear is this. We must make a sharp distinction between the treatment of Scotland and the treatment of Scotsmen. It is too often said, 'What has Scotland to complain of? Do not Scotsmen hold a larger proportion of the highest positions in England than they are entitled to by their numbers?' This used to be said more often in the past than it is to-day, but the fallacy is obvious. If Scotland, as we are told, is falling short of her past achievements and is always in need of English direction and English help, it is a poor consolation to be told that many of her ablest sons are doing very well for themselves elsewhere. Scotsmen have no complaint about the way they are received in England: quite the contrary. But this has no bearing on the fact that Scotland may be suffering both spiritually and materially from political treatment which is neither considerate nor even fair.

3. *Scotland and England*

What then, it may be asked, is wrong with the state of Scotland, and how can it be put right?

To these questions no simple answer can be given, but it is to be hoped that the answer will become clearer as we proceed. The problem lies deep in the long history of both England and Scotland and in a direct clash between the English and Scottish points of view. If an over-simplication may be forgiven, what is fundamentally wrong is that Scotland is being steadily deprived of control over her own destiny and even her own ideals. The only cure – so far as there can be a cure – is that she should be given more power to manage her own affairs.

Behind all this there lies, as I have said, a clash of attitudes or ideals. To many Englishmen Scotland is nothing but another province of England, a strange province perhaps, and even an irritatingly reluctant province, but in the last resort a province whose destiny is to become more and more absorbed in the glorious system of English government and civilisation. Every encroachment becomes an argument for further encroachment – the English attach more importance to precedents than to principles; and objections on the part of the Scots are put down to an irrational parochialism or even to that spirit of nationalism which is said to be the bane of the modern world. In many Englishmen this attitude may be unacknowledged or even unconscious; it may take the form of sheer indifference; but it is always liable to appear in action, or at least it seems to do so to those who belong to the northern kingdom.

The attitude of most Scotsmen is very different, whatever may be their political beliefs. To them it seems that the two ancient kingdoms of England and Scotland, after centuries of unhappy struggle, entered freely into one United Kingdom in which both the former kingdoms disappeared. But this did not mean that there ceased to be two nations in the United Kingdom, each entitled to a loyal partnership from the other. It has always been recognised by the Scots that the English nation because of its numbers and wealth must be the predominant partner; but few Scotsmen can regard their country as merely an English province. Even the Royal Commission on Scottish Affairs, whose report was published in 1954, recommended that Scotland should be treated as a nation, though it gave little help about the way in which this could best be done.

There are other nations in our one Kingdom. There were the Irish, and there are the Welsh. The Irish have now become independent through the political unwisdom with which they were governed, but the Welsh are still with us and appear to be as dissatisfied with their present position as the Scots are with theirs. It was the glory of the United Kingdom that it carried on so many different traditions – that it was enriched by so many varied types of men. But this does not alter the fact that the Welsh and the Irish were conquered nations and suffered the psychological wounds which come to the conquered. The position of the Scots, like that of the English, is different. These are the two free founder-nations of the United Kingdom and ultimately of the British Commonwealth and Empire. Why should it be a bad kind of nationalism in the Scots if they remember this, but no kind of nationalism in the English if they forget it?

The case for self-government in Wales may be very strong – I believe that it is. I will not attempt to pronounce on the view that the Welsh claim has stronger grounds than the Scottish one, for my judgement might be biased. There are certain principles which apply in both cases, but the Scottish claim is different in many ways, and it is only with this claim that I am here concerned.

4. *The Covenant*

It is hard to see how the position of Scotland can be improved without a radical change in the English attitude; but if we come down to matters of machinery, the aspirations of the Scottish people have been expressed in what is known as the Scottish Covenant. This was launched in 1949 and obtained over two million signatures. It runs as follows:

'We, the people of Scotland who subscribe this Engagement, declare our belief that reform in the constitution of our country is necessary to secure good government in accordance with our Scottish traditions and to promote the spiritual and economic welfare of our nation.

'We affirm that the desire for such reform is both deep and

widespread throughout the whole community, transcending all political and sectional interests, and we undertake to continue united in purpose for its achievement.

'With that end in view we solemnly enter into this Covenant whereby we pledge ourselves, in all loyalty to the Crown and within the framework of the United Kingdom, to do everything in our power to secure for Scotland a Parliament with adequate legislative authority in Scottish affairs.'

This document, and especially the final paragraph, deserves to be studied carefully on the supposition that it means what it says. What is asked for is asked 'in all loyalty to the Crown and within the framework of the United Kingdom'; and the Parliament which it demands is one which has adequate legislative authority 'in Scottish affairs'.

The demand is, on the face of it, a modest and reasonable one: it asks for nothing more than has long been enjoyed in Canada by Quebec, in the U.S.A. by the state of Nebraska, and in Australia by New South Wales. Why should it be dismissed as unworthy of serious consideration? Yet the leaders of the Labour and Tory parties – at that time Mr. Attlee and Sir Winston Churchill – refused even to see those who had drawn up this Covenant and won so much support for it in Scotland. It should in fairness be added that a too hurried approach by the organisers of the Covenant may have contributed to this unhappy result.

You may ask, 'How do I know that over two million people signed the Covenant?' The answer is that I know and respect the men who organised it, and I also know the mood that was prevalent in Scotland at the time. Large-scale dishonesty is not a Scottish vice. Various local plebiscites have more recently confirmed these earlier results. But even if you suppose that only half of those who signed the Covenant were serious people – an incredibly wild hypothesis – there would still be enough to deserve something more than a studied neglect of their opinions.

You may say that these signatures were not collected under strict supervision such as prevails at a general election. Strict supervision cannot be secured by an organisation of private persons with a limited amount of money. But the answer is obvious. If more evidence is wanted about the wishes of the Scottish people, let the Government itself organise a plebiscite under whatever conditions it may care to impose.

5. *Demand for a plebiscite*

After the signature of the Covenant the two main political parties, by a strange coincidence, gave almost the same answer to this demand. The first objection raised was that these matters are too complicated for a plebiscite, and the second was that a plebiscite was unconstitutional. 'Constitutional change', said the spokesman of the Labour Party, 'is considered and settled by the normal processes of Parliamentary democracy'.

The first objection springs from a confusion of thought. The principle of Home Rule is simple: it is its application which is complicated, and this would have to be the subject of elaborate negotiations. The representative of the Conservative Party went so far as to say that 'if the people of Scotland were ultimately to decide in favour of a Scottish Parliament, no one could gainsay them'. But he was as anxious as the Labour Party to make sure that no opportunity for such a decision could be given.

The objection that a plebiscite would be unconstitutional is no more convincing. If it rests on precedent, it means that Parliament has never consulted the people of Scotland on this topic in the past and has no intention of doing so in the future. If it rests on principle, the principle in question would seem to be that of the absolute supremacy of Parliament, a doctrine never accepted in Scotland. If we interpret this principle as meaning that Parliament can best decide the fate of Scotland by refusing to ascertain the views of its inhabitants, this is an inadequate ground for rejecting the only procedure suited to the situation.

In matters of dispute between political parties a referendum or plebiscite may be undesirable: it does not follow that it would be equally undesirable where a dispute transcends party politics. But the question of self-government for Scotland not only transcends party politics: it affects Scotland more intimately than it does the other parts of Britain.

What the Scots are being told is this. If they wish for self-government, they must renounce all other political interests and build up a new party confined to this one narrow issue. Only when it has won a majority of the parliamentary seats in Scotland can the question even be considered.

Why should Scotsmen have to make so irksome a renunciation and undertake so great an effort before their case can be examined? In Britain it takes years and years to build up a new political party till it can win a general election. The whole Establishment, the influence of money, the power of patronage, the mass means of communication, and even the electoral system itself stand in the way. These forces are still more formidable when the party in question is confined to one part of Britain and is supposed to have one interest and one interest only. When the two main English parties combine to smother serious consideration of the topic, their action is almost as overpowering as it is unreasonable. Is this high constitutional argument anything more than a device to postpone Scottish self-government for the time being and perhaps for ever?

It is in the light of such considerations that the organisers of the Covenant refused – perhaps unwisely – to form themselves into a political party. They had drawn their supporters from all political parties in Scotland, and they were simple enough to suppose that this strengthened rather than weakened their claim.

Even if a purely Home Rule party succeeded, after years of effort, in becoming dominant in Scotland, it would still be a hopeless minority in Parliament, and there would be no assurance that its claims would be met. The Scots know this only too well from sad experience. From the late eighties of last century, when electoral reforms first made it possible for the voice of Scotland to be heard, up to the defection of the Labour Party, when it came into full power after the Second World War, there had been Scottish majorities in favour of Home Rule, although there was no separate Home Rule Party. These had induced the Mother of Parliaments to accept Home Rule Bills in principle many times, but never to pass them into law. The Irish, on the other hand, who adopted the policy now recommended to the Scots, succeeded in winning Irish majorities for a party devoted exclusively to Home Rule, but in the end they found it more effective to take to shooting.

The plain fact is that the method of a plebiscite is ideally adapted to a problem of this kind and has habitually been applied by British Governments both outside and inside the British Commonwealth. It was used after the First World War to determine frontiers in Europe. It was used to decide whether Newfoundland should become part of Canada. It was used more recently to ascertain the wishes of the Maltese about self-government. What is more, the British Government has formally committed itself to the principle of plebiscites by signing the Bill of Rights sponsored by the United Nations Organisation; for in this 'all member States uphold the principle of self-determination of all peoples and nations and agree to facilitate this right through plebiscite or other recognised means'.

Whatever our opinions about the merits and demerits of a Scottish legislature or Scottish Parliament, should we not dismiss such weak objections to a plebiscite and agree as reasonable men that Scotland should at least be given an opportunity to pronounce upon her own fate? If, as some contend, the majority of Scotsmen have become so bemused and apathetic that they no longer want Home Rule, there is all the more reason why this should be made clear beyond any doubt.

6. *Federalism*

What the Covenant asks for Scotland is akin to a federal system such as is known and practised in many parts of the world. In a rudimentary form something like it already exists in this country for Northern Ireland, the Channel Islands, and the Isle of Man. Only to Scotland and Wales is it denied.

We might add that it is also denied to England, for it is sometimes alleged, perhaps in jest, that there are stronger arguments for an English Parliament – the only one that is never asked for. This would be the ideal arrangement, but it is hard to see why Scotland and Wales should have to wait for a contingency so remote. If the English do not want a Parliament of their own, why should this stand in the way of peoples who do?

Federal systems may vary in form and extent; but in the wide sense adopted here, a State is federal if, besides having one Supreme Parliament, it has also one or more regional Parliaments entitled to control regional affairs. If it is agreed, at least provisionally, that Scotland should have a regional Parliament, the extent of the control assigned to it would be a matter for future discussion and negotiation. My own view is that this control should be as extensive as possible.

It must not be thought that the English are against federalism for other States. Quite the contrary. After the last War the British Government pressed for federalism in Germany on the ground that this makes a country stronger. Some Germans were cynical enough to believe that the real aim of the proposal was the very opposite. I confess I was a trifle embarrassed to hear my German friends, friends too of this country, maintaining that the British attitude was sincere.

As I have said, the general character of a federal system is well-known. Yet the arguments used against it in the case of Scotland are often almost too irrelevant to be worth an answer. Thus a favourite contention is that it would mean a customs barrier at the Border. This is taken to be manifestly ludicrous and to provide a conclusive argument against any form of federation.

It may be observed that the British Government, when it suited them, had no qualms about setting up a customs barrier in Ireland. It may also be observed that there is something like a customs barrier between Savoy and the rest of France without any one suffering intolerable inconvenience. If Scotland were to be better governed as a result, we could perfectly well put up with a customs barrier. But the fundamental answer is that in a federal system there is usually no customs barrier at all.

Certainly no such demand was made by the supporters of the

Covenant. Its organisers drew up a blueprint for Scotland dealing with matters to be reserved for a United Kingdom Parliament, matters to be dealt with by a Scottish Parliament, and matters which would be the concern of both. The power to levy Customs Duties was reserved to the Government of the United Kingdom. All this can be found in the Memorandum of Evidence submitted to the Royal Commission. It has been published separately under the title '*The Case for Scottish Devolution*'.

It is not my purpose to discuss here the machinery of these proposals. Obviously they could at the most form a basis for discussions in which the interests of England would certainly not be neglected. Some Scotsmen would, I think, be willing to begin with almost any sort of Scottish Parliament or legislature so that the voice of Scotland might at least be clearly heard. It is ungracious to pretend that their aims are entirely different from what they say.

To refute triumphantly a position which your opponents do not hold is one of the less honourable ways of conducting a political argument.

7. *Independence*

At the beginning of this century most Scotsmen felt, perhaps a little sadly, that, in the words of Lord Normand, the Union of 1707 was 'an unequalled surrender of sovereignty for the greater good of mankind'. Some of them even hoped that one day the rest of the world might come to follow so good an example. The greater part of them supported the Liberal Party, which was committed to a policy of Home Rule, as indeed it is to-day. But they recognised that the claims of the Irish should be satisfied first, because Ireland had been treated so much worse. These hopes were frustrated by the War of 1914. No one who reads the great Parliamentary speech of Mr. Redmond on the Declaration of War can fail to be saddened by the thought of what might have been.

For reasons which may become clearer as we proceed, the feeling in Scotland is now less patient, but there seems to be little evidence that the demands of her people have greatly increased. It is unjust and ungenerous to maintain that the demand for a Scottish Parliament 'within the framework of the United Kingdom' masks a claim for complete independence. Nevertheless this claim has been raised in some quarters, notably by the Scottish National Party, which at one time succeeded in getting a member elected to Parliament and has recently won some success at the polls. Unlike most supporters of the Covenant it decided that the way to its goal lay in opposing the existing political parties and in concentrating on this single issue. It is true that it also has detailed proposals for reform in Scotland, but there does not seem to be very much point in this at present except for purposes of propaganda. The policy to be pursued in Scotland can be decided only when a Scottish Parliament comes into existence and not before.

It is not easy to be confident about political trends, but although the movement for independence is growing, it may still be some way from sweeping the country. The Scots are very sensible, very patient, very unrevolutionary. Yet it should be obvious that a continual blank resistance to moderate demands tends to produce demands that are less moderate. This result can in turn be used by the opponents of change to dismiss the whole movement as extreme. Such a hostile attitude can produce only more extremism and ought to be rejected by the good sense of the English, as well as the Scottish, people.

If we are not content to dismiss claims for independence with scornful silence or noisy hilarity or angry rebuke, it might be wise to refute them with intelligent arguments. The Scots are commonly regarded, even by their modern detractors, as capable of rational argument; and one of their crosses is to be fobbed off by criticisms which show as little respect for experience as for logic. Thus, for example, we are solemnly told that the setting up of new States is entirely against the modern trend, and that Scotland in particular is far too small and far too poor to be capable of independence.

It is unnecessary to waste time on such fantasies. Apart from the fact that Scotland is at least as old a State as England, we see new States burgeoning almost every day into independence with general approval throughout the world – they include even pygmy countries with less, sometimes much less, than half a million inhabitants. With over five million inhabitants Scotland is more populous than Norway, Denmark, and Switzerland, not to mention Ireland, and her revenue is more than double that of any of them. Even an opponent of Home Rule like Professor A. C. Turner of Toronto – in his book *Scottish Home Rule* – says there seems little doubt that Scotland is better able to support herself than England. He is one of the few who have taken the trouble to study the facts.

It is unnecessary here to discuss the case for and against independence. But it is not wise to bamboozle the Scottish people by arguments which will not bear examination. They are more likely to be moved by the plea that after long association in peace and in war, in government and in trade, it would be a pity for the two countries to separate. But such a plea involves a mutual obligation – the obligation to consider just claims with sympathy and understanding.

One thing more must be said. You cannot reasonably tell Scotland that every nation has a right to self-determination, but that one of the oldest and most democratic nations in the world has none. Whatever the circumstances that attended the Union in 1707, it was entered into freely by the standards of the time. Sixty years ago the question was never raised whether a nation entering into a free union was also free to leave it. The fact that this question is raised to-day shows that there has been political incompetence in British governments, an incompetence which cries out for a cure. Nothing could be more certain to foster a claim for independence than the brash assertion that no matter what the Scots may want, they are going to be tied to England for ever. It is hard to believe that our English brothers are capable of such injustice or such folly.

It should be added that even the kind of independence sought by the Scottish National Party is independence under the Crown.

CHAPTER II

HISTORY AND LEGEND

We are told that the Deity cannot alter the past.
But historians can and do.

Samuel Butler

1. *History*

The troubles of Scotland have their roots deep in past history –
that is, in the long series of events which have made Scotland
and England what they are. Unless we know something of
events in the past, we must fail to understand attitudes and
conflicts in the present.

We learn about past events mainly from the accounts given
of them by historians – that is, from 'history' in a different
sense. In this second sense history (sometimes given the rather
pompous name of 'historiography') is the writing of history or
history as written. This too may be a source of present
troubles, although in a different way.

No change in political machinery can alter either past events
or the way in which history has been written; and indeed
history as already written is itself a past event. Nevertheless it
remains true – and even trite – that we cannot understand a
present demand for political change without knowing something of its historical background. In the face of widespread
ignorance no apology is necessary for touching upon the history
of the relations between England and Scotland. As little will
be said about this topic as possible, but some misleading attitudes and assumptions must be challenged.

The English take a proper pride in their own history and are
prepared to justify all sorts of political oddities on historical
grounds. Yet too often they are inclined to resent appeals to
Scottish history and to charge the Scots with an unhealthy

C

33

tendency to dwell on the past. This used to be a still commoner accusation against the Irish. The cruder type of Englishman is even inclined to suppose that Scotland as an independent nation has no history worthy of the name.

This attitude does not make for good feeling or for political wisdom. Although the modern Scot is in fact strangely ignorant of his history – apart from some of its more romantic episodes – it may be true that a nation is inclined to dwell on its past when it is denied a future. If so, the remedy is to see that some future for it is assured. It is bad enough to say that Scotland does not exist as a nation, but it is still worse to pretend that it never did.

2. *History and Legend*

Every country has its own legends, and these are bound up with its patriotism. Legends do not cling too closely to historical facts, but they give a picture, generally an ideal picture, of how a nation appears to itself; and this is itself a historical fact. Horatius may never have defended the Tiber bridge against the proud Lars Porsenna, but he illustrates the ideal, and the fact, of Roman courage.

In the legends of a country, the country itself is always in the right and its enemies always in the wrong. In the Roman account of the long wars with Carthage 'Punic faith' is synonymous with the blackest treachery. The Carthaginians themselves may have used words rather differently.

As is suggested by these examples, the distinction between legend and history is not always so sharp as we are apt to think. Even modern 'scientific' historians are inclined to exaggerate the vices of their enemies and to condone or excuse or gloss over the misdeeds of their compatriots. They may be patriotic enough to see the best in their own country – and who can blame them? But if they portray their country as more ideal, and other countries as less ideal, than the facts warrant, if in short they are moved by national pride or by political and religious prejudice, their history contains an element which may be described as legend.

The best historians, though not necessarily the most popular, try to reduce the element of legend in their history. The best American historians, for example, are trying to portray the American Revolution with less bias than was shown in the past. Yet there is still some difference in American and British accounts of the same events, and this arises from bias on both sides, not merely on one.

A second characteristic of legend is that it is often stereotyped: it becomes so fixed that it is not easily corrected by an appeal to facts.

This second element of legend is to be found also in history as it is written. Errors and distortions are repeated by one writer after another till a kind of orthodoxy is established which continues to be a dogma even after it has been shown to be false. This is especially true in national and political history and perhaps most of all in the history of religion.

In this respect also the best historians try to reduce the element of legend: they are less bound by traditional accounts and better able to rise to a fresh and truer view of the facts. But even the best of historians are only human, and some element of legend must remain.

These elements of legend are more prominent in popular history than in the works of reputable historians. They seep through into novels and journalism and radio and television and are found even in what purports to be literary criticism. In this way they affect the beliefs of the common man and help to determine his political attitudes.

3. *English and Scottish History*

The English and Scottish legends, as is only natural, differ greatly: they differ at least as much as the British and American legends, for their roots go much deeper. In the Scottish legend England is the old enemy, and the problem is fairly simple. In the English legend Scotland is only one enemy, a small one in comparison with France or Spain; but in addition – as the legend goes – it is or ought to be or will be a part of England and so is judged, even more than other countries, by

35

English political and ecclesiastical assumptions. Scotland has the worst of it both ways, and the English legend about Scotland goes out to the whole world, too often under the name of British history. Even when it is called English history, it is assumed to be British.

Here also the best English historians endeavour to reduce the element of legend, and they would certainly shrink from any deliberate injustice to Scotland. Yet it is comparatively rare for an English historian to have a sympathetic understanding of the Scottish point of view. Some of them hardly pretend to conceal their impatience.

It may be replied that Scotsmen can have no cause for complaint since there is nothing to prevent them from writing history from their own point of view; if they fail to do so, this is their own fault.

This criticism hardly excuses a lack of sympathy in English historians, but in itself it contains an element of truth. Here, as so often, the Scots were pioneers, and in the Eighteenth Century David Hume and William Robertson were regarded as the founders of modern history along with Edward Gibbon; but since then Scottish historians have failed to maintain this early promise. Some Scottish historians, when they write about Scotland, seem too eager not to be thought provincial, while others have adopted or even exaggerated an English point of view. In any case the history of England will always have a wider public, and it is through English eyes that Scottish affairs are most commonly seen.

4. *The legend of Elizabeth*

Patriotic historians defend the misdeeds of their country by appealing to necessities of State and the moral standards of the time; but they are not so ready to show the same indulgence to countries other than their own. An illustration of this tendency can be found in a popular lecture which appeared in the *Listener* at the beginning of 1957. The lecturer was Sir John Neale, one of the outstanding authorities on the reign of Queen Elizabeth. His subject was the execution of Mary Queen of Scots.

In his discussion he glides over the illegality of her trial – this becomes merely 'a moot point'. He does not think that any dispassionate historian can question the truth of the verdict – perhaps Scottish historians are not to be regarded as dispassionate. He tells us that Elizabeth felt strongly the infamy and sacrilege of subjecting an anointed Queen to public execution and for this reason wanted to have Mary murdered privately – she in fact gave orders that Mary's custodians should be urged to bring about her murder, and we possess their reply. This was already well known to William Robertson in 1759, and if anything new has been discovered it can concern only the details.

What is most illuminating is this – Sir John appears to hold that knowledge of these facts will increase our respect for Elizabeth once we take into account the moral standards of the time. Yet on his own showing even the hardened custodians of the unhappy Mary were shocked at the proposal, and – to their credit be it said – they refused to carry it out.

By the nobility of her death the Queen of Scots atoned for many faults. In his anxiety to glorify Elizabeth at her expense, Sir John appears to forget that the blood of Mary runs in the veins of our monarchs and entitles them to be Kings and Queens, not only of England, but of the United Kingdom. He does, however, remember that the people of Scotland may have a different point of view, and proceeds at once to rule them out of court. 'In Scotland, where the people were Protestant, national sensitiveness roused Edinburgh citizens to paroxysms of anger on behalf of a queen whom they had once wanted to hang as a whore; and even today there are Scots who bear a grudge against the Sassenachs for the execution.'

The logic of this is as interesting as its emotional tone. Because the citizens of Edinburgh used harsh language against their Queen at a time when she was suspected of having conspired with her lover to murder her husband, they were therefore not entitled to protest against 'the infamy and sacrilege' of her execution many years later. There seems to be no point in saying that the people were Protestant unless Protestant subjects ought not to resent the wrongs done to a

Catholic queen. What is even more strange, Scotsmen of the present time apparently have still no right to express, or even to feel, disapproval. The argument, if it can be called an argument, is eked out by the use of emotive words like 'paroxysm' and 'grudge'. Is there not even perhaps a suppressed sneer in the use of the word 'Sassenach'?

Here we have one typical case where the glowing English patriotism of a historian shows little sign of being merged in a wider British loyalty. And this case is unfortunately not unique. There are others more extreme.

5. *The legend of Scottish intolerance*

It would be tedious to dwell on this tendency, but let us turn to another part of the English legend. In the seventh volume of *The Political History of England* the late C. F. Montague gives a very fair account of the arbitrary dealings of Charles the First with Scotland and her Church. He tells us of the ardour with which the National Covenant was signed in protest; and if he adds that sermons, solicitations, threats and even bodily violence, all were used to get signatures, until at length the nation seemed unanimous, this may be true under the conditions of the time. There seems to be little harm in sermons and solicitations, though he appears to regard these as examples of popular fanaticism; but if he is right about threats and bodily violence, these were not unknown elsewhere during this period, and he tells us nothing about their extent. He adds that the king 'had called forth a spirit which, heroic as it was, was also narrow, dogged, bitter, and intolerant almost to madness'. He seems to assume that this typically English view is common knowledge. So far as he gives any evidence for it, it appear to be found in the fact that the Scots sought to be loyal to the Stuart kings as well as to their own Church. This goal may have been unwise and even unattainable, but it seems very far from an insane intolerance. The plain fact is that in the Seventeenth Century all parties were intolerant. Even those which, like the Scots, had a passion for freedom seem curiously blind to their own inconsistency. Was it not John Milton, the exponent of English liberty, who insisted that bishops should not only be condemned to death, but should also be among the lowest slaves in hell?

Professor Montague himself seems a little uneasy about a view which holds that although the Scots are generally supposed to be shrewd and reasonable men, they become madly intolerant when they approach the subject of religion. Yet the terms he uses, together with others like 'dour', 'rigid', 'extreme', and even 'rabid', are stock epithets in the English legend of the Scottish Church. These hardly attain the standard of politeness which might be expected between sister nations or even between Christian denominations.

The real question is whether the Scots have been more madly intolerant than other people. This may perhaps be tested roughly by the number of those who have been martyred for their religion.

It is hard to get exact figures, and it is often possible to maintain that martyrs were punished for sedition rather than for their faith. But it has been estimated that before the Reformation the number of Protestant martyrs in Scotland was only twenty one. The Church of Scotland claims that it made no martyrs, but the Roman Church maintains that there was at least one, the Jesuit John Ogilvie: the highest estimate appears to be that there were three. According to the *Dictionary of National Biography* Ogilvie was tried and executed for stirring up rebellion; and if the account of his trial given by Archbishop Spottiswoode deserves any credit – for this happened under the bishops – he was certainly asking for trouble. But even if we suppose the worst, the persecutions originating in Scotland, shameful as they were, are mild in comparison with the record of other nations. The 'Killing Times' under Charles II and James II were imposed by absentee monarchs whose rule was absolute so far as Scotland was concerned. Even so, the Scottish Privy Council, arbitrarily appointed by the King, had to be enriched in 1674 by English members who, together with Lauderdale, were deputed to conduct Scottish affairs from London. It requires some ingenuity to ascribe the resultant savagery to the intolerance of the persecuted Scottish Presbyterians.

We are all aware of the Protestant martyrs in England under Queen Mary ; but if we visit the English College in Rome, we can see – or at least could see some years ago – a large number of not very good pictures portraying the horrible tortures of the Roman Catholics under Queen Elizabeth. The English legend that insane intolerance is peculiarly characteristic of Scotland seems to find little support in the facts.

It is easy enough to pick out intolerant utterances from the records of the Scottish Church (as also from those of others). These should be compared with similar aberrations elsewhere if we are to have a balanced judgement. But above all we should set beside them other Scottish statements which breathe a different spirit – one which I should judge to be characteristic of the Scottish temper at its best. I choose one example from the preface to the *Confessio Scotica* of 1560, and translate it – not without loss – into modern English. This Confession was drawn up by John Knox and five other ministers, and it continued to be the standard of the Church of Scotland till the Westminster Confession of 1649.

'Protesting that if any man will note in this our confession any article or sentence repugnant to God's Holy Word, that it would please him of his gentleness and for Christian charity's sake to admonish us of the same in writing; and we upon our honours and fidelity by God's grace do promise unto him satisfaction from the mouth of God, that is, from His holy scriptures, or else reformation of that which he shall prove to be amiss.'

Similar sentiments were repeated by Scottish divines even when tempers had been frayed by years of arbitrary interference from the South.

6. *The Wars with England*

The legend of Scotland lies outside the scope of our present plea and can be touched upon only in passing. It is no part of our present purpose to dwell on ancient wrongs, but it would give a false impression if the more sombre side of Scottish history were passed over in complete silence.

The Scots and the English fought each other off and on for some six centuries until the Union of the Crowns in 1603. A period of six centuries is quite a long time. In the earlier years war may be accepted as, so to speak, all in the day's work, with gains and losses on both sides. At the end of the thirteenth century Edward I of England made a ruthless and treacherous and temporarily successful attempt to reduce a friendly Scotland to complete subjection. The Scots rose against him under Sir William Wallace, who defeated the English at Stirling but was himself defeated later and was in the end betrayed and captured. It was not till the victory at Bannockburn in 1314 under Robert the Bruce that Scotland recovered her independence, which was finally assured by the Treaty of Northampton in 1328. But for nearly three more centuries Scotland had to resist the aggression of the kings of England, and her only times of relative prosperity were when the English were too much engaged in foreign conquest or domestic strife to occupy themselves with their northern neighbours.

To-day we are better acquainted with the horrors of war, cold and hot, than were our Victorian grandfathers; but, even so, it is hard for us, who have not been invaded by our enemies, to conceive the brutalities of these times. According to the Scottish Declaration of Arbroath in 1320, no one who had not experienced them could describe or fully understand the wrongs inflicted by Edward I – 'the slaughter and violence, the pillage and burning, the imprisonment of prelates, the burning down of monasteries, the robbing and killing of their inmates, and all the other outrages he perpetrated on the Scottish people, sparing neither age nor sex nor religion nor holy orders'.

You can say that this Scottish version of events may be exaggerated; but it differs little from the explicit orders given by Henry VIII to the army which invaded Scotland some two centuries later, when the Scots had, for good reasons, denounced a treaty providing for the marriage of the infant Mary with the future Edward VI.

'Put all to fire and sword, burn Edinburgh town so used and defaced that when you have gotten what you can of it it

41

may remain for ever a perpetual memory of the vengeance of God lightened upon it for their falsehood and disloyalty. . . . Sack Leith and subvert it and all the rest putting man, woman and child to fire and sword without exception when any resistance should be made against you.'

These and other humane instructions from the Defender of the Faith were conscientiously carried out.

It will be said that similar horrors occurred in the retaliatory raids which the Scots perpetrated from time to time in England; and these do not escape the well-merited condemnation of English historians. But the chief responsibility must belong to the more powerful and aggressive State which sought for so long to destroy its neighbour.

7. *The Trial of Wallace*

To Englishmen Westminster Hall in London is an ancient court of justice, where freedom has broadened down from precedent to precedent. To Scotsmen with any imagination it must appear as a place that is sinister and even dreadful. It was there – to give only one example – that Sir William Wallace, who had fought loyally for his country, was condemned as a traitor by an extraordinary parody of a more sacred trial – the details may here be spared – and was sentenced to an obscene and cruel death even more horrible than crucifixion.

The Scots are a long-suffering people: they refer to England almost with affection as 'the old enemy'; and they even described the outrages of Henry VIII with dry humour as 'The Rough Wooing'. Yet they must feel a great gulf set when a liberally-minded paper like the *Manchester Guardian* asks the question 'Could any Englishman doubt that justice was done, if brutally, when Wallace was executed?' It should not be too difficult to understand why, with their different ideas of justice, the Scots still find it hard to swallow the bland assumption that the English brought the blessings of civilisation to a barbarous and strangely reluctant people.

It is a pity it should be necessary to write like this, but the innocence of the English in regard to their political misdeeds is almost beyond belief. Although perfectly genuine, it is one of the reasons why they have come to be regarded so widely as hypocrites.

8. *The Union of the Crowns*

The century between the Union of the Crowns in 1603 and the Union of the Parliaments in 1707 was a most unhappy time for Scotland. When her king, James VI, became also James I of England, the Scots were still able to defend themselves with some effect; but they were now under absentee rulers who, instead of being limited monarchs, claimed to be absolute by Divine Right, and who, at least after the Restoration of Charles II, could get enough English support to enforce these claims in Socotland. From the victory of Cromwell at Dunbar in 1650 the Scots were under a military tyranny ensured in the best tradition by a massacre at Dundee of the same type as the better known one at Drogheda. In other ways the tyranny of Cromwell was mild in comparison with what came after him. The religious persecutions under Charles II, to whom the Scots had been so desperately loyal, and under his brother James II and VII have already been mentioned. But even apart from these the Scots had the worst of both worlds: they had all the disadvantages and few of the advantages of this limited Union. They were expected to fight in England's wars, but to have no say in foreign policy; and their trade with Holland was destroyed, while they were excluded from trade with England and the English colonies. By the time of the Union of Parliaments they were facing financial ruin and were in a weak position to maintain their independence.

It is true that Presbyterianism was restored in Scotland in 1690 after the accession of William and Mary, and it was possible to show what a free Scottish Parliament could do in passing some admirable laws. But this period was sadly brief.

9. *The Treaty of Union*

However unpopular the Treaty of Union was at the time and for many years afterwards, it was accepted freely by the standards of the age, and it was a blessed relief from the horrors of the past. Thereafter the Scots ceased to suffer from the cruel wars with England. Some Englishmen and many foreigners cherish the illusion that the Jacobite Risings of 1715 and 1745 were attempts on the part of Scotland to recover her independence. These risings were, on the contrary, civil wars in which the Scottish Jacobites displayed more valour than discretion, while the English Jacobites displayed more discretion than valour. The Old and Young Pretenders were indeed willing to promise anything to the Scots for their support – this was in the family tradition – but, although there was wide-spread dissatisfaction with the Union, it was too late to hope that the Lowlanders or even all the Highland clans would trust a Stuart who was also a papist. The Jacobite movement was a minority movement, and Scottish regiments took part in the Hanoverian victory at Culloden. On the other hand, the savagery with which the Highlanders were treated after the battle, and the repressive measures directed even against the many clans loyal to the House of Hanover, shocked the whole of Scotland and helped to make the Scots the united people that they are. The misfortunes of Bonnie Prince Charlie, like those of Mary Queen of Scots, have given him a place of honour in the Scottish legend far beyond any personal merits. A good judge of character like the old Earl Marischal of Scotland, who knew him well, had no use for him.

In the negotiations for the Treaty of Union the desire of the Scots to have a kind of federal union – that is, one which would allow to Scotland a subordinate Parliament for purely Scottish affairs – was swept aside by the English, who insisted on what is known as an incorporating union, a union in which there could be only one Parliament. Even this did not mean that Scotland was to be incorporated in England. What is was supposed to mean was that the two ancient kingdoms of Scotland and England were to disappear in one kingdom – the United Kingdom of Great Britain.

In the Treaty of Union and the accompanying Acts of the Scottish and English Parliaments, three things were guaranteed to Scotland, her Mint, her Law, and her Church. The rights of the Church in particular were a fundamental and essential condition of any Treaty or Union.

The Church of Scotland had long had her own democratic machinery of self-government in her General Assembly, which had expressed the spirit of Scotland far better than her hampered Parliament; but it is hard to see how a system of law could be properly maintained without any special machinery for Scottish legislation. In any case the Union Parliament proceeded to break the Treaty on all three conditions of Union. The Scottish Mint disappeared – its only relic is that the Scottish Lion is still to be found on some of the shilling coinage. The Church had imposed upon her a system of lay patronage which was alien to her traditions and was the prime source of the secessions so commonly attributed to a quarrelsome spirit peculiar to the Scots. As to the Law, it had been stipulated that there was to be no appeal from Scottish Courts to the English ones, a list of which was carefully given, 'or to any other of the like nature after the Union'. This was evaded by insisting on appeals to the (unmentioned) House of Lords, where English lawyers who knew no more of the laws of Scotland than of the laws of Japan had the final say. This system imposed a heavy financial burden on Scottish litigants and resulted in many injustices.

In both Houses of the Union Parliament Scotland was greatly under-represented relatively to her population at a time when the ratio of Scotsmen to Englishmen was one to five. In those days property was more important than men.

For the House of Lords, which had one hundred and ninety English peers, the numerous Scottish peers were allowed to elect only sixteen representatives. Those not elected – and at first also their eldest sons – were debarred from sitting in the House of Commons and even from voting in the election of its members. What is more extraordinary, Scottish peers who had been made also peers of Great Britain were denied seats in the House of Lords till 1782. The election of representative peers continued till 1963, when all the holders of ancient Scottish peerages, now sadly reduced in number, became entitled to sit in the House of Lords as the result of a Bill initially devised to enable a popular young English politician to abandon his seat in the Upper House for one in the House of Commons.

In spite of their small numbers the Scottish representative peers in 1712 had some chance of holding the balance between the two English parties in the House of Lords and so of doing something in the interests of their country. The danger was averted by the large-scale creation of new peers, the so-called 'Tory dozen', in order to make the Government majority safe. Till 1832 the elections were successfully, and even scandalously, manipulated through the influence of the Court.

In the House of Commons the Scots were allowed forty-five members as against five hundred and thirteen from England. The favoured county of Cornwall had as many. In spite of improvements under the reforms of 1832 and later, it was not till the Reform Bill of 1884 that the number of Scottish representatives became proportionate to the population. The original electoral system was in any case so gerrymandered that in 1790 – to take one example – the Government could secure a majority in every Scottish constituency by the votes of three thousand individuals (some of them fictitious) out of a total population of one and a half million. Scottish writers on politics and economics might be respected throughout Europe, but in the British Parliament the voice of Scotland was effectively gagged for some hundred and seventy years after the Union. No wonder that nothing could be done to cope with the dire results of the industrial revolution. Proposals for reform in Scotland were received by Lord Melbourne with something which it is hard not to describe as insolence. Scotland had been reduced to one vast 'Rotten Borough', and her interests could be ignored with impunity.

Injustices of this kind may be trivial in comparison with the sufferings of Scotland during the previous centuries, but they placed serious obstacles in the way of her progress. Without understanding this the present system of administration in Scotland is unintelligible. It consists of a series of make-shifts devised to soothe Scottish opinion when that opinion at long last acquired some power to make itself heard in Parliament.

The English did not argue a great deal about the Treaty –

they had too much to gain; but even before it was signed they had already begun to describe Scottish opposition to it as illogical, unreasonable, and fanatical. Perhaps their attitude was best expressed in the words of one enthusiast: 'We have catched Scotland; we will never let her go.'

10. *A double loyalty*

This potted history, or potted legend, is intended only to make one thing clear. The English have not displayed so much wisdom and benevolence in their dealings with Scotland as to justify the assumption that they know what is good for that country better than the Scots do themselves.

To some Scots it seems as if the English are still, with their customary innocence, carrying on by gentler, but more effective, measures their traditional policy of reducing Scotland to an English province. This Scottish suspicion might be understood more sympathetically by our English brothers if they had a better informed and less one-sided view of British history. Is it too much to ask them to remember that in the United Kingdom two ancient kingdoms became freely one? The Scots have faithfully developed a double loyalty, loyalty to their own country and to the United Kingdom as a whole. Is it impossible that the English, instead of condemning this as parochial, should begin, even at this late day, to do the same?

CHAPTER III

IN ALL LOYALTY TO THE CROWN

Should such a man, too fond to rule alone,
Bear, like the Turk, no brother near the throne –

Alexander Pope

1. *The Crown*

The Crown is to most Scotsmen the symbol of an ancient
kingdom which had to fight through so many centuries for its
very existence. This is why their loyalty has a special colour and
even passion. They are loyal to their Queen as Head of the
United Kingdom and the British Commonwealth; but she is
this Head for them – whatever she may be for others – because
she is descended from a long line of Scottish kings going back
and back till it is lost in the mists of antiquity. The fact that she
is also descended from the kings of England is not the basis of
Scottish allegiance – how could it be? To any one with some
sense of history it should be obvious that this is a claim about
which Scottish feeling is bound to be sensitive. It is also one
which could so easily be met by a little courtesy and consideration.

The kings of Scotland bore also the title 'King of Scots':
they were kings, not merely of the land, but of the people.
Although the loyalty of the Scots to their kings has been pas-
sionate, it has not been abject or servile. Its authentic note rings
out in the letter of protest sent in 1320 to the Pope and known as
The Declaration of Arbroath. Speaking of King Robert the Bruce
six years after he had won the battle of Bannockburn it says:
'He has been made our Prince and King by the Providence of
God, by the right of succession in accordance with our laws
and customs which we are resolved to maintain even unto
death, and by the due consent and assent of us all. To him, as

to one through whom salvation has been achieved for our people we are bound alike by law and by his services in the preservation of our liberty, and we are resolved to adhere to him in all things. But if he should abandon the task he has begun and should seek to subject us or our kingdom to the King of England or the English, we should instantly strive to expel him as our enemy and the betrayer of his rights and ours; and we should appoint as our king another who should be equal to our defence.

'For so long as a hundred men survive, we will never in any way submit to the domination of the English. It is not for glory or for riches or honours that we fight, but simply and solely for freedom, which no good man surrenders but with his life.'

This Declaration was presumably made in King Robert's presence and with his approval – he was not the kind of man to be lightly crossed. The Scots have believed that kings under God hold their crown subject to the laws of the realm and the consent of the people and on the condition that they are faithful to their trust. They have never accepted the doctrine that kings are absolute by Divine Right and that subjects have a duty of non-resistance in the face of tyranny; nor have they hesitated to say so bluntly in the presence of the monarch. The English have been more polite; but it was they who shocked Scotland and the world by putting their king to death.

It may be noted in passing that when this Declaration was quoted by the B.B.C., it had to be toned down. The Scots were made to declare that they would never submit to the domination of the enemy. Who the enemy were was veiled in decent obscurity.

2. *The Coronation*

It is not unreasonable that the predominant partner should conduct the ceremony of crowning the ruler of the United Kingdom; but it might be expected that every effort would be made to show that the coronation is not an exclusively English affair, and that England is acting for Scotland – not to mention the other members of the British Commonwealth – as well as for herself. What do we find?

In the 'approved souvenir programme' for the Coronation of our present Queen there was a genealogical table showing 'the descent of the Crown'. It starts from William the Conqueror and is entirely English. There is no mention of the long line of Scottish kings which is the source of the Scottish allegiance. It is true that Sir Arthur Bryant, a historian who shows respect for the composite character of the United Kingdom, mentions, in his article on *The Queen's Majesty*, that she is a descendant of Robert the Bruce; but so far as the official genealogy is concerned there is no indication that Scotland existed before a daughter of Henry VII married a Scottish king in the early Sixteenth Century. In a description of the ceremony itself the Garter Principal King of Arms, who might be expected to be punctilious in these matters, tells us bluntly that it is the coronation of a Queen of England.

The Church of England is prevented by its theology from allowing a minister from a non-episcopal Church to function jointly in a religious service, and particularly in a service of Holy Communion. As the Communion Service forms part of the Coronation Ceremony, it was a great concession in 1953 to invite the Moderator of the General Assembly of the Church of Scotland, almost a quarter of a millennium after the Treaty of Union, to join the Archbishop of Canterbury in presenting a copy of the Holy Bible to her Majesty. This concession after so many years was gratefully welcomed in Scotland. The gratitude did not become warmer when it was revealed later that the Archbishop, in spite of his own more liberal views, felt obliged by the law of his Church not to offer to the Moderator the bread and wine which he gave to his fellow bishops during the Communion Service. But if Scotland cannot be represented further on the ecclesiastical side, there might be all the more reason why she should be represented on the secular side. There seems to be no such representation, and the peers who pay homage to her Majesty are exclusively English. As was remarked by *The Times*, few could object if the peers of Scotland were given a separate place in this ceremony.

Apart from the very recent official presence of the Moderator of the General Assembly Scotland might as well never have existed so far as the Coronation Ceremony is concerned. The royal obligation to maintain the settlement of the Church of England forms part of the Oath. The equal obligation to maintain the settlement of the Church of Scotland receives no mention whatever.

3. *The Title*

Although it is occasionally admitted that at the Union there ceased to be a Queen of England just as there ceased to be a Queen of Scots, yet in practice this is far from English usage even in the highest quarters. Some Englishmen go so far as to resent being reminded of the legal position and regard Scottish criticisms as petty or even grotesque.

There might be something to be said for reviving the old titles. There is still a sad lack of royal magic in titles like 'King of Britain' or 'King of the United Kingdom of Great Britain and Northern Ireland'. Provided the monarch were both King of England and King of Scots, there could be no objection if he were referred to generally by his English title, but in Scotland he would be described and welcomed as the King of Scots. From the Scottish point of view there is nothing to be said for using the title 'King of England' without using also the equally ancient title 'King of Scots'. This would seem to be another example of the pretension that Scotland, if it ever existed, has disappeared for good and that Britain is just England and nothing more.

It was unfortunate that in her Christmas Day broadcast from New Zealand in 1953, the Queen referred to herself as the first Queen of England to visit the Dominion. This caused pain to some Scotsmen: they would have felt less unhappy if she had also said that she was the first Queen of Scots who had visited Dunedin, the Edinburgh of the southern hemisphere. It was, however, realised that this was a mistake of her advisers, and it affected in no way the loyalty of her Scottish subjects. Yet the depth of Scottish feeling was shown by one exception. Two maiden ladies, the Misses Alison and Karleen Macintosh, refused to pay their pitifully small income tax on the ground that the Queen had chosen to be Queen of a separate kingdom, had dissociated herself from Scotland, and so had rendered the Treaty of Union null and void. Needless to say, their case, which one of them pled in an impassioned speech, was not accepted by the Sheriff in spite of his observation that this was a somewhat interesting constitutional point. If reports are to be trusted, they avoided future claims by getting rid of their taxable income.

A further source of Scottish protest concerns the numeral to be attached to the reigning monarch when he or she has had predecessors of the same name. William III of England was known also as William II of Scotland – this was before the Union of 1707 – but the next William was known simply as William IV. Her present Majesty was proclaimed Elizabeth II as a successor to Elizabeth of England. The Scots have never had an Elizabeth as a Queen Regnant, and they resented this numeral as a slight to Scotland. They resented it all the more because at this time changes were made in the royal title to meet the desires of the Dominions, while the wishes of Scotland were ignored.

At the suggestion of an ingenious Scottish M.P., the Prime Minister – Mr. Winston Churchill, as he was then – asserted that since the Act of Union the principle had 'in fact' been followed of using whichever numeral in the English or Scottish lines happened to be the higher. He even affirmed that this would be reasonable and logical. 'Thus', he said, 'if a King Robert or King James came to the throne, they might be designated by the numeral appropriate to the Scottish succession, thereby emphasising that our Royal Family traces its descent through the English Royal Line from William the Conqueror and beyond, and through the Scottish Royal Line from Robert the Bruce and Malcolm Canmore, and even further back'.

Such a principle would certainly satisfy Scottish claims; but it was noticeable that Sir Winston declined to commit his successors to it. It is greatly to be feared that the suggestion was merely another example of the political dust that is thrown in the eyes of the Scottish people. If practice has 'in fact' accorded with this principle, this, as the Americans say, is purely coincidental. The principle that was really followed is well known. The numeral is determined by the names of the Kings of England from the time of William the Conqueror, and the Scottish Royal Line is – and is likely to be – ignored.

The common answer to the Scottish protest was that the Dominions raised no objection to the title Elizabeth II, although they never had an Elizabeth I. This is not surprising because in her time they did not even exist – let alone have their own monarchs. There is no parallel here whatsoever. The argument ignores, as usual, the fact that Scotland is not, and never was, an English Colony or Dominion or Dependency, but is, along with England, one of the two co-founders of the United Kingdom. The argument in short does not even begin to meet the Scottish case.

What is really interesting is this: the name of Edward is manifestly more obnoxious to the Scots than the name of Elizabeth; yet when the titles 'Edward VII' and 'Edward VIII' were proclaimed, this gave rise only to sporadic protests, whereas the title 'Elizabeth II' occasioned something which might almost be described as a burst of anger. To this day the Post Office dare not put the inscription E II R on pillar-boxes in Scotland. This is almost the only affair in which the Scots have not been content to restrict their protests to rational argument, which has so little chance of being heard. If politicians would try to understand why there has been this surprising change of temper, there might be some hope that the interests of Scotland would get more consideration than they do.

4. *The Honours of Scotland*

The regalia of Scotland – the Crown, the Sceptre, and the Sword of State – are older than the regalia of England, since Oliver Cromwell destroyed the original English regalia but was foiled in his attempt to confer the same benefits on Scotland. They are known as 'The Honours of Scotland' and were carried before the Scottish kings at what was called 'The Riding of Parliament'. At the Union of 1707 they were hidden away in a chest and were rediscovered only in 1817, a few years before the visit of George IV to Edinburgh, the first British monarch to see Scotland since the reign of Charles II.

It was a gracious thought on the part of the present Queen when she decided to pay a Coronation Visit to Scotland and to attend a national service in St. Giles' Cathedral. By her express desire the Honours of Scotland were carried to the Cathedral, and there they were presented to her by three Scottish peers in full ceremonial dress. She received the Crown from the Duke of Hamilton and gave it back to him after holding it in her hands. This unique acknowledgement of Scotland's place in history aroused feelings of loyalty which it would be hard to describe without appearing to exaggerate.

It may seem niggling to mention even a breath of criticism, but the full picture must be given. It had been hoped that she would wear her coronation robes and perhaps even place the Crown on her own head; and there was a feeling of disappointment when she appeared in ordinary dress and carrying a handbag, which got in her way during the course of the ceremony. This feeling was perhaps increased when later she did wear her coronation robes for the opening of the Canadian Parliament. It was known that among her English advisers were some who were exercised at the thought of what might happen in Scotland without English supervision – there might be a second Coronation! – and it was commonly believed that they intervened at the last moment to prevent her Majesty from carrying out her original intention.

The warmth of loyalty shown on this occasion seems to have taken some Englishmen by surprise: they apparently imagined that the outcry against the royal title meant a lack of respect and affection for the Queen herself. Nothing could be farther from the truth. The protests had never been personal; and indeed as her mother's daughter her Majesty enjoys, as it were, an extra loyalty and affection in Scotland, where she is regarded by her subjects as their own specially Scottish Queen.

5. *Symbols and ceremonial*

There are many other matters of symbolism and ceremonial in which Scottish sentiment is ignored and sometimes outraged.

They cannot be discussed in detail here, but some reference must be made to them, although it is very easy for the non-expert to fall into error.

Whether by accident or by design, there is now no Earl Marischal of Scotland. But Scotland still has her ancient College of Heralds, which has the powers of a Court of Law and is headed by the Lord Lyon.

The Royal Arms, as authorised by the Scottish College of Heralds and used on government documents, differ from these used in England, where the three lions passant guardant of England occupy the first and fourth quarters. In Scotland it is the lion rampant of Scotland which occupies these quarters; and this would seem to be a proper recognition that at least within her own borders Scotland, as a partner in the United Kingdom, is in no way subordinate to England. Some Scotsmen wish that the Royal Standard could be used in its Scottish version when the Sovereign visits Scotland, and they resent the use of the English version on these occasions as a symbol of English encroachment.

The form of the Royal Standard is for the Sovereign to decide. It would certainly give pleasure to her Scottish subjects if when she is resident in her Northern Kingdom she adopted the version of the Scottish, rather than of the English, heralds.

If we turn to the 'supporters' of the Royal Arms, these are the lion of England and the unicorn of Scotland. In the English version the lion of England alone is crowned – is this in order to cock a heraldic snook at Scotland and the Treaty of Union? With greater courtesy the Scottish version gives crowns to both the unicorn and the lion. The Scottish version is used on the official papers of the Scottish Office, but it is the English version which is printed on Acts of Parliament passed exclusively for Scotland.

In matters where regard for Scottish tradition and rights would gain so much and cost so little, dismal discourtesies are hard to understand. From 1820 onwards even the tabards supplied at coronations for the Lord Lyon and his Heralds were quartered English fashion. It was only by the command of the King himself that the Scots quarterings were restored in 1928.

The Scots have also grievances in regard to the Army, which plays so great a part in ceremonial and pageantry. It has been said that the British soldier can stand up to anything except the War Office, and the War Office is resolute in ignoring Scottish sentiment. In dealing with the Scottish regiments, who have won so much glory for an army that is supposed to be British, advice seems to be taken only from the English heralds, and the display of Scottish arms in regimental colours is forbidden.

To give one example. The Queen's crest for England is used on the Colour pikes of all English regiments, and the flag of St. George is used as a second Colour by many of them. We might expect that the Colour pikes of Scottish regiments would bear the Queen's crest for Scotland, and that the second or regimental Colour would be the flag of St. Andrew, as it was in the past. Such ceremonial equality, which could injure nobody, is not allowed. If Scottish soldiers ask why their ancient Colours should be taken away and replaced by English ones, the answer is 'My dear fellow, these are not English Colours, but the Colours of the British Army'. Thus a plain injustice is defended on the ground that it has already been committed.

A similar temper is shown in questions of precedence. The Royal Scots Fusiliers, so far as the date of their original formation is concerned, are the fourth among the British infantry regiments, but they are reckoned as the twenty-first. Why? Because precedence is reckoned, in the case of Scottish regiments, not from the date of their formation, but from the date on which they first came upon the English establishment.

The whole attitude is reminiscent of the English peer who said of the Dominion troops, during the First World War: 'These fellows act as if they were allies, when they are only parts of the English army.'

It would be tedious to elaborate further complaints. The War Office does not hesitate to impose its own English ideas on the uniform of Scottish regiments and at one time even proposed to design a common tartan for them all. Regiments of utterly different traditions are amalgamated in spite of protests, and it is said to be official policy in recent years never to allow more than one Scottish regiment at a time to be quartered in Scotland. Mr. Hore-Belisha did his best to abolish the Scots Greys – the sole Scottish cavalry regiment – and was prevented from doing so only by the ferocity of the snarls which greeted his orders. More recently the records of the Black Watch – together with the men who kept them – were removed from Perth to England in direct breach of the Treaty of Union. A rule had been introduced that the smaller record offices of the Army should be amalgamated and it was impossible to make an exception for Scotland. There had been no difficulty about making an exception for the Guards.

There may be a rational defence for some of these practices, but as a whole they reveal the same curious disregard of Scottish sentiment and tradition that we find elsewhere.

6. *The Stone of Destiny*

At their Coronation the Kings of Scotland sat on a very unusual throne covered by a silken cloth woven with gold. It was a block of stone called the 'Lia Fail', or 'Stone of Destiny', because of the belief that no one could rule in Scotland unless he had sat on it at his crowning and that so long as this stone was in Scotland the Scots would possess the land. According to a legend which need not be taken too seriously it was the stone which had been Jacob's pillow when he saw the angels in a dream at Bethel.

It was this stone – if we may ignore some evidence to the contrary – that Edward I carried off to England as loot along with the Holy Rood of St. Margaret and any documents which might show that Scotland had been independent. It was placed in Westminster Abbey as a memorial of the subjugation of Scotland. At the time of the Treaty of Northampton in 1328 a promise was made to return the Stone, though this was embodied, not in the Treaty itself, but apparently in some accompanying document now lost. This promise was never kept.

The Scots, as so often, had to make the best of a bad job.

They recalled – or composed – a Latin epigram, which has been translated, not too elegantly, as follows:

Unless the Fates be faithless found,
And prophet's voice be vain,
Where'er this monument be found,
The Scottish race shall reign.

This prophecy was supposed to have been fulfilled when James VI of Scotland ascended the English throne.

On the early morning of Christmas Day 1950 the Stone of Destiny was removed from Westminster Abbey by three students from Glasgow University and a Highland girl. After a series of misadventures they succeeded in bringing the Stone to Scotland in spite of all the efforts of the police. There it was hidden for some time, and a petition was sent by them to King George VI stating that they were able, willing, and eager to return the Stone, but asking that it should be allowed to remain in Scotland except at the time of future coronations. In the end the Stone was solemnly placed before the high altar of Arbroath Abbey. There it lay covered by the Scottish flag till it was summarily seized by police officers and whisked away to a police cell. It was then taken back unceremoniously to London and Westminster Abbey. There was no prosecution of the culprits.

It was most unfortunate that this affair happened at a time when King George VI was suffering from an illness which proved to be fatal. When this became known later, it was a source of the utmost regret to every one, and not least to the perpetrators of the deed itself, especially when it was reported that he had taken it as a personal affront. If his advisers had had any understanding of Scottish feeling, they would have known that this was far from being intended. The petition addressed to him was from 'certain of His Majesty's most loyal and obedient subjects', and one clause of it ran as follows: 'That His Majesty's petitioners, who have served him in peril and peace, pledge again their loyalty to him, saving always their right and duty to protest against the actions of his Ministers if such actions are contrary to the wishes or the spirit of his Majesty's Scottish people'.

There can be no doubt that this escapade, even if light-hearted and irresponsible, sprang from a spirit of patriotism, however misguided. In England it was fiercely denounced as vandalism, theft, and sacrilege with no redeeming features whatsoever. The then Archbishop of Canterbury, if he was correctly reported, said that 'There could be no simpler, more elementary illustration of the spiritual causes of the world's evil than the stealing from Westminster Abbey of the Coronation Stone'.

In Scotland feelings were more mixed. Many Scotsmen were as much shocked and outraged as were the English. The crime of sacrilege is unknown to the civil and ecclesiastical law of Scotland; but the Church of Scotland condemned it as 'a violation of the sanctuary' and passed sadly from the subject – perhaps because by this time there was news of the King's illness – without making any recommendation about the future fate of the Stone.

There were others who felt differently. They thought that charges of theft and sacrilege would be more appropriately directed to those who had first seized the Stone by treachery and violence and had kept it in a holy place as a perpetual insult to another nation. When they were told that two blacks cannot make a white, they declined to regard the recovery of stolen property as on the same level with the original theft; nor could they easily accept the doctrine that if an injustice is perpetrated for a sufficient length of time it becomes a legal and moral right.

Between these extremes there were many shades of opinion, but one emotion seemed to be as widely shared as it was strongly felt. This was the feeling that the Stone ought to be returned to Scotland for safe-keeping in St. Giles' Cathedral; and that at a coronation it should be transported with due ceremony – perhaps with an escort of Scots Greys – to Westminster Abbey, where it might function, no longer as a symbol of English pride in what the Garter King had patriotically described as 'the spoil of war', but as a symbol of the free loyalty of the Scottish nation.

This reasonable wish was silently but resolutely ignored.

7. *The bears of Berwick-upon-Tweed*

Perhaps we may be excused if we turn from these high matters and seek a little light relief in the history of Berwick-upon-Tweed, not so much for its own sake as for the tendencies which it reveals.

This ancient little town on the north bank of the Tweed was made a Royal Burgh of Scotland some six hundred years ago. The English in the course of their many wars captured it and used it as a bridgehead, just as Calais was used by them in France. But they did not cease to regard it as part of Scotland – even when it was the only part of Scotland they held, they gave the titles of the Scottish Officers of State to some of the local inhabitants as a symbol of the English claim to subjugate Scotland as a whole. At the Union of 1707 it would have been a gracious act to return it officially to Scotland; but this was not done, and the town enjoyed an ambiguous position right into the Nineteenth Century. It is said that the Crimean War was declared in the name of the United Kingdom and Berwick-upon-Tweed, but in the Treaty of Peace Berwick-upon-Tweed was forgotten and so remains at war with Russia until this day.

Whatever be the truth of this tale, Berwick-upon-Tweed is now administered as part of Northumberland. Even if we set aside historical claims, this is unfortunate geographically: the town is cut off from its natural hinterland. A large proportion of its rates is paid to Northumberland County Council, but if the shops paying these rates were dependent on the economy of Northumberland many of them would disappear. Berwickshire, on the other hand, is deprived of its natural county town, as can be seen by a glance at any map. To restore the town now to its natural status in Scotland might mean something of an administrative upheaval, and this may be considered an adequate excuse for letting things stand as they are, in spite of their unfairness and inconvenience. The only point to be made here is that the status of the town was abolished, not after a consultation of the inhabitants, but as an administrative consequence of the introduction of County Councils.

Now for the light relief. English officials do not always

display a superabundance of tact in dealing with those who have been brought under their control. The inhabitants of Berwick-upon-Tweed decided to have a properly authorised coat of arms, and for this they dutifully applied to the English College of Arms. Since they had used a wych-elm and a bear in their arms for at least six hundred years, they expected to have these as part of the new design, but this was refused. The English do not give reasons, or at any rate not the real reasons, for their actions; but the real reason was suspected to be that this was a Scottish bear. The inhabitants were outraged by this refusal; and, remembering their Scottish origin, they applied to the Lord Lyon of Scotland for a coat-of-arms. This he duly granted, bear and wych-elm and all.

The inhabitants were delighted, but the English Heralds were shocked beyond measure and regarded the proceedings as Scottish aggression. Their spokesman was even driven to appeal to the Treaty of Union, which is so commonly ignored and which in any case did not assign Berwick-upon-Tweed to England. He contended that whatever was the status of the town in the past, its present status was decisive; and since it was now an English town, it was therefore not entitled to the insignia of a Royal Burgh of Scotland. He found the proceedings of the inhabitants and of the Lord Lyon alike beyond his comprehension, and he even went so far as to suggest that in granting, not merely the original bear, but two other Berwick bears (as supporters) the Lord Lyon had sold the inhabitants a pup.

A spokesman for the Lord Lyon replied with some coldness that the English Heralds had failed to understand the situation. The Lord Lyon had been acting in his judicial capacity; and since ancient arms in Scotland are a form of heritable property, he could have come to no other conclusion. When a person becomes English he does not abandon his rights to any Scottish heritable property, and the town of Berwick had established its legal right to the heritable property which it had held for centuries as a Scottish Royal Burgh.

Fortunately for its inhabitants, while the Lord Lyon has the power to enforce his decisions in Scotland, the English College of Heralds has no corresponding power in England, and the town of Berwick is able to flaunt its traditional arms with impunity.

8. *Psychology*

Where symbols and ceremonials are concerned, we might perhaps not unreasonably expect some semblance of equality between free nations joined in a common union. Yet it is the common practice to dismiss Scottish complaints under this head as petty and trivial or even as the manifestation of an inferiority complex. The very fact that a plea for Scotland should begin with grievances of this kind may be taken to show how sentimental the claims of Scotland are.

This argument is hardly convincing. Symbols, and especially symbols of status, play a far from negligible part in the life of individuals and nations. The argument comes strangely from Englishmen, who attach so much importance to ceremonies and symbols so far as England herself is concerned. It would seem difficult to sustain the thesis that in Britain English patriotism is truly noble, but Scottish patriotism merely absurd; or even that while English patriotism is properly manifested in traditional symbolism, the desire of the Scots to retain their own national symbols is parochial and childish. The demand that the Scottish case should be examined on such assumptions is – to put it mildly – a trifle steep.

Disregard of Scottish sentiment in ceremonial matters cannot but be a potent source of irritation, and it is important also as itself symbolical – or symptomatic – of an English attitude manifested in other spheres. Its significance is all the greater because here no obvious English interest is concerned. I make no apology for beginning with this topic. It will help us to understand the treatment of Scotland in affairs which may be thought to be of more practical importance.

To dismiss Scottish complaints as the product of an inferiority complex hardly conforms to the decencies of polite discussion. Instead of meeting a serious argument it uses a cheap cliché to rule the arguer out of court. It is itself an instance of that very disregard of Scottish feeling which is the subject of complaint. This clumsy incursion into depth psychology merely strengthens the Scottish case. If the present system is able to give Scotsmen an inferiority complex, it must be about as bad as it is possible for a system to be.

CHAPTER IV

FRUSTRATION IN PARLIAMENT

Magnanimity in politics is not seldom the truest wisdom
Edmund Burke

1. *The supremacy of Parliament*

The new Parliament of Great Britain, as set up by the Treaty of Union, acted from the first as a continuation of the English Parliament. This could hardly have been otherwise so far as matters of procedure were concerned, but it raises questions as to the character of the British Constitution.

On the Scottish view the Treaty of Union is an essential part of the British Constitution. This means that a breach of the Treaty by Parliament would be unconstitutional. Some Scottish Nationalists go so far as to argue that a breach of the Treaty would mean a cancellation of the Union and that the rights of the independent Scottish Parliament would be revived – and indeed have been revived.

The English take the Treaty of Union more lightly. It has even been argued by cynics that since Scotland as an independent kingdom disappeared as a result of the Treaty, there now exists no entity which can seek redress on the ground that the Treaty has been broken. The Treaty, so to speak, conveniently cancels itself out.

Apart from such extreme arguments there is a real conflict of traditions and attitudes. It is sometimes said that the English, when they rejected the absolute supremacy of Kings, immediately replaced it with the absolute supremacy of Parliament, as is most obvious in the claim to enforce Parliamentary privilege without the safeguards of legal trial. The absolute supremacy of Parliament, if taken literally, would be incompatible with any constitutional checks. On this theory it could be held that

Parliament has the unquestionable right to abolish Scots Law and disestablish the Church of Scotland even although these are stipulated to be essential conditions of the Treaty of Union.

As against all this is has been argued that Scotland never accepted either the supremacy of Kings or the supremacy of Parliament, but has supported the supremacy of law and the supremacy of the people – or rather the supremacy of the people under law. Hence the right of Parliament to impose whatever measures it may choose upon the people of Scotland is hotly denied. This right could not be acquired by the Treaty of Union since the Scottish Parliament which adopted the Treaty had itself no authority to do away with the fundamental liberties of the Scottish people.

These may seem academic questions. In actual practice the people of Britain as a whole are a strong check on Parliament, whatever may be the constitutional theory. But the conflict of attitudes is a real one, and many Scotsmen resent the doctrine that the wishes of the Scottish people can legitimately be over-ridden in all matters by an English Parliamentary majority. In this attitude, curiously enough, they had at one time the support of Sir Winston Churchill, when he claimed that the Scots were not bound to accept the kind of slavery imposed by a Socialist Government. There is no evidence that his support survived when his own Party came to power.

2. *Legislation for Scotland*

The Treaty of Union, besides promising the independence of Scottish courts of law, stipulated that no alteration should be made 'in Laws which concern private Right, except for the evident utility of the subjects within Scotland'. Scots Law, it must be remembered, differs from English Law both in its principles and in its terminology and is more akin to Roman Law and to the systems of Law prevailing on the continent of Europe. Hence there are many matters in which it cannot be amended or developed merely by adding to it the incompatible laws of England. By the nature of things as well as by the spirit of the Treaty there ought to be some machinery for special Scottish legislation.

There are two obvious ways of dealing with this problem. One is to pass laws for England and then to translate these laws into Scottish terms. This is known as legislation by appendix and, like most translations, is almost bound to be inadequate and can even be unintelligible. The other way is to pass special laws for Scotland; but how can enough time be found to do this in an over-burdened and predominantly English Parliament?

There is also a third way – the special needs of Scotland can be ignored altogether or at least for an indefinite time. The fact that a reform would require legislation is often considered an adequate ground for doing nothing. It is sometimes even said of the most necessary reforms that there can be no legislation for Scotland unless there is unanimity of opinion. How can a modern country be governed on such a principle?

A system of this kind is bound to be unsatisfactory and becomes intolerable in a Parliament where sufficient time cannot be found even for necessary legislation in regard to England. The words of one wise Englishman, Sir James Headlam Morley, sum up the position very well:

> 'I should have thought that the experiment of a unitary parliament for the whole of the United Kingdom had in fact broken down. . . . It seems to me impossible to maintain that the House of Commons under modern conditions can exercise any intelligent control over the affairs, whether of Ireland, Wales, or Scotland.'

Since these words were written the congestion of Parliament has become very much worse, and the problem becomes more and more insoluble – insoluble, that is, so long as the English refuse even to consider the obvious solution of setting up a Parliament in Edinburgh to deal with exclusively Scottish affairs. How desperate they are to avoid the obvious can be seen by a proposal once made in 'Crossbow', the organ of the Bow Group of Young Conservatives. This had the merit of recognising Scottish dissatisfaction and asked 'Could Scotland have, not a separate Parliament, but a separate House of Lords?' This House, they suggest, could meet in Edinburgh and could have the power of initiating Scottish legislation or of considering it in committee.

It would be hard to find any proposal more contrary to the Scottish tradition of democracy; but at least it was welcome as a rare gesture of goodwill.

3. *The Scottish Grand Committee*

One concession has been made to Scottish legislative needs by setting up a piece of Parliamentary machinery commonly known as the Scottish Grand Committee. This was introduced in the early part of this century when Sir Henry Campbell-Bannerman was Prime Minister, and its powers were extended after the Second World War. It is composed of all the Scottish members of Parliament with the addition of ten to fifteen others to act as watch-dogs and to see that all decisions are in accordance with the policy of the party in power. At present it may be permitted to discuss Bills on the second reading as well as at the committee stage, and it may also be allowed to discuss the Scottish estimates for six days instead of the former two. As it has no powers of initiative, it can only affect matters of detail and help to remove the worst anomalies. The time allowed it for discussion is narrowly limited, and the subjects it can deal with are in effect determined by the Government of the day. Its mere existence does at least recognise that Scotland has special legislative problems.

The inadequacy of this machinery is freely recognised by Scottish members, and even by some English members, especially when they are in opposition. Thus the time allowed in 1954 for the Scottish Town and Country Planning Bill was said by spokesmen for the Labour Party to be 'an outrage on Parliamentary democracy'. In 1958 the Local Government and Miscellaneous Financial Provisions (Scotland) Bill was said to be opposed by all the local authorities in Scotland, and one speaker declared that the majority of English members had not the slightest idea of what the measure meant. The Bill was none the less forced through by the guillotine, and by this gagging of the Opposition the Government were declared to be guilty of gagging the whole of Scotland.

When the Scottish Town and Country Planning Bill was passed on to the House of Lords, Lord Silkin pointed out that it was substantially in the same form as the corresponding English Bill *before* this had been changed by 212 amendments: it was, he said, quite unrealistic to expect that any amendments could be made in the Scottish Bill which were in conflict with the English one. This he very properly described as a legislative farce, and he appeared to hint that the only solution was to get rid of special legislation for Scotland.

This dog in the manger attitude is the main source of all the trouble. The British Parliament cannot begin to deal adequately with Scottish legislation, yet the two main political parties consistently refuse to set up any machinery which can. Even the creaking machinery that exists already is not used to its full capacity, nor is it always lubricated by the necessary expert advice from the Lord Advocate or the Solicitor General for Scotland. In 1963, for example, neither of these officials had a seat in Parliament, and this was recognised to be 'an inconvenience'. It was, however, an inconvenience that could be defended on the ground that it had happened before. By 1966 it seemed to be comfortably accepted that the absence of the Scottish law officers in Parliament is normal, no matter how many anomalies may be imposed on the laws by which Scotland is governed. Parliament apparently cannot even afford the money to pay an adequate number of draftsmen properly skilled in Scots Law.

4. *The political parties*

Of the two main political parties each assures us that its opponents are of doubtful honesty and proved incompetence. Whatever be the truth of this in general, they are both right so far as the treatment of Scottish affairs is concerned.

The Conservative Party developed in its present form as an opponent of Home Rule for Ireland. Although political parties have little regard for consistency, the Conservatives opposed Home Rule for Scotland as well, even if the situation there was very different. In spite of occasional verbal salutes to the principle that the people of Scotland have a right to decide in favour of a Scottish Parliament, like the Labour Party they refuse to allow a plebiscite and do so on precisely the same grounds. In a letter authorised by Mr. Macmillan in 1959, we were told the old old story once again: a plebiscite could not be held without legislation, which would be controversial; in any case it could not offer any reliable guide; and a true reflexion of considered judgement could be expected to emerge only through normal Parliamentary processes, and in particular through open debate in an elected assembly. Why a predominantly English Parliament could judge the needs of Scotland better without a plebiscite to discover Scottish opinion he did not condescend to explain.

The queer thing is that the Scottish Conservatives, who supported all this, not only demanded, but also enjoyed, something very like Home Rule within their own party. They did not even call themselves Conservatives but Unionists, and they rejected English interference. Yet they refused to allow their fellow-countrymen the kind of rights they claimed for themselves. This autonomy they now seem to have abandoned – or was it taken away from them? – after a series of electoral defeats. Nowadays they do call themselves Conservatives and have adopted English methods of organisation. As a result they have foolishly issued public notices which assume that English Courts already govern electoral procedure in Scotland. It is hardly surprising if they find less and less support at the polls.

The Labour Party has a different history. It was founded originally by a Scotsman, Mr. Keir Hardie; during its early struggles much of its impetus and most of its liveliness came from the so-called Clydesiders led by Mr. Maxton; and its first Prime Minister was Ramsay Macdonald. During all this period Home Rule for Scotland was part of its official policy, and even Mr. Attlee favoured 'the principle' up to the General Election of 1945. As soon as the election was won and the Party obtained real political power, he dropped the whole idea like a hot brick.

Mr. Gaitskell later showed a little more grace – he at least recognised that a political betrayal merits some semblance of excuse. Addressing the Scottish Council of the Labour Party in

1956 he declared blandly that there is a form of Scottish Parliament in existence already, only it sits at Westminster. This form, incredible as it may sound, is the Scottish Grand Committee – did he expect any one to believe that the only Labour promise to the Scottish people was to give them something they already had? He was also good enough to assert that he was not closing his mind to further changes, but there was one proviso – these changes must not conflict with the true interests, realistically assessed, of Scotland herself. This meant presumably that they must be assessed by Englishmen.

Mr. Gaitskell also professed to explain why the Labour Party had changed its mind. He recognised that under Tory rule between the Wars practically the whole of Scotland had become a distressed area through the drift south of industry – this process was known as 'rationalisation'. At that time it was only natural to think that Scotland should have control over her own affairs. Now that they had nationalisation and economic planning the grounds for such a claim had disappeared.

Curiously enough, Mr. Macmillan had answered this piece of sophistry two years earlier at a Unionist rally in Edinburgh. On his view it was Socialist rule which justified the Scottish claim. Under the Socialists, he told us, the control of Scottish affairs had slipped steadily and mercilessly southwards; and all this injured the material interests of Scotland, offended her nationhood, and touched her pride. Now that the Conservatives were in power, everything in Scotland was improving so much that as an English minister he was sometimes rather jealous, though as an exiled Scot he rejoiced at Scotland's share.

Both of these gentlemen were dead right in what they said of their opponents, however unduly they may have flattered themselves. Conservative 'rationalisation' and Socialist 'nationalisation' have precisely the same effect – the control of Scottish affairs slips steadily and mercilessly southwards and so does her industry and wealth.

It should not be forgotten that there is also a Liberal Party, which has been committed to Home Rule since 1886. Unfortunately when it was in power it never found time to pass a

Home Rule Bill for Scotland. There may have been excuses for this such as the opposition in the House of Lords; but if Scotland has to postpone its hopes of self-government till the Liberal Party returns to power, the prospect is pretty bleak.

5. *Party discipline*

When English Party leaders make speeches north of the Border, they are full of solicitude for the Scottish interests so badly neglected by their opponents. Even if the goodwill is most marked when they are in opposition, and even if it cools a little when they get back to London, it may still be asked why the Scottish members of Parliament cannot do more to meet the special grievances of Scotland.

One answer is that their efforts are restricted by Parliamentary machinery – they are given neither the time nor the opportunity. Another answer is to be found in the nature of Party discipline.

It is hard to be precise on this topic, but there is no doubt that members of Parliament enjoyed more independence in the Nineteenth Century than they do to-day. The congestion of Parliamentary business itself demands more Party discipline, and it is a serious matter for a recalcitrant member if he falls foul of the Party Whips. His position is weak if his electoral expenses are paid by the Party, and especially if he is a poor man dependent on his Parliamentary salary. If he is obdurate, he may lose his seat at the next election. He will certainly have to abandon all hope, not only of the glittering prizes which mark political success, but also of the minor offices and honours which proliferate under present conditions and give the Party in power an extent of patronage only less formidable than that enjoyed in the Eighteenth Century.

This Party pressure applies to Scottish members as well as to others. If they devote too much time to defending the interests of Scotland, they are likely to be looked on with disfavour. If they were to commit themselves to self-government for Scotland, especially when their own Party is in power, they would be regarded as men of bad judgement: their chances of a successful political career would, to say the least, be greatly diminished. Considerations like these are almost bound to affect men who are able and ambitious. Those who lack ability and ambition will in any case be ready to toe the Party line; and even if they refused to do so, their own weakness would make them ineffectual.

It is noticeable that the most outspoken defence of Scottish interests is apt to come from the Scottish peers in the House of Lords. Although nearly always educated in England, they are not entirely oblivious of the history of Scotland in which their ancestors played a part; and unless they are bent on a political career they have less reason to be influenced either by the favours or by the disapproval of their Party.

The members for Scottish constituencies are sometimes described as the representatives of the English Parties in Scotland. This is unfair. Many of them are patriotic Scotsmen, and all of them try to do their best for their constituents. Without their efforts the treatment of Scotland would be worse than it is, and we owe them a debt of gratitude. If they are relatively ineffective, this springs, not from moral obliquity, but from the system of which they form a part.

In both political parties the English point of view must predominate by sheer weight of numbers, and this is generally hostile, or at least indifferent, to any real self-government for Scotland. Yet in lesser matters we may find interesting variations. If we collected the speeches made by professional politicians, irrespective of party, when they are out of office, we might get a tolerable statement of at least the minor injustices under which Scotland suffers. When power changes hands after a general election, it is almost comical to observe how often and how quickly the two parties also exchange their attitudes. The new opposition brings up the old grievances which they ignored or belittled when they were in power; and the new government produces the same specious answers, supplied by the same civil servants, which its members had condemned when they were in opposition. This superficial and apparently unconscious comedy is for Scotland almost tragic as a permanent obstacle to necessary reform.

6. *Frustration*

It should not be thought that there is any deliberate attempt to oppress Scotland or to neglect her interests. Sometimes her special needs may be met – as, for example, in 1921 when the Church of Scotland was granted the spiritual liberties that had been sought through so many centuries. But inevitably it is English interests that are considered first. If Scottish interests are similar, well and good. If they are different, they have to suffer. Sometimes there may come a readjustment if the outcry from Scotland is fierce enough. Even if it comes, it may come very late. Often it may never come at all.

Let us try to sketch summarily an outline of the kind of treatment that Scotland may, and too often does, receive. Later we shall have to discuss some of these grievances in rather more detail.

If Scotland produces mainly oats and England mainly wheat, it is wheat that will receive government support. If Scotsmen drink whisky and Englishmen drink beer, whisky will be taxed till it is beyond the reach of a working-man: to do this with beer would cause a revolution. Highland games will be subject to entertainments tax, while English cricket matches will get special exemption. Indeed cricket, as a game sacred to the English, must have very special privileges: its implements will be freed from purchase tax. Golf-clubs, however, will not, although golf is almost equally sacred to the Scots.

The reasons advanced for this last discrimination were that cricket was a democratic game for the poor man, while golf was a game for the rich. This reasoning was hard to bear. In Scotland golf has always been, and still is, a game for poor men and is democratic in a sense unknown in England. It is only the English – and still more the Americans – who have made it a rich man's game.

These discriminations may be dismissed as trivial, but they display the prevailing pattern. If Scotland builds ships, and England builds aeroplanes, it is aeroplanes that will get lavish government support. If Scotland has beds of shale oil capable of producing precious petrol for her needs and even of saving

73

foreign currency, this industry will be taxed out of existence – it will certainly receive no help. If Scotland has many inlets of the sea which require special bridges, the building of these bridges will be held up for years and even then will have to be financed by tolls, while money is poured out on special English motorways, which are entirely free. If the Highlands and Islands are uniquely dependent on ships for their transport, the necessary piers will be allowed to sink into disrepair and subsequently closed to the detriment or destruction of one community after another. Indeed the Highlands as a whole have no counterpart in England, and this may explain, at least in part, their melancholy history of depopulation and decay.

When a system of equalisation grants was introduced under the Labour Party in order to help struggling municipalities, it was so well suited to English conditions that the prosperous city of Birmingham received over £1,000,000, while the city of Glasgow, which was in much greater need, got nothing. This continued for some years till the Conservative party came into power. Only then was some adjustment made to remedy this injustice, and the Conservatives preened themselves as the friends of Scotland; but it would never have occurred to them to make up some of the money lost.

Unfortunately changes are sometimes made in the other direction. There was at one time a measure for the support of what are known as 'marginal lands', and the grants given under this measure really did help the Highlands. Unfortunately they did not do much for small farmers in England, where there is relatively little marginal land. It was decided to abolish these grants, and a new system was suddenly introduced to help the English farmers. This, as sometimes happens, aroused so many protests from Scotland that the grants for marginal lands were reduced gradually instead of being abolished outright. A later measure – the so-called Winter Keep Scheme – failed to restore anything like the original benefits.

Since Scotland is a country of deep sea-inlets and of many islands it is to her interest that territorial waters should extend beyond the three mile limit, and that the limits should be drawn from headland to headland instead of hugging the land. This is in fact the law of Scotland. England is a country of few inlets and few islands, and so the Scottish view was rejected – on the ground that it was contrary to international law. Up till 1964 the British Government continued to maintain this attitude even after the International Court of Justice ruled (in the case of Norway) that the view held in Scotland is in accordance with international law. The damage done to inshore fishermen and to the Scottish fishing grounds during the present century has contributed to the ruin of the Highlands; but unlike Norway or even Iceland Scotland has no power to defend herself.

And so the dreary catalogue goes on. Even where no English interests are involved, Scotland has to wait year after year for legislation recognised to be necessary. Acts, for example, have been passed to give adopted children in England various rights, including the right of succession. Yet, as a Scottish Sheriff had to complain, 'In Scotland the years dragged on and nothing was done. That neglect was evil.' The same evil neglect was shown in regard to the Scottish rating system, which, though reasonable in itself, had ruinous effects under a system of continuous inflation. To this topic we shall have to return, but enough samples – and they are only samples – of the methods of legislation from which Scotland suffers have been given already.

If it is painful to read about such grievances, it is still more painful to endure them. Even if some of them may seem trifling, they show how unfair the present system is, and the continuous accumulation of them may be compared, if not to the Chinese water torture, at least to a continual dropping on a very rainy day. They are not made easier to bear by English legislators who congratulate themselves on their ignorance of Scottish affairs and resent the time that is set aside for their discussion. Such discussions, so obviously necessary under the present system, have even been attributed to the chauvinism of the Scots; and on one occasion an English member exclaimed indignantly, 'Is not Scotland England?' Let us hope that such attitudes are confined to a minority of Englishmen; but so long as they prevail, the most serious problems of Scotland will continue to be neglected.

On the other hand, the Imperial Parliament does waste

75

precious time in discussing the most trivial of Scottish affairs. Thus, for example, on one day in June 1965, three Scottish Bills were considered by the House of Lords. The first provided for the maintenance and control of salmon fishing on a stretch of the river Annan. The second extended the municipal and police boundaries of the burgh of Coatbridge. The third corrected a previous oversight in the Order governing the Widows' Fund for Writers to the Signet. Such a waste of Parliamentary time is necessary, not because Scotsmen are irrational, but because English politicians are resolute to prevent them from exercising any control over their own purely national concerns.

7. *A change of heart*

It may be true that not all Scotland's grievances could be removed by the creation of a Scottish Parliament, for some of the affairs in question might remain under the jurisdiction of the Parliament in Westminster. It may be true that a Scottish Parliament would be hemmed in on every side, though magnanimity would here be the truest wisdom. Yet even if it were unnecessarily restricted, its very existence would have a psychological effect. The feeling that Scotland has so little control even over minor matters is a sickness spreading apathy into all walks of life. If only it were possible to do something, however little, there might be a revival of energy and hope. And even in matters not under its control, a Scottish Parliament might at least be able to speak with an authentic voice. Whether this voice were listened to or not, it would be able to speak in a way that could not wholly be ignored; and it would no longer be possible to pretend that no one knows what the Scottish people want.

What is needed is a change of heart in England, where a centralising government impoverishes 'the regions' both materially and spiritually in spite of spasmodic efforts to undo some of the damage already done. We may think that such a change of heart is impossible, but it is sometimes forgotten that a Home Rule Bill for Scotland has at times gained a first, and even a second, reading in the British Parliament, when self-government was perhaps a less crying need than it is to-day.

Between 1889 and 1914 the subject had been before the House of Commons thirteen times; and on the last eight occasions the principle had been accepted by a general majority of the House. In 1919 a *Speakers' Conference* was set up to consider a plan of federal devolution. Moved perhaps by a war fought for the rights of small nations and possibly mindful of the streams of Scottish blood shed in this cause, the Conference approved a scheme of devolution by 187 votes to 34. The vote of its Scottish members was as high as 35 to 1. Nothing practical came of it; but it is strange that Scotsmen should be consigned to a 'lunatic tartan fringe' because they venture to suggest that a principle not only rational in itself, but also accepted from time to time by the Mother of Parliaments, might reasonably be translated into action.

CHAPTER V

BUREAUCRATS IN THE SADDLE

A criticism of administration is as much part of the policy as administration itself

Walter Bagehot

1. *Administration in Scotland*

The administrative system of Scotland was not reserved under the Treaty of Union, and the Scottish Privy Council was speedily abolished; but for a brief period the Scottish Secretary of State continued to function under the new dispensation. As early as 1711 Daniel Defoe, that master of English fiction, was denying that the office was necessary, and using arguments of the type with which we are now all too familiar: Scotland no more requires a Secretary than Yorkshire; the office is only a source of needless expense; and so on. The office in fact lasted, with some interruptions, only till 1725, but was revived briefly from 1741 to 1745. Otherwise, right up to 1885, the sole official Officer of State in Scotland was the Lord Advocate, although until 1827 he had to share the real power with some noble but unofficial 'Scottish Manager' who happened to have influence in the Cabinet and was given an uncontrolled exercise of patronage in Scotland. After 1827 the English Home Secretary took over Scottish affairs, but was supposed to act with the advice and help of the Lord Advocate.

So far as London was concerned, the Lord Advocate functioned from a small and dark room in the Home Office, and there was some doubt if it was even wholesome. Every Lord Advocate had, so to speak, to start afresh since he had no Department and no permanent staff. According to one story it was essential for him to be a tall man so that in Parliamentary voting the submissive Scottish members could be sure of following him into the right lobby. The poor gentleman had to move continually between Edinburgh and London at a period when Edinburgh was farther in time from London than New York is to-day by one of the slower liners. The coming of the railways made his lot a trifle easier, but by no means enviable.

This strange and irresponsible system, or lack of system, may have worked in some ways to Scotland's benefit, for it was sometimes too inefficient to place obstacles in the path of progress. It was still possible, for example, to deepen the Clyde and turn Glasgow into the greatest ship-building centre in the world; and again to construct the Forth Railway Bridge as the first of the great bridges which are one glory of the modern age. Even so – the quotation is from a book by Mr. W. C. Smith in 1885, though it might have been written to-day –

'A feeling grew up in Scotland that national interests were neglected in Parliament; that the actual wants of the country were not understood by London departments; that necessary legislation was abandoned or delayed; that injustice was done in the matter of imperial grants.'

In 1885 through the influence of Lord Rosebery the office of Secretary for Scotland (now Secretary of State for Scotland) was revived. In 1919 he was allowed for the first time a Parliamentary Under-Secretary; and by 1964 he was assisted by a team of four – the Minister of State and three Parliamentary Under-Secretaries. When in that year the Labour Party came into power they continued the same system of organisation, which looks is if it may be relatively permanent.

The proposal that Scotland should have a Secretary of State was regarded in 1853 as a romantic extravagance and was dismissed contemptuously on the usual grounds. Yet after many vicissitudes it was accepted in 1885 almost without debate. Perhaps the proposal for a Scottish Parliament will have a similar destiny.

2. The Little King

The Secretary of State for Scotland has under him four separate departments – Agriculture, Development, Education, Health and Home – which constitute the Scottish Office and have their headquarters in St. Andrew's House in Edinburgh. Apart from him these departments have no legal existence or independent functions. The six symbolic figures outside St. Andrew's House would represent the real position more accurately – as has been suggested by Sir David Milne in his book *The Scottish Office* [1]– if they could be replaced by statues showing the same man clad symbolically in different ways. The Secretary is responsible for administrative matters which in England are the concern of eight separate and independent Ministers. But even this is far from exhausting his functions. His office exercises a magnetic attraction on other administrative organisations concerned with Scotland, such as the Forestry Commission and the Office of the Crown Estates Commissioners. As 'Scotland's Minister' he has to defend decisions made by English Ministers with regard to Scotland – decisions for which he has no responsibility except as a member of the British Cabinet.

This is a system of one-man government reminiscent of Pooh Bah in the *Mikado*, and the Secretary is sometimes described as the Little King of Scotland. No wonder his job is freely admitted to be quite impossible – certainly in private, but also in public, as by Lord Alness, who held the office as long ago as 1916–22. What is surprising is that the Scottish people should be expected to submit indefinitely to a system whose impossibility is admitted.

The Secretaries of State are always men of good intentions and sometimes of more than average ability. In the over-burdened British Cabinet they are supposed to defend the interests of Scotland – a task too difficult for the less able and too compromising for the more ambitious. It is widely recognised that the best work in this office was done by Mr. Thomas Johnston – an unusually able man with no ambitions south of the Border. In 1941 he instituted an unofficial Council of State, as it was called, composed of all the ex-Secretaries from whatever party. By getting general agreement he was able to do a great deal for Scotland, notably by setting up the North of Scotland Hydro-Electric Board, an independent Scottish

[1] London: George Allen & Unwin Ltd.

institution which has been of real help to the Highlands, in spite of continual sniping from the South.

A Council of State of this type, though eminently desirable, is possible only under a Coalition Government, such as existed during the Second World War. As soon as Party strife was renewed, this experiment had to be abandoned.

The Secretary of State has both too much power and too little. He is responsible for duties far beyond the compass of one man, yet his freedom of action is narrowly restricted. His every footstep is dogged by a watchful Treasury in London, and his decisions must be adjusted to what has been done, or is about to be done, in England. If he has to deal with some problem unknown in the South – such, for example, as the modest subsidy required to help the production of a much needed Gaelic dictionary – the restrictions laid upon him are made painfully clear. The whole system, besides being incompetent to meet the needs of Scotland, is flatly opposed to the age-old tradition of Scottish democracy, which has always been hostile to one-man rule imposed from above.

3. *The Scottish Office*

Little need be said about the workings of the Scottish Office itself. The tales about telephone enquiries being greeted with the answer, "oskins 'ere', may apply to the outposts of the invading Ministries from London, but the four Scottish Departments are in the main manned by Scotsmen familiar with the conditions of the country they have to govern. These gentlemen are as competent and well-meaning as civil servants normally are, but creative minds are not usually attracted to this profession; and if they are, the system itself may be counted upon to see that they become less creative. Civil servants are, and ought to be, if not 'yes-men', at least safe men: it is not their business to make revolutions, but to carry out scrupulously regulations imposed on them by others. As was once said – I think by Lloyd George – their proper place is between the shafts and not on the dickey.

Pioneer reforms in accordance with Scottish traditions are no more likely to receive an impulse from conscientious civil servants than from an over-burdened Secretary of State. What is needed to supplement both is the breath of fresh air that would come, if it can come at all, from a Scottish Parliament directly concerned with the needs and ideals of the Scottish people. Without this the existing system is manifestly incomplete, and its working is determined far too much by quite other considerations than the interests of Scotland. The claim sometimes made even by Members of Parliament for Scottish constituencies that in virtue of such a bureaucratic organisation Scotland already enjoys Home Rule is too grotesque to merit serious consideration. There can be no Home Rule without an elected body of representatives to determine policy and to keep the administration up to the mark.

4. *Control from London*

If the story ended there, it would be easy enough to understand, but in fact administration in Scotland forms a kind of maze in which only the most expert can hope to find their way. More and more of the London Ministries have come to be directly responsible for affairs in Scotland, particularly economic affairs; and there is a wide-spread belief that they know little and care less about the special needs of that country. Even if this belief is sometimes exaggerated, it is only natural for civil servants in London to take the line attributed to one of them: 'Surely you don't expect to be treated any differently from the rest of the country.' To the more tidy minds among them the very existence of Scots Law appears to be an anachronism and an offence.

This is not the place to expound the details of the present system. They may be found, if not always too easily, in the Report of the Royal Commission on Scottish Affairs (1952-54).

Before 1914, as the Commission recognises, the Government interfered little with the concerns of the individual, but since then its encroachment on private activities has mounted with ever increasing velocity.

'Restrictions arising from two world wars, steps to meet the depression and unemployment in the inter-war period, the allocation of scarce materials, the rationing of capital investment, the need to channel production – all these have called for regulations and controls, most of which have been organized on a Great Britain basis with ultimate authority resting in London.'

However inevitable these regulations and controls may have been in time of war, they enabled the Central Government to get a firm grip on the economic life of Scotland, and this grip they show no inclination to relax. I am inclined to think that the movement began even before 1914. Many years ago a very sweet and gentle old Oxonian, who – as I discovered to my surprise – had spent most of his life in the Scottish Office, assured me that Scotland had received a very raw deal ever since Lloyd George had insisted on his reforms being administered from London; and he also complained, as bitterly as was possible for a man of his nature, about the lack of understanding shown by English civil servants in Scotland.

At the time of the Commission the most powerful London Ministries determining the economic fate of Scotland were the Board of Trade, the Ministry of Supply, and the Ministry of Transport and Civil Aviation. Since then some have been renamed; some have been amalgamated; and some have been split up; but all this in no way affects the general position, though it does make precise description difficult. They invaded the country with a series of subsidiary offices headed by gentlemen sometimes called 'Regional Controllers' and only too ready to act as such. Their need to refer matters to Whitehall was and is the cause of frustrations and delays. It also means, as the Commission itself remarks, that any one who holds a leading position in either public or private business in Scotland has to spend too much of his time in London. It said nothing about his money, though this too is a consideration, and sometimes British Railways takes its share of the swag by perversely charging heavier rates of fare to long-distance travellers.

We need not concern ourselves here with the long list of other London Ministries which – like the Ministry of Works and the Ministry of Fuel and Power – take a hand in domestic matters that should be decided in Scotland itself; but it may be observed that the Secretary of State for Scotland is sometimes given joint responsibility with a London Minister. Even then it is to be feared that the ultimate decision still rests with Whitehall.

It is the big decisions of powerful economic Ministries in London which affect most seriously the life of Scotland; but continual interference on minor details is also a fruitful source of irritation. Some of the complaints concern matters so ludicrous that it is hard to credit them, but at the very least they illustrate the unhappy atmosphere which has been spread so thickly over Scotland. For example, it has been solemnly alleged – and I have seen no contradiction – that it is forbidden to send a haggis to Russia unless it first goes south to be packed by a London firm, and even then it cannot be sent in the same parcel as a Tam-o'-Shanter. And perhaps here it may not be out of place to put in a plea on behalf of Scottish dogs. In England the money paid for dog-licences goes to the local authority, but in Scotland it is whisked resolutely over the Border to London. It looks as if no loose Scottish revenue, however small, can escape the clutches of the Treasury; and even the most patriotic West Highland terrier, unlike English dogs, is prevented from contributing to the welfare of his own country.

A more dignified depredation affects the emoluments of the Lord Lyon and his Court. Formerly these came from the 'profits of the Lyon Court', though the Lord Lyon himself had a small salary as well. In 1867 the profits were transferred to the Treasury. At the same time the six Heralds were reduced to three, as were also the six Pursuivants. To this day the Heralds have been paid an annual sum of £25 each, and the Pursuivants £16 13s. 4d. In comparison the Lord Lyon enjoys the princely salary of £1,200 – much less than is paid to a Clerk of Assize in the County Courts of England. No wonder that the Treasury is said to make a substantial profit.

Let us turn to an example of the consideration which Scottish requests may meet in Whitehall. This concerns what was at the time the Ministry of Transport and Civil Aviation.

At the beginning of 1960, even before the era of Dr. Beeching, the usual policy was being extended of closing branch lines in the Highlands on the ground of expense. As this was, and is, devastating to thinly populated counties with inadequate roads, a large deputation was sent south at considerable expense to interview the reigning Minister – at that time Mr. Marples. According to newspaper reports, he first put the meeting forward by a quarter of an hour, and then kept them waiting for twenty minutes. When at last he arrived, 'sucking a sweetie' according to one version, he refused to see them unless two Members of Parliament left the room, although they were members of the deputation. He then spent a lot of time telling them how hard he was working in other fields and cut short their attempts to state their case. Finally he informed them that it did not matter what they said to him because the power to deal with the subject did not lie in his hands. It may be surmised that the deputation proceeded to tell him exactly what they thought of him, for he was reported to have finished by saying 'I am going to listen to no more. I will listen again to delegations from England, Wales, and even Northern Ireland. But this is the last bloody Scottish delegation I will ever hear'.

It is only fair to add that he later denied the use of the offensive adjective, but his attitude was inconsiderate enough even apart from the precise terminology in which it was expressed. The incident illustrates the worst side of the treatment that can be meted out to Scotland and also the difficulty of finding out the real source of oppressive decisions. If the Minister had no power to deal with the subject, why was the deputation not informed of this before setting out on so fruitless a journey? Is it really perverse of Scotsmen to want matters so intimately Scottish to be decided in Edinburgh, or does the perversity lie on the other side?

5. *Wheels within wheels*

As government intervenes more and more in every-day life, so the mechanism of administration becomes ever more complex. Scotland has to plead her cause, not merely with government Departments, but with other bodies centred in London. The most conspicuous of these we may perhaps call 'Corporations' – such as the British Broadcasting Corporation, British Railways,

British European Airways, the Coal Board, and so on. The fact that they are given different titles does not make the discussion of them any easier. Generally speaking, each is responsible to a government Minister; but they have a certain measure of independence, and their day-to-day working is commonly protected against questions in Parliament.

Apart from the increased possibility of 'passing the buck' – the occupational disease of civil servants – and the added difficulty of finding who is responsible for what, such a system tends to work against the interests of a country like Scotland, which has special problems in need of special solutions. Ministries are at least aware that too much neglect of Scottish claims may lead to political trouble. Corporations are less directly affected in this way, especially when they regard themselves, not as social services, but as enterprises for the making of profits. They sometimes seem, at least to a jaundiced eye, to prefer their own interests to those of Scotland. If they take special circumstances into account, it is to insist on Scotland paying higher charges than the rest of the country (as in the case of fuel). When Scotland enjoys natural advantages they may prevent her from reaping the full benefit.

We may take the Forestry Commission to illustrate this tendency, although it is a Corporation for which the Secretary of State for Scotland is supposed to have a joint responsibility. More than half the land to be afforested lies in Scotland, but the Commission's headquarters and its main research centres are kept resolutely in the South. When its headquarters were obliged to leave London, they moved no farther away than Basingstoke. The treatment of staff seems even more revealing. In 1955 the Professor of Forestry in Edinburgh wrote to the press saying that 'it seems to be the policy to send Scottish graduates to England and Wales and English and Welsh graduates to Scotland, irrespective of whether they are trained at a Scottish, Welsh, or English University'. In spite of demands for clarification no answer, so far as I know, has been given.

These Corporations perform so many functions that it is difficult to generalise about them, though they seldom fail to congratulate themselves on the many benefits they confer on

Scotland. Some of them, in the course of nationalisation, have taken over Scottish enterprises, and we may attempt a rough outline of what seems to happen in such cases (and also in take-over bids by large private businesses from the South). These Scottish enterprises, whether owned by private companies or by town-councils or by co-operative societies, usually have – or rather had – relatively larger reserves than corresponding enterprises in England. First of all, these reserves are swept over the Border to London, never to return; and protests are silenced by the familiar rebuke; 'Don't you realise, brother, that we must all learn to sacrifice ourselves in the interests of the wider whole?' When the take-over is complete, the staff is doubled, and two men are made to do the work that was efficiently done by one man before. Grandiose schemes are started at great expense with a flourish of trumpets and a lack of elementary caution. Then some genius in London discovers that the new branch office is no longer profitable. The formerly prosperous Scottish enterprise is closed down; the best of the workers are offered jobs in England; the less good become unemployed; and Scotland is deprived of necessary services – not to mention skilled men – which she can ill afford to lose.

You may say that this is a one-sided caricature; but there are more than enough happenings of this kind to make it a recognisable caricature.

Besides the Ministries (with their many Departments) and the Corporations responsible to them, there may also be intermediate organisations exercising control in Scotland. Let us take a comparatively simple example, though I cannot be sure of getting even this right. If the Scots consider an air-service inadequate, they have first to persuade British European Airways or some other line that they should fly an additional route. The Air Transport Licensing Board has to hear proposals from airlines wishing to fly particular routes, and must either accept or reject. There is an appeal to a Commissioner who advises the Board of Trade. The Minister can refuse to accept his advice, though in practice he seldom does so except where international routes (which may be the most important for Scottish business) are concerned. Thus a whole series of London hurdles may have to be surmounted. It is hard to see why there should not be an independent Scottish airline which could do for Scotland what Aer Lingus does so successfully for Ireland.

One further point should be noted. There are also other organs of administration which we may call 'Consumers' Councils' (though they go by different names), and it looks as if these might enable the Scots to exercise some influence, at least on the 'regional' outposts of the London Ministries and Corporations. Such a hope would be in the main illusory. In the last resort – I have to speak very generally – the members of these Councils are themselves chosen by London; and their chairman may be partially silenced by being made a director on the board of the Corporation he is supposed to criticise.

There is yet one other device which can be used for the thwarting of Scottish influence on the administration. This is the 'Committe of Enquiry', as we may call it, though in its most august form it may be dubbed a Royal Commission as, for example, the Royal Commission on Scottish Affairs. The members of these Committees are chosen by the Government, and judicious selection may often, though not always, be able to secure whatever result is desired. Unwanted recommendations, and even undesired evidence, can be ruled out by carefully restricted terms of reference. If these devices do not wholly succeed, the enquiry itself takes a long enough time for outraged feelings to die down; and in any case its report can be pigeon-holed for consideration later. If some constructive enterprise is being examined, the delay may mean the dispersal of skilled staff and machinery, and so may make the project itself less profitable, and consequently more easy to condemn.

Besides all this elaborate machinery we have enjoyed since 1965 a supreme 'Overlord' – the Board of Incomes and Prices. However this may function in the future, it is in a position to ensure that Scottish workers – and even teachers – will never get higher remuneration or earlier increases than English ones. No doubt it could also do the reverse; but this would be a breach of the ordinary practice.

This vast structure of administration has not been devised in order to subjugate Scotland. On the contrary – apart from the

Secretary of State and the Scottish office – it has been imposed on Britain as a whole. What I am saying is that in fact it has given London an increasingly powerful strangle-hold on the life, including the economic life, of Scotland. No wonder that the Scot – if I may quote again from the report of the Royal Commission – begins to criticise 'what he regards, however erroneously, as the English government'.

It may be objected that since this new and vast machinery is applied to all parts of Britain, the more remote regions of England – that is, remote from London – might also be expected to suffer and complain. Why does all this outcry come from Scotland alone?

In actual fact the outlying regions of England – the North-East, the North-West, and even Cornwall – have suffered while London and the Midlands have grown ever more prosperous; and Lord Hailsham, now Mr. Quintin Hogg, was deputed to meet some of their complaints, at least in the North, by what was claimed to be an entirely new effort of 'regional planning'. But these regions have not enjoyed a long history of political independence, nor have they had, like Scotland, to battle against alien encroachments for centuries, both before and after the Union of the Crowns in 1603. History cannot be arbitrarily swept aside – least of all by English critics who attach so much importance to their own. Even geographically the situation in Scotland is very different from that in England and offers different problems to be solved. Besides, the myopic vision of the London official appears to descry the land very dimly north of Stratford-upon-Avon, while Scotland seems at times almost to be out of sight.

It may be added that in unofficial British or 'national' organisations, such as the Trade Unions or the corresponding bodies representing employers, or even the British Federation of University Women, claims from Scotland are apt to be received with disfavour. When the Government decided to transfer the headquarters of the Post Office Savings Bank to Glasgow, the Trade Union concerned, not only opposed the decision fiercely, but also threatened to expel a Scottish branch which refused to support the view of the English majority.

6. *The Royal Commission*

The terms of reference given in 1952 to the Royal Commission on Scottish Affairs were drawn up so as to exclude any discussion of self-government for Scotland. The only topic to be considered was 'administrative devolution'. Even under this head the working of the nationalised industries could not be examined, and there is nothing in the Report on the burning question of railways. 'Parliamentary devolution', as it was called, was expressly ruled out by the Secretary of State on the ground that this was a matter, not for a Commission, but for Parliament itself.

Here again we meet the assumption that a predominantly English Parliament can deal best with the future of Scotland if no attempt is made to discover and examine the opinions and desires of the Scottish people. The decision was particularly bitter because the Commission itself was set up after two million Scotsmen had signed the Covenant demanding 'a Parliament with adequate legislative authority in Scottish affairs'. Feeling at the time was running high, and it was generally believed, and only half-heartedly denied, that the Commission – like the earlier Catto Committee on Scottish Financial and Trade Statistics – was primarily a device to let this feeling die down and to postpone the problem indefinitely.

Within the limits of their remit the Commission did reasonably well. They claimed that unless there was conclusive evidence to the contrary, Scottish business should be disposed of in Scotland. When it had to be dealt with by English Ministers, these Ministers and their officials should recognise that Scotland is a nation and that she entered voluntarily into union with England as a partner and not as a dependency. Furthermore, Scotland's needs and point of view should be taken into account at all stages in the formulation and execution of policy, that is to say, when policy is being considered, when policy is decided, and when policy is announced. Effective arrangements should be made to ensure that Scotland's voice is heard at all these stages.

The principles laid down by the Commission are in themselves impeccable, but do they do more than express a pious hope that quantities of oil may be poured into our creaking and top-heavy administrative machine? The very hope itself, if we are to trust past experience, would seem to be out of touch with reality. Only a very holy simplicity could expect over-burdened English Ministers and their officials to stop at every stage in their already difficult task in order to ascertain and weigh the peculiar needs of Scotland. It would seem so much more natural to let the Scots decide these matters for themselves.

7. Northern Ireland

That this would in many cases be possible is shown by the example of Northern Ireland, where a local Government and a local Parliament have privileges which Scotsmen can only envy. Ulster is neither a viable country nor one which had a long history of independence as a kingdom. Yet it was given these privileges with the utmost expedition because, as it seems to some Scotsmen, special English – or, if you prefer it, British – interests were at stake. Besides, although Ulstermen had a reasonable case (not unfamiliar to Scotsmen) against being dominated by a larger country to the south with different traditions, they had not let their case rest merely on rational arguments. They had loudly proclaimed that 'Ulster will fight, and Ulster will be right'.

There are eight Government Departments under the control of Ministers responsible to the Parliament of Northern Ireland. The mere fact that they are so responsible is a great advantage denied to Scotland. Furthermore, although some of the Departments perform functions similar to those exercised by the Scottish Office, there are others which have much more extensive powers. In particular, Northern Ireland has a Ministry of Commerce responsible for industry and trade inside its own territory. It has also a Ministry of Labour and National Insurance. The functions of these important Ministries are in Scotland controlled from London.

This topic was a delicate one for a Royal Commission narrowly restricted by its terms of reference. It could do little more than utter the platitude that these differences had their origin in past history. It also declared that in Scotland devolution was exemplified by the presence of her Secretary of State in the British Cabinet – although manifestly the word 'devolution' is here being used in a totally different sense. Finally it referred in a gingerly way to the forbidden topic of Home Rule by mentioning what it called 'a form of devolution more readily apparent'. If this were adopted, the Commission 'felt' – and 'felt' rather than 'thought' seems to be the appropriate word – that this would inevitably reduce the prestige and standing of Scotland and her representation in Parliament at Westminster, and would thereby weaken her voice in British and world affairs. Why this surprising result should be inevitable was not explained.

The burden laid on the unfortunate Secretary of State is indeed heavy. In addition to his other innumerable duties he should defend the special interests of Scotland in the British Cabinet wherever these may be involved – that is to say, in almost everything. We can picture his heroic efforts to do this in a body of Englishmen impatient to get on with business that is already beyond the capacity of finite human beings. If he is not to become an intolerable nuisance, he will have to select very carefully the questions that are of paramount importance to Scotland and let the rest go by default. If this system is to be regarded as a form of devolution, it must be admitted – to adopt the language of the Commission – that it is not a 'readily apparent' one.

The voice of Scotland should be heard loud and clear if she is to be worthy of her past. The voice of one man, however able and courageous, in the secret meetings of a British Cabinet can never be any kind of substitute.

8. *Local Government*

We are sometimes assured that the voice of Scotland requires no special organ: it is adequately heard in the instruments of local government, in town councils and other local authorities.

This is a strange suggestion: it puts forward one of those principles which no one would dream of applying to any other nation in the world, even the most primitive.

The local authorities contain some able, and a few supremely able, men, but their official concern is with local, rather than national, interests. Even in local matters their powers are being steadily curtailed. Former functions have been taken over either by Government Departments or through newer agencies for gas, electricity, and so on. Other functions, such as housing and education, are shared with Government Departments from which the local authorities receive sums of money necessary to supplement the rates. So far from being able to criticise civil servants, it is civil servants who, quite properly, are able to criticise them – and even within limits to control them.

In any case what is badly needed is an elected national body which would be in a position to check and control the local authorities. To give one minor example, some local authorities are working havoc with the old stone houses of Scotland and replacing them with gimcrack erections which have no place in Scottish tradition and are doubtfully suited to the climate. They are said in these matters to take the advice of sanitary engineers; and the training of these gentlemen, at least in Scotland, does not commonly include a course in aesthetics. It has been widely alleged that some sanitary engineers are so hostile to traditional buildings that they prefer to drive roads precisely where this gives them an excuse for pulling down a row of stone cottages which could easily be remodelled at very little expense. This seems to be part of the campaign to iron out local differences and make every place look like every other. Every day we seem to hear of some old building being destroyed in the name of progress, and it is melancholy that such decisions should be in the hands of local authorities without any further appeal. We have not so many treasures in Scotland that we can afford to lose them.

So far from being substitutes for a Scottish Parliament, local authorities need to be supplemented by such a Parliament if they are to work in the interests of Scotland as a whole.

9. *Lamp-posts in Ecclefechan*

It may be replied that Scotland has her own representatives in the British Parliament and so should be able to deal efficiently with the vagaries of local authorities and of any other authorities alleged to work against the interests of Scotland as a whole. Is it not precisely the function of question-time in Parliament to deal with matters such as these?

The members for Scottish constituencies try their best to make use of these opportunities, which occur, I believe, as often as one day in six weeks; but what they do in this way is not welcomed enthusiastically by the House of Commons. Some years ago the Speaker himself protested against the number of their questions, and in this respect contrasted Scotland unfavourably with – you will have guessed it – Yorkshire. More recently Mr Emanuel Shinwell, to the delight of many English members, chided the Scots for their parochialism and expressed contempt for questions dealing with 'the construction of a lamp-post in Auchtermuchty or Ecclefechan'. But this alleged parochialism, however irritating, does not spring from any innate petty-mindedness in Scotsmen as such. It arises because they are deprived of any suitable body in which necessary questions about the administration of Scotland can appropriately be asked.

Scotsmen are put in such a position that they can get their special problems considered only by making themselves unpleasant, and this leads to what may be called government by snarls. Then their procedure is condemned as unreasonable. They have been charged, for example, on the B.B.C. with what was elegantly called 'griping' – a recent addition to our polite vocabulary. But what is the alternative? The gentleman who brought these charges told Scotsmen that instead of this they should get to know the right people and work behind the scenes. Apart from the fact that back-stairs intrigue is alien to the Scottish temper, this is a strange substitute for open and responsible government.

10. *The fundamental complaint*

Although something has been said here of the economic evils from which Scotland suffers under the present dispensation, it should not be thought that these are the only, or even the main, source of dissatisfaction. In the few discussions of Home Rule permitted by the B.B.C. in Scotland, the opponents of self-government have sometimes contrived to give the impression that it is all a matter of pounds, shillings, and pence. As a result we had to listen to tedious and inconclusive arguments showing that if a change were made, a sixpence might be lost here but would be gained there, and so on indefinitely. This reduces the whole subject to a farce. Even in their most depressed state few Scotsmen can believe that they would manage their own affairs less economically and efficiently than is done by the present system of remote control; but the question is one that goes much deeper. The fundamental complaint is that Scotland is being insidiously deprived of all control over her own destiny. The spiritual effects of this may be more disastrous than the economic ones.

CHAPTER VI

THE LAW

The Law is the true embodiment of everything that's excellent.
It has no kind of fault or flaw,
And I, my Lords, embody the Law.

W. S. Gilbert

1. *Scots Law and English Law*

Under the Treaty of Union, as has already been noted, Scotland was guaranteed the preservation of her Law (so far as this concerned Private Right) and the independence of her Courts of Justice. Alterations were to be made in her Laws only for 'the evident utility of the subjects within Scotland'. We have seen how inadequate for this purpose is the legislative machinery of a predominantly English Parliament, whose members can even boast that they know nothing of the Law of Scotland. Although it is perhaps less obvious, the institution of appeals to the House of Lords, besides undermining the independence of the Scottish Courts and imposing heavy expenses on Scottish litigants, worked also as a device for altering the Law of Scotland and adjusting it to English models. With the best will in the world – and this was not always present – English judges, interpreting a law of which they knew nothing, could hardly be expected to do anything other than assimilate the Law of Scotland to that of England, even when the result was inconsistency and confusion. Scots Law, like so many other Scottish institutions, was denied its own natural development in accordance with its own principles. As was said by the late Lord Cooper of Culross, we have confided the last word on a Roman system of law to a court whose members are drawn predominantly from the opposite camp of Anglo-American law. Indeed for a century and a half the situation was much worse, since during this period the members of the court were drawn, not predominantly, but exclusively, from the opposite camp.

It must again be emphasised, since there is so much ignorance on this subject, that Scots Law, like other European developments of Roman Law, differs from English Law in its fundamental principles; and that to assimilate it to English Law must inevitably produce internal incoherence (sometimes glorified as 'greater flexibility').

Continental lawyers have suggested that if Britain were to enter the European Common Market, Scots Law might be used as a sort of bridge between English and European Law. Such a suggestion awakens no echo in London: when a committee was set up to consider the legal implications of the proposed political change, it was composed entirely of English lawyers. There is a fear in Scotland that closer connexions with Europe might be used to substitute English for Scots Law in Scottish dealings with continental countries. This is presumably one of the reasons why a Scottish judge remarked that if Britain were to enter the Common Market, it might be necessary to have a new declaration of Scottish independence. In any negotiations for such an entry Scottish legal interests should be represented in order to ensure that no agreement should prejudice the system of Law guaranteed by the Treaty of Union. But there seems little hope that these (or any other special Scottish interests) will be represented at all.

2. *Differences in practice*

Apart from differences in their theoretical approach the two systems of law differ fundamentally in their practical working; and Scots lawyers are apt to claim that their system is, not only the more logical, but also the more just and more merciful: it is said, for example, when compared with English Law, to show more concern for the liberties of the individual and less for the rights of property; to be more bound by principles and less tied to precedents; to lay more stress on matters of substance and less on questions of technicality. Indeed in certain respects, few perhaps in number but of fundamental importance, it is even claimed that until recent years the Law of England was centuries behind the Law of Scotland.

The Crown, for example, has in Scotland always been responsible for breaches of contract and is more strictly bound by statute than it is in England. Landlords have had weightier responsibilities to their tenants and less protection against trespassers. Divorce has been allowed on two grounds since the Reformation, and in this respect women have been given equal treatment with men, whereas in England divorce (except by a Private Act of Parliament) was forbidden till the Nineteenth Century and women have gained equality of treatment only in very recent years. Illegitimate children became legitimate through the subsequent marriage of their parents – a measure introduced in England as late as 1926. Wives and children were protected against being completely disinherited by the arbitrary will of a husband and father – another measure only recently introduced into England in a more limited form. Cheap and speedy justice has long been within the reach of any one through the Sheriff Courts in a way said to be still unknown in England.

Similar differences are to be found in the Criminal Law of the two countries. The strange crime of attempted suicide was never recognised in Scotland; and until recently any one anxious to drown himself in the river Tweed was well advised to try this from the northern bank; for there the most he could ever be charged with is a breach of the peace. In Scottish criminal trials the prosecution has to build up its case gradually from evidence without the initial speech which in England may colour the mind of the jury in a way from which it never recovers; and the defence is allowed the last word after the final speech for the prosecution. Until the recent softening of the public attitude to crime and its punishment, the penalties inflicted on the guilty were less than those imposed in England for the same crimes. It is noteworthy that immediately after the Union one of the first changes made in Scots Law by the new British Parliament was to bring the Law of Treason into line with the harsher law of England.

In Scotland the right to prosecute for crime has long been

almost exclusively in the hands of public prosecuting authorities – England appears to be unique in the civilised world in leaving this right mainly in the hands of private individuals and the police (who themselves were supposed to act as private individuals). In murder cases the Scottish system avoids the premature publicity which arises in England from the preliminary trial before the magistrates, where the case for the prosecution becomes known often without any statement of the case for the defence.

In England the coroner's inquest often adds yet a further complication to a subsequent criminal trial, and even apart from this may cause unnecessary pain to the relatives of the deceased. The fact that there are no coroners in Scotland, though too often unknown to writers of detective fiction, means that painful publicity at a time of tragedy is avoided, and there seem to be no great counterbalancing disadvantages.

These brief allusions to a complicated and controversial subject are not made in order to decry the laws of England, but simply to suggest that the assimilation of Scots Law to English models may not necessarily be for 'the evident utility of the subjects within Scotland'.

3. The House of Lords

It was this un-English system of Scots Law that was put, immediately after the Union, under the paramount authority of a purely English House of Lords. Even the counsel who pleaded before it were at first mainly English. The proceedings were carried on in the pure language of the English Law – the only language the Court understood – and the decision had in the end to be translated, whether well or ill, into Scottish terms unless, as sometimes happened, they were set forth in terms which were meaningless in Scotland and consequently incapable of being carried out. In their difficulties the House of Lords sometimes referred questions of law to the English judges, as they did in purely English cases. At other times they sent the decisions under appeal back to the Scottish courts in order to have them restated – a procedure which added to the already oppressive costs of litigation. For a short time Lord

Chancellor Lyndhurst, rightly feeling himself incompetent, delegated his work to two so-called 'Speakers', who also knew nothing of Scots Law. The gentlemen so entitled were not permitted to speak, but at the close of an argument they made a sign and retired in silence. In an adjoining room they expressed their opinions, and having done so returned to the Woolsack to resume their taciturnity. Then a lay figure, who need not even have heard the argument, would rise to his feet and might gravely move that the judgement complained of be reversed. This method was more suited to a comic opera than to a court of law. Fortunately it did not last long, but it lasted long enough to bring discredit on the highest tribunal in the country.

Even if we discount the contention that appeals to the House of Lords were instituted in breach of the letter and spirit of the Treaty of Union, it can hardly be denied that the method of conducting these appeals was indefensible from the start. The situation was aggravated by the fact that the members of this august tribunal were as ignorant of Scottish conditions and traditions as they were of Scots Law. Because English lawyers seemed unable to conceive a Church except as either a department of State or a trust company, the Church of Scotland had to wait until 1921 before it could realise an ideal of liberty which had been pursued continuously since the Reformation.

The system threw a very heavy additional burden on successive Lord Chancellors of England, and the best of them were well aware of their ignorance and sometimes oppressed by their responsibilities. Thus Lord Erskine, although himself a Scotsman, could say: 'I know something of the law, but of Scots Law I am as ignorant as a native of Mexico; and yet I am quite as learned in it as any of your Lordships'. Similar remarks could be quoted from Lord Chancellor Brougham and Lord Chancellor Chelmsford. As to the burden, we need only quote Lord Eldon's observation about Scottish appeals: 'When I became Chancellor the duty of deciding such causes was most extremely painful and requiring infinite labour.'

In spite of these inevitable hardships Lord Chancellor after Lord Chancellor faced his impossible task with true bull-dog courage. Some, like Lord Lyndhurst, and even on occasion

Lord Cranworth, showed a becoming tendency to hesitate about reversing Scots decisions. Others were less modest, and their attitude is revealed in some memorable observations.

In 1830 Lord Wynford made the following statement: 'I protest against what has been said in another place, namely that English lawyers are not competent to advise your Lordships on a question of Scots Law. As well might they say that one who had studied logic in Edinburgh would not be able to reason on any question of morality or policy that arose in England'.

In 1802 Lord Alvanley remarked: 'Here we have no question peculiar to the law of Scotland. The law as to nuisances must be the same in both countries'. In actual fact the case being considered did not purport to be concerned with nuisance, and the laws as to nuisances differ very greatly in Scotland and England.

In 1845 Lord Campbell, in spite of his Scottish origin, expanded this bold generalisation. 'The law', he declared, 'must be the same in all countries where law has been considered as a science'.

But perhaps the gem of the collection is to be found in a statement by Lord Cranworth in 1858. Having first reviewed a series of English cases in accordance with the usual practice, he turned finally to the Scottish authorities and said this: 'But if such be the law of England, on what ground can it be argued not to be the law of Scotland? The law as established in England is founded on principles of universal application, not on any peculiarities of English jurisprudence'.

Attitudes of this kind could not but be adverse to the rational development of law in Scotland. They also illustrate in a limited sphere a more general English failure to recognise Scotland as a partner with traditions and problems of her own.

4. *Legislation by English judges*

One example of the way in which the House of Lords could in effect legislate, and legislate badly, for Scotland may be taken from the case in which Lord Cranworth produced the remarkable statement that has just been quoted. The problem to be considered was whether a master could be held responsible for

damage incurred by one of his employees through the careless-
ness of another. This was denied in English Law on the rather
odd principle that servants must be supposed to have contem-
plated the risks of their employment before they undertook it.
Scots Law took the opposite view and held that the master was
responsible in the case of a servant just as he would be where
damage had been incurred by any third party. In the case of
Bartonshill Coal Co. v. *Reid* this principle had been followed by a
unanimous Court of Session; but its judgement was reversed
by Lord Cranworth on the ground, as we have seen, that the
English rule was founded on principles of universal application
and so could not but be the law of Scotland. The result was
that an irksome rule plagued Scotland for nearly a hundred
years until English lawyers woke up to the badness of their own
rule and procured its abolition in 1948 to the general satisfaction
on both sides of the Border.

There was another case even odder, if less harmful in its
effects. The question here was the standard of care owed by an
occupier to persons entering his premises – care to secure that
they did not come to any injury as a result of the state of the
premises or of anything done on them for which the occupier
was in law responsible as occupier. English Law distinguished
different categories of persons entering an occupier's premises
(as 'invitee', 'licensee', or 'trespasser'). These categories were
not recognised in Scots Law, but they were imposed on it in
1929 by a decision of the House of Lords reversing a decision of
the Court of Session. Here again the English rule was finally
recognised to be unsatisfactory and was abolished in England in
1957. The absurdity then arose that while England now
enjoyed the former advantages of Scots Law, the Scottish
Courts continued to be troubled with the irksome English
rule imposed on them arbitrarily by the House of Lords. It was
not till two years later that a measure was introduced to
restore what had always been the Common Law of Scotland.

These two examples – one of them very recent – are instances
of changes in Scots Law made directly by decisions of the House
of Lords. Not unnaturally under the circumstances, there were
also changes made indirectly by the House of Lords through its

influence on Parliament. One of the best known of these was the introduction into Scotland of juries in civil cases. This was done in 1815 on the English model, mainly, it is alleged, in the hope that the work of the House of Lords would be made easier. This innovation was bitterly regretted by Sir Walter Scott, and it has irked Scottish lawyers right down to the present time; it has to-day the curious result that civil juries are drawn exclusively from the citizens of Edinburgh and the Lothians. As the civil jury has now been almost abandoned in England except for one or two special types of action, there may perhaps be some hope that in the course of time Scotland may be freed from an alien system which should never have been imposed on her. Here too England may ultimately catch up with the old Scottish system, but why should Scotland have so long to suffer?

5. *Reform*

It would be tedious to go on piling up grievances or claiming further advantages for the Scottish legal system. Enough has been said to suggest that Scots Law has been humane and rational and in certain respects pioneering: it reveals the liberal spirit of Scotland and certainly is in no way to be despised; and indeed it does credit, not only to Scots lawyers, but also to the old Scottish Parliament, which is too often dismissed as wholly ineffective. Enough has been said to suggest also that Scots Law has received very ill treatment in the past and even in the present, and that the English attitude to Scotland has not always shown that consideration which is due to a partner in a free union.

Perhaps we may add one brief illustration of the pioneering spirit of Scots Law. From A.D. 1425 onwards the Faculty of Advocates met annually to appoint 'Counsel for the Poor' to defend for love of God any poor creature who 'for fault of knowledge or expenses cannot or may not follow his cause'. This ancient ceremony came to an abrupt end in 1965. After more than five hundred years the English had at last caught up and introduced a Legal Aid Scheme of their own, and the Scots instead of having their own venerable law amended where this was necessary were obliged to adopt the latest model from London in its place.

There has been no attempt here to make a balanced comparison between the Scottish and English systems, which is obviously a matter only for experts; and in any case it is not necessary to disparage one system in order to praise another.

But what are we to say of the present situation as a whole? Some eminent Scottish lawyers accept it with satisfaction while others do not; but it may be observed that elderly gentlemen who have risen to great eminence in their profession may be a little too ready to defend the excellence of the *status quo*. There is no doubt that Scotland requires some highest court of appeal, though it is hard to see why this should not have been purely Scottish from the beginning. At present there are Scottish judges who, as members of the House of Lords, usually, though not necessarily, sit for Scottish appeals so that the House of Lords is no longer without the indispensable expert advice which was lacking for so long.

The main suggestion for improvement is that for Scottish appeals the House of Lords should sit in Edinburgh. It is difficult to see why it should not then have a majority of Scottish judges, though this possibility seems not to have been considered. A move of this kind would certainly do much to placate Scottish feeling and to reduce the expenses of Scottish litigants. The Faculty of Advocates would be deprived of jaunts to London at the expense of their clients and might be expected to regard the proposal with mixed feelings. Otherwise it would be very welcome in Scotland and would do something to make up for injustices in the past.

Such a reform, however, would still be incomplete. What is required is a Parliament in Edinburgh which would be familiar with Scottish conditions and would be able to develop the Law of Scotland in accordance with its own traditions and with the spirit of the Scottish people.

CHAPTER VII

THE FRAMEWORK OF TAXATION

In this world nothing can be said to be certain,
except death and taxes
Benjamin Franklin

1. *Economic grievances*

For many years before the First World War Scotland was in certain respects one of the richest countries in the world – even richer than England according to some estimates of wealth per head of the population. On the same basis England at that time was thought to be richer than America. Whether these estimates are accepted or not, it seems certain that since then Scottish wealth has steadily declined in comparison with that of England. This is not an agreeable situation when the disparity seems likely to increase. But Scotsmen are inclined to flatter themselves that they are not without a capacity to meet the hardships inevitable in a difficult and changing world. Their fundamental grievance in economic as in other matters is that they are no longer able to control their own progress or regress, as to some extent they could in an age of Free Trade and *laissez-faire*. Now that governments determine more and more the economic progress of a country, it is widely believed that the economic troubles of Scotland spring at least in part from the policies of a London Government whose main concern is always with England, and primarily with the South of England.

A good man may learn to content himself with a modest estate. What he finds intolerable is that his estate should be mismanaged at great expense, and without any proper audit, by a trustee who insists on doling out to him his own money in small packages and on controlling every detail of his expenditure. This is the position of a ward, and not of a grown up. What is resented in Scotland is the continual expansion of an English tutelage whose incompetence, if it is nothing worse, is sufficiently established by its results.

It is impossible to examine economic grievances here in a way that would be even remotely adequate. The subject is full of pitfalls and would require an elaborate discussion of statistics, which are too often incomplete or even unobtainable. The most that can be done is to sketch very crudely the sort of framework within which a detailed discussion should be carried out.

2. *Government revenue from Scotland*

It is not possible to determine with precision the revenue which the British Government draws from Scotland. All surtax is collected in England; and Customs or Excise Duty on articles consumed in Scotland may be collected in England (and *vice versa*). Apparently too where income tax is collected 'at the source', as it is on the income from almost all investments, 'the source' is taken to be London. Obviously enough, if calculations depended solely on the place where taxes are collected, the contribution of Scotland to revenue would be underestimated. Hence there has to be what is called an 'adjustment' to give the 'true contribution'. The method of adjustment must be rough and ready at the best, and no one need be surprised if these adjustments have sometimes been received in Scotland with scepticism. If they are ignored altogether as not 'identifiable' – to use recent jargon – the result can only be a travesty.

Nevertheless returns, such as they are, of the revenue from Scotland were in fact published from 1893 to 1922, and again in 1932 and 1935. In 1952 the Catto Committee on Scottish Financial and Trade Statistics concluded, after prolonged investigations, that it was practicable to do what had so often been done in the past – to make a return segregating government revenue and expenditure in Scotland: they even recommended that this should be done annually. A return was in fact made for the year 1952-3. Since then the silence has been unbroken.

Thus we have had no official figures since 1953, and it must be unconvincing to base precise conclusions on imprecise unofficial estimates. For 1952-3 the official estimates of revenue drawn from Scotland was £409,694,000, while the revenue from England was £3,817,401,000. It is unlikely that the Scottish revenue was overestimated. But even as they stand, the figures show how feeble is the argument that Scotland is too poor to support Home Rule, or even independence. In comparison with the smaller nations of Europe, let alone of other continents, she is still relatively rich.

Between 1935 and 1953 the revenue drawn from Scotland increased from £67,000,000 to £409,000,000, and to-day it may be more – perhaps very much more – than £600,000,000. This increase may arise partly from depreciation in the value of the pound, and partly from the general increase in taxation. In any case a great part of the whole national income of Scotland – some say as much as a third – is now at the disposal of the British Government. Nothing like this has ever happened before. It is not surprising if some Scotsmen think Scotland might fare better if she had more control over her own money.

3. *Government expenditure in Scotland*

The fundamental question to be asked is how much of the revenue raised in Scotland is also spent in Scotland. Does Scotland get her fair share? To this we can get no clear answer.

Here again we must go back for general principles to the last official estimates – those of 1952-3. These distinguished between 'local expenditure' and 'general expenditure'. Local expenditure is, for our present purpose, expenditure on Scottish services; but there is of course similar local expenditure on services to England and Wales. General expenditure is expenditure on what are known as 'general services'.

'Local services' in Scotland may be taken to cover such services as health, housing, roads, forestry, food and agriculture, national insurance and assistance, and so on. The expenditure on these Scottish services in 1952–3 was estimated at £207,000,000 – that is, at slightly more than half the revenue from Scotland. The other half went on 'general services' for the benefit of the United Kingdom and its people as a whole. Among these are included, for example, the defence services and the service of the National Debt.

These over-heads, if we may so term the expenditure on general services, may seem at first sight to be rather heavy; but it is right that Scotland should pay her share of the defence services and of the interest on the National Debt. This she has never grudged.

In the light of these distinctions the question we are asking breaks down into two separate questions.

Firstly, as regards 'local expenditure' is a fair proportion of this allotted to Scottish services?

Secondly, as regards 'general expenditure' does Scotland get her fair share of the benefits provided by the general services?

The second question may seem obscure and even unanswerable, yet to answer the first question and ignore the second would be to give a false picture of the situation. We all benefit alike – to take only one example – from the money spent in the defence of our common country; but if in spending this money a preference were given to England in assigning government contracts, maintaining naval establishments, and so on, Scotland would get less than her fair share of the benefits from this part of government expenditure. If a similar preference were commonly shown throughout the whole field of general services, the total treatment of Scotland might be grossly unfair even if she received a fair proportion of government expenditure on her local services. This is why our second question has to be answered as well as the first. The British Government, however, does not supply us with the figures necessary to give a satisfactory answer. Information on this subject – to quote the words of the Royal Commission on Scottish Affairs – 'is not available'.

There is a further difficulty. How do we decide what is fair treatment as between England and Scotland? If we may keep a firm grip on the obvious, it would be unfair to Scotland if all her revenues were spent in England; and equally it would be unfair to England if all Scottish revenues were spent in Scotland without any contribution to general services for Britain as a whole. But how do we strike a fair balance?

The nearest thing to a principle for distributing government expenditure is to be found in what is known as the 'Goschen formula'. According to this formula Scotland should receive eleven-eightieths of what is spent in England and Wales. This was fixed in 1888, when Scottish votes had begun to exercise real influence in Parliament. We must here assume that it is reasonably fair. In regard to the Scottish local services its present application is obscure. As for the general services, it seems to have no application there at all.

4. *Expenditure on Scottish local services*

If eleven-eightieths of government expenditure on local services in England – that is, in England and Wales – were assigned as a lump sum to a Scottish Parliament empowered to use it in accordance with Scottish needs, this might do substantial justice between the two countries, so far at least as local services are concerned. Unfortunately this is the one solution which politicians in Westminster are resolute to reject.

On the other hand, if the Goschen formula were to be strictly applied under each separate heading of expenditure on Scottish local services, the position would be most unsatisfactory. First of all you would decide in every case what is appropriate to the needs of England, and then assume that a fixed proportion of this will meet the needs of Scotland, although these, for geographical and other reasons, may be very different.

Something like this seems to be the accepted ideal, but a system so absurd could not be strictly imposed in practice. Hence the application of the formula is modified in ways that are arbitrary and obscure.

Sometimes the formula seems to be used as a maximum beyond which Scotland is not allowed to go. In education, for example, the Goschen formula is applied in a way far too complicated to be explained here; but the result appears to be that Scottish teachers, even if more highly qualified, must not be paid more, but may be paid less, than their counterparts in the State Schools of England. In some fields, notably in that of law and order, Scotland is allowed considerably less than her due proportion: it is a little hard to see why Scottish judges (including sheriffs) should be paid so much less than comparable judges in England. In other fields, sometimes as a result of past neglect, Scotland may for a time receive more than her due proportion, especially if we include loans at a high rate of interest – loans which may themselves be derived from Scottish taxation or Scottish savings. Sometimes the formula is used to show how well Scotland is treated, as when Scottish roads are allowed slightly more than the Goschen proportion. It seems to be forgotten that Scotland is more than half the size of England and Wales put together. No doubt other considerations must enter in: sparsely populated mountainous areas require fewer roads, though these are more costly to build and to maintain; and so on. But, broadly speaking, this is one field where the Goschen formula may well be inadequate to Scotland's needs. Over large areas the Highlands have to suffer from narrow single-track roads which would not be tolerated anywhere else: in some places they have no roads at all. Even if we supposed the present road system to be satisfactory, the needs of Scotland, which has 18 per cent. of the road mileage in Britain, cannot be adequately met by a slight improvement on the Goschen formula.

To an impartial observer all this must seem a strange way to finance local services in Scotland. If we apply the Goschen formula strictly, we, as it were, compel one brother in a family to wear clothes designed for another of a very different build. If we modify it, we lose even the apparent guarantee of justice and are at the mercy of arbitrary decisions taken in London.

A further source of dissatisfaction is to be found in the arbitrariness of the distinction between local and general services. One might have expected that the cultural interests of Scotland would count as a Scottish service and be supervised by a Scottish authority, even if it were only by the Secretary of State. For some unknown reason these interests (apart from school education) count as a general service, and so expenditure on them is controlled from London without regard to the Goschen formula.

There are bitter complaints that art collections, museums,

and libraries are starved in comparison with those in England and that the national galleries in Edinburgh are not given the special consideration they ought to have. Valuable works of art accepted in lieu of death duties, even if they come from Scotland, are ear-marked for London. Grants from the Arts Council change from year to year, but apart from some improvements made by Miss Jennie Lee in recent years the percentage allowed to Scotland has fallen steadily; and the whole of Scotland received in 1961–2 less than a quarter of the grant to Covent Garden. Even if we ignore the huge expenditure on London opera, Scotland is still allowed less than the Goschen proportion. When a vast sum was set aside to subsidise a history of the English Parliament, Scottish historians had to fight, and to fight hard, to secure a pittance for the history of the Scottish Parliament. No one would pretend that the two histories were of equal importance, but why should it be necessary for Scotsmen to struggle hard in order to get their modest needs met at all? And why should even culture be doled out to them by men whose interests are centred in the South?

The position of Scotland is naturally worse where her special needs have nothing corresponding to them in England. When the Secretary of State was requested in 1963 to grant a small subvention of some £800 a year for a badly needed English-Gaelic dictionary, it was at first ruled that he had no power to to give grants for such a purpose. Later on it was said that a grant could be given only by an Order in Council passed by the British Parliament, though this too was questioned and subsequently denied. So far as I know, no grant was ever made; but the whole incident shows how little power Scotland has to use her own revenues in her own cultural affairs.

These are only samples of the treatment from which Scotland suffers in matters deeply affecting her national pride. The sums involved may be relatively insignificant; but this makes it all the more strange that she should be humiliated so unnecessarily. She is put, as it were, in the position of a wife compelled to go to her husband pleading – or nagging – for every sixpence of her own money that she wishes to spend on her own concerns.

5. *Expenditure on general services*

When we turn to the general services and ask whether Scotland receives a fair share of the benefits from them, the problem becomes even more complicated and more obscure.

First of all, there is what may be called the inflow of revenue to London. Every capital draws wealth from the whole country of which it is the capital, and the Treaty of Union was bound to be London's gain and Edinburgh's loss. The chief government offices and the bulk of government officials – to take the most obvious example – must be in the capital, and Scotland must pay her share for their support.

It may seem that expenditure on the central machinery of government is sometimes unduly high. More than two million pounds were spent in repairing three houses in Downing Street, yet after the repairs were completed the floor of the Prime Minister's drawing room was found to be worm-eaten. Several ministers enjoy official houses in London, maintained, equipped, and furnished at the expense of the tax-payers. The Secretary of State for Scotland is less fortunate. Only in 1966 was he assigned for the first time an official house in Edinburgh. This had come to the Government from death duties on the estate of a Scottish nobleman; but it was left to some Scottish peers to pass round the hat for private contributions to its equipment and furnishing. Such meanness in relatively little things may be a sign of similar tendencies in graver matters; but this topic cannot be pursued further here.

The fundamental question is whether the outflow from London, particularly for the general services, is fairly distributed throughout the United Kingdom. It is widely believed in Scotland that the answer is in the negative. This belief has been held ever since the Union, but the question becomes more crucial when the Government absorbs and spends so large a part of the national income as it does to-day. It has been argued that every year as much as £100,000,000 or £150,000,000 – some say £200,000,000 – of Scottish revenue is drained off to be spent in England to the impoverishment of one country and the enrichment of the other.

Such an estimate must obviously depend on a vast mass of detail, and it is difficult to see how it can either be established or refuted without far more evidence than we are permitted to have.

An attempt to refute it was made in the winter of 1966–67, when the Conservatives circulated widely, and almost gleefully, some figures obtained from the Chancellor of the Exchequer. These purported to show that Scotland was subsidised by the central government to the tune of £80,000,000 a year.

The figures supplied have been condemned in detail as inaccurate and as inconsistent with other official statistics, but fundamental criticism of them must go deeper: they profess to deal only with 'identifiable' revenue and expenditure, and the expenditure examined is only what is spent on 'local services' in Scotland. As a picture of the whole situation they are valueless. If politicians do not face the fundamental questions I have tried to outline, they merely show that they do not even begin to understand what the problem is.

It is most unfortunate that these matters should be shrouded in mystery. Although the calculations might be complicated one would imagine that with a little trouble it would be possible to give at least a rough estimate of what actually happens, and even this might be revealing. Busy officials, especially those who find the claims of Scotland irritating, are naturally reluctant to make the necessary investigations; but it is not surprising if some Scotsmen suspect that refusal to supply information on this topic springs, at least in part, from a desire to conceal the truth.

Amid all this obscurity certain things are clear enough.

The very obscurity itself constitutes a kind of smoke-screen under which the wealth of Scotland can be steadily drained away for the benefit of England. This is bound to happen if London administrators out of sheer ignorance and indifference tend, however unconsciously, to favour the South when conflicting claims are evenly balanced. Indeed we might almost say it is what is bound to happen in any similar situation unless steps are taken to prevent it. A distinguished historian like Professor Trevor-Roper has no difficulty in seeing that if

Portugal had been governed from Burgos or Toledo, 'its economic life would no doubt have been drained away into the Spanish monarchy'.

There is certainly nothing in the present machinery of government to prevent this happening to Scotland – certainly not the Goschen formula.

Perhaps we may be allowed an illustration of what could happen, and may seem to happen, although the prevailing obscurity makes it impossible to be certain whether it does happen or not.

For many years the Westminster Parliament has borne the excessive unemployment in Scotland with commendable equanimity. When in 1963 the same unhappy fate – not for the first time – struck the North of England with almost equal force, the equanimity was disturbed. Lord Hailsham, as he was then, was deputed to do some regional planning – which, as he himself explained, had never been done before. This happened to coincide with the need for building new Polaris submarines. Two of these were assigned to the North-East of England, and two to the North-West. None was given to the Clyde, but a sop was thrown to Scotland by assigning their maintenance and repair to Rosyth, whose naval establishments had been allowed to run down between the two World Wars.

No private person is in a position to say that this was not a fair decision on commercial grounds. If doubts arise, they arise from memories of the way in which Scotland has to fight, too often unsuccessfully, for a fair share in government distribution of strip mills, research centres, and so on. What is indubitable is that this was a heavy blow to Scotland with effects continuing far beyond the moment. Apart from the immediate loss of contracts which would have helped unemployment on the Clyde, where the art of building submarines had long been practised, it meant that new skills would be developed in England which would constitute a compelling claim for all similar contracts in the future.

The effect of big decisions about government contracts is obvious, but the effect of a whole series of small decisions may be hardly less damaging. Even the long delays in coming to a decision may seriously affect Scotland's economy. Furthermore, if government ineptitude or indifference is one of the main factors that drain Scotland's wealth to the South, this has further consequences far beyond its immediate effects. A prosperous region acts as a magnetic field to attract more and more prosperity away from regions less prosperous; and it is generally recognised that this is what is happening now.

The Royal Commission on Scottish Affairs recommended that Departments should review at intervals the distribution of their expenditure on contracts as between the different component parts on the United Kingdom. Without special machinery to enforce it the recommendation can be only the amiable expression of a pious hope.

6. *The balance of payments*

If we may try to sum up the position, what we want to know is in the first place, the difference between the revenue drawn from Scotland and the total amount of government expenditure in Scotland, whether this is described as local or general. We may call this the balance of payments as between Scotland and England on government account. Unfortunately we have no means of knowing what this balance of payments is. The necessary figures are not available, nor does it seem likely that they ever will be.

What we want to know in the second place is whether this balance of payments is fair to Scotland. If we do not know what the balance of payments in fact is, we obviously cannot answer this question with any pretence at accuracy. Even if we did know the balance of payments, we should still have the problem of deciding what is fair treatment as between the two countries; and we should have to remember that Scotland ought to pay her share of government expenditure abroad. It is fair enough that a considerable part of Scottish revenue should be spent in England – this is the inevitable price of Union, a price that increases as government becomes more centralised. The case for Scotland is that, even if we make due allowance for all this, the amount of Scottish revenue spent in England is a great deal more than can reasonably be called fair.

If we are given neither exact figures nor an accepted standard of fairness, the obstacles to a rational discussion of the Scottish case become very great. It may be unjust to suspect that these obstacles rise from a desire to conceal the unfairness from which Scotland suffers. It is hardly unjust to say that they arise, at least in part, because London politicians are not interested in asking whether Scotland is fairly treated or not.

In all this obscurity one thing is clear. In matters of revenue and expenditure, as in administration generally, the system of government, so far as Scotland is concerned, is simply a muddle – it could never have been devised spontaneously by any one with any pretension to rationality. It almost looks as if it were designed to ensure that the interests of Scotland can never be considered as a whole. Such a system is almost bound to work out to Scotland's loss and England's gain.

This sad conclusion may seem to be confirmed – it is certainly not contradicted – by the way in which Scotland becomes relatively poorer as control increases from the South. It is confirmed more strongly, if we find the interests of Scotland neglected and thwarted in many spheres of action, both great and small, where detailed information is available. Examples of this treatment might be multiplied indefinitely, and a limited selection of them will be found in various chapters of the present book. In the absence of comprehensive figures these examples can never demonstrate the Scottish case with mathematical certainty; but their cumulative effect may be persuasive and even convincing, except to those who are determined not to be convinced.

It should not be forgotten that besides the method of taxation there are other financial controls by which the economic welfare of Scotland can be affected for the worse. If some trivial examples of these may be given, they may perhaps serve as straws to show which way the wind is blowing and may afford some relief from arguments that are painfully abstract.

7. *Straws in the wind*

One of the complaints made is concerned with Scottish savings. By savings banks and in other ways the Government borrows money at a low rate of interest and transfers it to London. Some of the money is later returned to Scotland at a higher rate of interest through loans which politicians too often describe as 'grants'. It is hard to see why the Scots should have to pay such heavy charges to London before their own savings can be used to meet the needs of their own country. This is all the more galling because even to-day the Scots save more per head of the population than is the practice in the affluent South. This ancient virtue is sometimes counted against them, as in the case of a benevolent gentleman from the Home Counties who wrote to a Scottish paper explaining that Scotland was doomed to poverty by saving money instead of spending it freely, as they did in England. He showed no awareness of the real reason why this might to some extent be true.

Other methods of extracting money from Scotland may be found in *Memories* by Mr. Thomas Johnston. I confine myself to a couple of samples.

In the year 1925 the city of Glasgow wished to extend its boundaries. In those days, though things may be better now, the claims of Glasgow and the opposing claims of other local authorities had to be examined in London. A tribunal was set up in Westminster Hall. It was made up of Members of Parliament, none of whom was a Scot, although it was reported that one of them had once visited a grouse moor and might therefore have been supposed to sin against the rule of absolute freedom from bias. So profound was their ignorance of the local conditions that another of them is said to have imagined the town of Yoker in Dumbartonshire to be a kind of drink. Over twenty advocates took part, and a large number of witnesses, skilled and unskilled, had to be examined at great expense. The entertainment lasted several weeks and, according to one account, is supposed to have cost Glasgow about £25 a minute. Mr. Johnston himself mentions an estimate of some £200,000 in all.

This extravagant method of dealing with local problems by way of private bills in Parliament was of long standing. In the early eighties of last century the Great Northern Railway Company had to spend £763,077 for obtaining leave to construct 245 miles of railway, or over £3,000 per mile. It seems not unreasonable to suppose that such affairs could have been arranged more economically in Edinburgh. Yet we are told to-day that the cost of a Scottish Parliament would be an impossible burden.

The second sample involves very little money, but is even more revealing. It is concerned with government attempts to bring tourists to Britain.

The story goes back to 1930, when Mr. Johnston was Under-Secretary at the Scottish Office. There then existed a British Travel Association, which received a subvention from the Treasury but, in his opinion, did less than justice to Scotland. He succeeded in forming a separate Scottish Tourist Development Association and even in securing its Goschen proportion of the Treasury grant, but only on one condition – it had to hand over to the British organisation 25 per cent of whatever money it raised by voluntary subscriptions and donations. Nobody seems to have observed that Scotland was already paying her full share of the Treasury grant through taxation. In return for surrendering 25 per cent of these voluntary contributions Scotland received from the Treasury the colossal sum of £345 18s. 7d.; and even this grant became less and less till in 1939 it was only £250. The fact that such an arrangement was accepted by Mr. Johnston and other distinguished Scottish Members of Parliament shows how even the most hard-headed Scots can allow themselves to be bemused by English claims.

The further adventures of the Scottish Tourist Board, though too variegated to be examined here, illustrate the difficulties of any similar Scottish Agency – including even the Scottish Council (Development and Industry), which struggles to perform the functions of a Ministry of Commerce such as is granted to Northern Ireland – in dealing with the British Government. There is usually a similar 'British' Agency to which the Scots must contribute by way of taxation. If they are content to merge completely with this, their interests will be neglected. If, on the other hand, the Scots set up an Agency of their own, they will have to support it by voluntary contributions bound to be insufficient. If they succeed in getting for it some special government grant, this will not only be inadequate, but will be tied up with arbitrary and hampering restrictions.

At one time the Scottish Tourist Board was granted as much as £41,000; but not a penny of this could be spent in England where so many potential tourists are to be found – it could be used for overseas publicity only. In 1964 the grant allowed was £15,000 a year, but it had to be spent exclusively for the advantage of the Highlands. Even this was suddenly withdrawn by a Conservative Secretary of State, who was presumably too intelligent to have done so except under pressure from the London Treasury. His Labour successor substituted a grant of a possible £25,000 a year for three years – but on condition that it should be devoted solely to research. When the Board was starting on its new job under Lord Kilbrandon, a chairman whom everybody trusted, the Conservative ex-Secretary suddenly declared during the General Election of 1966, apparently on his own initiative, that if he got back to office, he would appoint a full-time paid professional chairman, on the ground that Scottish Tourism – commonly supposed to be worth some £65,000,000 a year (much of it paid in dollars) – was 'big business'. The immediate result was that Lord Kilbrandon felt obliged to resign.

All this arbitrary chopping and changing is bound even by itself to produce inefficiency; and if we are really concerned with big business, why should the pittances allowed (to which Scotland contributes her share by taxation) be so pitifully small? And why after thirty-six years of existence should the Scottish Tourist Board be compelled to spend its dole on a three-year programme of research before it can even begin to do its proper work of attracting tourists to Scotland?

The contrasting advantages of genuine autonomy may be indicated by some recent figures.

About this time the Tourist Board of Northern Ireland was receiving some £166,000 annually; the Board of the Isle of Man £143,000; and the Board even of Jersey £107,000. The Irish Tourist Board enjoyed an income of £1,900,000 – 97 per cent by way of government grant. Besides spending £108,000 on general publications it was able to devote £158,000 to publicity in the United Kingdom – precisely where the Scottish Board was forbidden to spend a penny.

It is not surprising if tourists are being siphoned off to these autonomous areas of the United Kingdom, but especially to Ireland. What is surprising is that the Scottish tourist trade is able to survive and even to expand. Here where a small corner of the financial veil is for a moment lifted, we can get some ideas of the way in which Scotland is hampered in one limited sphere; nor have we any reason to suppose that she is not similarly hampered when much larger sums of money are involved.

8. *The rating system*

Although rates may seem to be a matter of purely local taxation, they are determined more and more by policies of the central Government; and the system which prevailed till 1961 had for many long years disastrous and permanent effects on Scotland's economic life. After 1961 it became more like that in England.

In England the occupier pays the total rates on his house, whereas in Scotland half the rates were paid by the occupier and half by the landlord. The Scottish method might appear to be the more equitable so long as the rates were small in relation to the rent – if they amounted, for example, to £20 on a rent of £100 a year, £10 paid by the tenant and £10 by the landlord. When the rates exceed the rent and may even go up, as in some rare cases they do, to 30s. in the pound, the landlord and the tenant had in Scotland *each* to pay £75 in rates on the same house. The obvious result in this extreme case is that the landlord now received a net income of £25 (£100—£75) from a house which formerly brought him £90 (£100—£10). From this £25 he still had to pay landlord's repairs. If we add to this a wave of inflation such that the cost of repairs is three or four times what it was before, it is obvious that repairs become impossible if he is to have any profit at all.

The problem was further complicated by the Rent Restrictions Act of 1915, which, however necessary as a temporary measure, was allowed to become almost permanent and has recently been renewed. This may be ignored for our present purposes – it certainly was no help to the landlord, and it applied also in England. Even if we suppose the Scottish landlord free to raise the rent of his house to £200 a year in order to cover the swollen rates and the inflationary costs of repairs, he was still no better off. Since in Scotland, though not at that time in England, rates were levied on the actual rent of the house, the total rates have now gone up to £300 a year, of which the landlord, like the tenant, has to pay £150. If he were to raise the rent again so as to cover the extra burden, the same thing will happen; and so on *ad infinitum*.

It may be held that landlords as an exploiting class have forfeited their claims to be treated justly; but this system, even where the rates are only twenty shillings in the pound, affects far more than the pockets of the landlords. Houses will inevitably fall into disrepair, and in the long run will become uninhabitable as well as unprofitable – there was one notorious case where a landlord offered to sell a large house for 2½d. and found no takers. It was said at one time that for every new house built an old house was condemned. What is more, private building became so unprofitable in Scotland that it was bound in the long run to cease altogether unless for some one who could afford to build his own house. This in turn placed an even greater burden of building on the local authorities with the inevitable result that the rates had to be still further increased. This vicious spiral is one of the main reasons why the housing situation is so much worse than it is in England, and why Scottish labour is so much less mobile: a man who loses his job cannot find a new job and a new house somewhere else unless he joins the weary trek to the South. Attempts to make good the damage have so far been ineffective.

Why should so oppressive a system have been allowed to last for so many years? The answer appears to be the usual one. Reform would require legislation, and Parliament was too busy with other things. The legislation might also be controversial, since although every one agreed that the system was wrong, there might not be agreement about the best way of putting it right. Apparently in Scotland, and in Scotland alone, unless opinion is unanimous there can be no reform – at least not for a very long time.

There is no such painful delay where English interests are directly involved. In order to meet an emergency the British Parliament in 1928 introduced a system of derating for industry and agriculture – a system which, however defensible as a temporary measure, has meant that at least in the country districts of Scotland the richer members of the community have been permanently subsidised by the poorer. Since the method of levying rates in Scotland did not fit in with this derating system, a change was introduced almost in the twinkling of an eye. Against the vote of a majority of Scottish M.P's the control of education was suddenly transferred from reasonably efficient *ad hoc* bodies to local authorities dominated by party politics. There was certainly no demand for this in Scotland, and its effects on Scottish education have been far from satisfactory. Education is a permanent Scottish interest, and it is hard to see why it should have been so hurriedly sacrificed in order to ease administrative difficulties in meeting a temporary emergency.

One further point should be noted. In England no rates are levied on an unoccupied house, but in Scotland they continued to be exacted unless the roof was taken off. The regulation now may be rather more humane, but its effects are there for all to see. Everywhere throughout Scotland the traveller will find these tragically roofless houses sinking defencelessly into ruin. To some they seem a standing symbol of Scotland's helplessness and decline.

9. *Fiscal reform*

In spite of many examples of indifference and even hostility to reasonable Scottish complaints, it would give a false picture if we failed to record that some Englishmen at some times can be helpful and friendly. Thus, for example, the Liberal Assembly which met in Edinburgh in 1961 carried by an overwhelming majority a resolution supporting the claim for a Scottish Parliament to deal with Scottish Affairs. They demanded the maximum amount of fiscal power for such a Parliament so far as this was consistent with close co-operation in the United Kingdom and the Common Market. In particular, a Scottish

Treasury should be responsible to the Scottish Parliament for the levying of direct and indirect taxation in Scotland and should contribute to the United Kingdom Treasury the Scottish share of expenditure for defence, foreign, and Commonwealth affairs. Excise duties should be levied by the Scottish Treasury.

This would give to Scotland far more than was asked by the two million signatories of the Scottish Covenant.

A more modest reform suggested above would be to allow Scotland a fair proportion of her total revenue and to let a Scottish Parliament decide how this is to be expended in accordance with her special interests and ideals. Why, for example, should her expenditure be cut to an English pattern in transport, where her needs are so different, or in education, when for centuries she has had a distinctive tradition of her own?

There are bound to be differences of opinion about the rights and powers that should be given to a Scottish Parliament; but it is hard to see how a system so incompetent, not to say so crazy, as the existing one can be defended on its own merits. Apart from the special claims and problems of Scotland the logic of events appears more and more to demand legislative devolution for what are called 'the regions'. Resistance to this demand may spring partly from the instinct of administrators to extend, rather than to abandon, whatever powers they have acquired. In the case of Scotland and Wales this resistance seems to be fortified by English unwillingness to weaken in any way English control over the other British nations. Here we can glance only at some of the arguments explicitly put forward against any change.

One argument is that a central authority can do more good to an outlying part than the part can do to itself. Even if we accept this doubtful proposition, a central authority can also do more harm.

A variant of this argument is that a local parliament must be incapable of planning. It is hard to see why local knowledge should make planning more difficult; but in any case the existing system has consistently failed to plan for Scotland as a whole.

A further argument put forward is that if government money is to be spent in Scotland, this must obviously be done under government control. But the case to be answered is that if this money is drawn from Scotland, its expenditure would be more usefully controlled by some form of government in Scotland itself.

This further argument against Scottish self-government does not become more palatable when politicians of the less tactful variety speak as if the revenue from Scotland becomes English property when it is taken South of the Border. Too often they treat Scottish claims as if they were appeals for charity and must be balanced against the needs of under-developed countries in Africa. Even loans at a profitable rate of interest they seem to regard as gifts. Their kindly condescension is most conspicuous with regard to the Highlands – the contribution to the revenue from the duty on Highland whisky is conveniently forgotten. In extreme cases they almost give the impression of holding that the English alone are disinterested enough to distribute some part of English wealth among their poverty-stricken neighbours. All this belongs more to psychology than to economics, but it may help to explain the belief, or even the fact, that the treatment of Scotland is unfair.

The extent to which the wealth of Scotland is drained away to the South may be a matter for dispute, but one thing is indubitable. It would be hard to devise a system – if it can be called a system – more likely to produce this result without fear of discovery.

10. *Sir Walter Scott*

Sir Walter Scott is commonly regarded as a man who was eminently sane, and a summing up from him, even if it is a trifle heated, may serve to indicate that the complaints of Scotland are of long standing, though the grounds for them are much stronger to-day.

His protest was occasioned by an attempt to deprive the Scottish banks of their right to issue their own notes and so to influence in some slight degree the economy of Scotland. The attempt was fortunately unsuccessful, although to this day the sight of a Scottish £1 note in Scotland can make even the most sympathetic of Englishmen begin to think it high time that such an anomaly should cease. The quotations from Sir Walter are not continuous.

After a tribute to the kindness with which individual Scotsmen are received in the South, the author of *Waverley* goes on to say:

'But, on the other hand, if the English statesman has a point of greater or less consequence to settle with Scotland as a country, we find him at once seized with a jealous, tenacious, wrangling, overbearing humour – not only insisting upon conducting the whole matter according to his own will, but by no means so accessible to the pleas of reason, justice, and humanity as might be expected.

There has been in England a gradual and progressive system of assuming the management of affairs entirely and exclusively proper to Scotland, as if we were totally unworthy of having the management of our own concerns.

All must centre in London. We could not be entrusted with the charge of making our own roads and bridges, but these labours must be conducted under the tender care of men who knew nothing of our country, its wants, and its capabilities, but who, nevertheless, sitting in their office in London, were to decide, without appeal, upon the conduct of the roads in Lochaber!

But I may perhaps be answered that these operations are carried on by grants of public money, and that therefore the English – undoubtedly the only disinterested and trustworthy persons in the universe – must be employed to look after its application.

Public money, forsooth! I should like to know whose pocket it comes out of. I should like still farther to know how the English are entitled to assume the direction and disposal of any pittance which may be permitted, out of the produce of our own burthens, to revert to the peculiar use of the nation from whom it has been derived.

For God's sake, sir, let us remain as Nature made us, Englishmen, Irishmen and Scotsmen! We would not become better subjects, or more valuable members of the common empire, if we all resembled each other like so many smooth shillings.'

CHAPTER VIII

THE TAKE-OVER BID

The good old rule . . . the simple plan,
That they should take, who have the power,
And they should keep who can.

William Wordsworth

1. *The take-over bid*

We live in an age of take-over bids: small companies are continually losing their identity and being amalgamated with larger ones. When this trend continues far enough it results in monopolies: more and more power is concentrated in fewer and fewer hands. The process may be said to make for economy and efficiency, at least for a time. In the long run it may produce a less healthy society and be less favourable to consumers as a whole.

The Treaty of Union has been regarded by some Scotsmen as a take-over bid effected on terms more favourable to England than to Scotland. The process of taking over has gone on ever since 1707 and has been greatly speeded up in recent years, particularly in the economic field. You may say, if you like, that this accords with modern trends. Such a view is cold comfort to Scotsmen who see their country being subjected increasingly to control from London and who become ever more conscious of losing power to determine their own economic progress.

Remote control is bad in itself so far as it undermines initiative among those who suffer from it. It may become disastrous if it is exercised by men who are unable to see beyond their own limited horizon. Such parochial blindness may be revealed in non-official utterances. We may illustrate this by two trivial examples.

127

Many years ago – I speak only from memory – a gentleman from the neighbourhood of London wrote a letter to *The Times* about the North of Scotland Hydro-Electric Board. Whatever – he asked – were things coming to? If they went on like this, people in the Highlands would have electricity before the inhabitants of the Home Counties!

This is a crude example, and *The Times*, let us hope, may have published it as a type of what ought not to be said – or even thought. But did it perhaps, like a slip of the tongue, reveal something of an attitude that is not unknown in the South, even if it is seldom so bluntly expressed?

A more significant revelation of this self-centredness was produced by the Church of England Commissioners. For some reason they had been buying up land in the south of Scotland, and there had been complaints that they were absentee landlords and out of sympathy with their Scottish tenants. Their spokesman was kind enough to answer these criticisms in the *Scotsman*. 'The Church Commissioners', he said, 'do not consider themselves out of touch or out of sympathy with any of their tenants.' He failed to observe that those most deficient in sympathy are precisely those who are least conscious of their defects. But his way of meeting the second charge was still more enlightening: 'When you have a large block of flats in London, you can hardly be called "absentee landlords".'

English politicians and administrators seldom express themselves quite so obtusely; but too often they also seem equally insensitive, and even hostile, to Scottish criticisms and claims. If in their actions they are sometimes affected by similar prejudices even in the slightest degree, it is not surprising that Scotland is full of complaints about the neglect of her interests. What else could you expect?

2. *Stop-and-go*

One result of control from London is that Scotland has to come last in the queue. The nation which can claim, perhaps with the exaggeration common to all patriotism, that it not only pioneered the Industrial Revolution, but also provided it with a philosophy in Adam Smith's *Wealth of Nations*, is now condemned to be always behind the times.

Being last in the queue has peculiar disadvantages when the economic policy of the country is governed by the principle of stop-and-go. The unfortunates at the tail of the procession are stopped suddenly by the red light; and by the time the green light is turned on, they are expected to fall still farther into the rear since future advances are to be made on a percentage basis. When the South of England suffers from over-employment, there is a sudden clamp down on the credit urgently needed to meet the very different problem of permanent under-employment in Scotland. Scotland – to change the metaphor – is expected to swallow the medicines, certainly distasteful and probably harmful, which are devised to cure ailments other than her own.

The stop-and-go policy is well illustrated by what happened to the Scottish members of the National Association of Local Government Officers (commonly known as N.A.L.G.O.). In England such officers were awarded a salary increase of 7 per cent before the freeze deadline of July 20th, 1966. Their Scottish brethren were caught by the guillotine. Not only could they receive no similar increase, but even after the period of restraint they would have to start fresh negotiations with no promise of priority.

This caused a near-revolt in Scotland even among some members of the Labour Party. The Government met this with a torrent of abuse and insisted that the unhappy local government officers in Scotland were in no different position from that of millions of other workers caught by the freeze. Scotland could not be allowed special privileges.

In all this they blandly ignored the real point of the complaint. This was that by Government policy Scottish local government officers – like Scottish teachers – must wait for salary awards till the claims of their English equivalents have been settled. The only special privileges allowed to Scotland are to be paid later and to be paid less.

A Minister of State for Scotland, if correctly reported, allowed the cloven hoof to appear, if only for a moment.

I   129

According to him the trouble 'stemmed' from the effect of different negotiations in England and Scotland, and the possibility of U.K. negotiations would have to be borne in mind in the future. Scotland, in short, is offered the usual painful choice: either you must lose yourself in a so-called British association, where your interests will be neglected in favour of the English majority; or else you must suffer the unhappy consequences of being last in the queue, when you will be told that you have only yourselves to blame.

3. *Transport and the Forth Road Bridge*

One glance at a map of Scotland should suggest to any intelligent man that here is an economic problem of a very special kind – all these islands, all these mountains, all these inlets of the sea. Especially in the matter of transport it should be obvious that the problem ought to be looked at as a whole. Steamers, ferries, roads, railways, and aeroplanes should be so co-ordinated as to supplement one another and keep costs down as far as possible. The failure to do this has contributed to the depopulation of the greater part of the country; and this depopulation in turn makes the problem ever more insoluble. Without some attempt at a flat, or at least a special, rate for transport it seems inevitable that under present conditions the remoter areas will become entirely uninhabited; but apart from postage the only flat rate is said to be confined to stout and cigarettes. Such special rates as I have been able to find in transport charges seem all to be in favour of England.

The small but rich industrial area of central Scotland, with the bulk of the wealth and the bulk of the population, could, even in its present difficulties, do much to help the other parts of the country. Everything depends on treating the problem as a whole, but this is what is never done, or at least never done effectively.

In the crisis of a general election party politicians may occasionally get a brief glimmering of the truth. Thus in the 1959 election the Conservative Party promised a measure of local control over transport which might have led to some real improvement; but this promise, in accordance with the traditional practice, was dishonoured. London bureaucrats cling jealously to their powers, and they can always exercise pressure on politicians as soon as votes cease to be important. Judging in their own cause, they have a good chance of getting their own way by insisting that experience – their experience – shows central control to be absolutely necessary for efficiency. Unfortunately the experience of other people is rather different.

This history of the project for a Forth Road Bridge may be taken as a sample – it became almost a symbol – of the delays and frustrations imposed by control from the South. The deep estuary of the Forth cuts off the capital of Scotland from Fife and the counties to the north. In the nineteenth century, when the hand of London lay less heavy, it was possible to build the Forth Railway Bridge, which in its time was one of the wonders of the world. With the coming of the motor-car, traffic by road had either to make a long and awkward détour or to use ferries which were inadequate and costly. The need for a Forth Road Bridge was recognised in Scotland as early as 1923. In spite of unremitting agitation it took forty years to get the Bridge built.

Here, as always, there were many changing excuses for the delay. At first the Government regarded the Bridge as solely a matter for the local highway authorities, although it serves the whole of the East of Scotland. In 1936 the Minister of Transport considered that the traffic figures supplied him did not justfy any grant. Thereafter nothing could be done because of the rearmament programme, and the War naturally put a stop to all such projects. After the War a Provisional Order for its construction was approved, but the Government still found reasons for inaction: there were always other claims to be considered first. As late as 1953 it was officially maintained that if a road bridge were to be constructed, every road project in Scotland would have to be abandoned.

At this juncture an attempt was made in Scotland to form a company which would build the bridge from private investment, but this project was efficiently strangled in its cradle. Finance was not the only consideration; there were other demands for steel and cement; the claims of the Forth Road Bridge had to be considered in comparison with other schemes which the Government was pledged to assist 'both in this country and overseas'. It has been said with some bitterness that there was no difficulty in providing steel for a Fun Fair at Battersea – and even that if Scotsmen could only blacken their faces they would be better treated than they are. In any case the stranglehold exercised by London became beautifully obvious. It applied to the use of private capital in Scotland as well as to the allocation of the revenue provided by the Scottish taxpayer.

In the end the Road Bridge cost £20,000,000 – five times as much as would have been needed to build it earlier. English politicians sometimes speak of this as a great favour conferred on Scotland by the British government or even by their own political Party. What they really did – apart from delaying it for so long – was to allow a so-called 'grant' of £14,000,000: the remaining £6,000,000 was contributed by the local authorities. The 'grant' itself was merely a loan to be repaid, together with interest, during the comparatively short period of thirty years. The transaction has to be financed by tolls such as no one dreams of imposing on the costly motor-ways and fly-overs constructed in the south of England. How much of the money for the original 'grant' came from Scottish taxation and savings we shall never know.

During this period the Government was trying, successfully or unsuccessfully, to promote industrial development in Fife while at the same time denying or delaying an efficient outlet to the South. Government departments appear to be concerned only with their own particular problems, and to co-operate as little as possible with one another. They not only find it difficult to see objects clearly at a distance, but have a blinkered or 'tunnelled' vision unable to look either to the right hand or to the left.

4. *Railways and Dr. Beeching*

The British Railways Board too suffers from this blinkered and myopic vision. It is unable to look beyond its own immediate profit or loss; and it is so far from Scotland that it fails to descry any special problems there. It has no truck with wider economic and social considerations. It is, in short, dominated by the profit motive – the motive which nationalisation was supposed to replace by the nobler motive of social service. Its treatment of Scotland was so typical and aroused such violent opposition that we must be forgiven if we examine this at some length.

The method favoured for making profits or avoiding loss is to reduce services and increase charges. This is sometimes described as 'increasing productivity'. Whether successful in its immediate aim or not, such a policy raises the cost of living and speeds up the process of inflation.

We cannot expect a nationalised service to be purely philanthropic, and the railways have to face real difficulties from the competition of motor transport – difficulties not diminished by perversely allowing ever bigger and heavier and faster lorries to run on roads ill-adapted to withstand such traffic. But we might expect that a Ministry of Transport, before taking drastic action, would ask whether immediate gains for the railways may not be overbalanced by a loss of national income and so of national revenue. We might even expect it to enquire about the time and money necessary to supply alternative means of transport: might not the cost of this in some regions be greater than that of a railway subsidy?

The actual practice of those in authority does little to encourage such expectations. If we may confine our attention to Scotland, the Railways Board, besides removing locomotive repair shops to the South, has been steadily running down the railways ever since it got really going. Its ideal apparently is that every part of the system should either make its own profit or be abolished. On this basis branch lines have been abandoned, stations have been closed, trains have been cancelled, through carriages have been taken off, no matter what inconvenience may be caused to passengers, and no matter what economic damage may be done to vast tracts of the country – and perhaps even to the lines that are allowed to remain.

The principles adopted may seem too narrow and too rigid, but it is possible they might work not too harshly in prosperous, thickly populated regions round London and Birmingham with many roads and alternative means of transport. Perhaps

the same might be said of the Scottish central industrial belt.
Yet these principles may do immense harm if they are applied
mechanically to poor and thinly populated regions with
miserable roads, severe winters, and no adequate alternative
means of transport.

But are these principles in fact applied uniformly? It came as
something of a shock to be told that London 'commuters'
would have to pay 50 per cent more for their fares if the railways
they use are not to be run at a loss. This is said to be true
particularly of the Southern Railway, where express trains
leave for Haywards Heath nearly every twenty minutes with
passengers who must be among the most opulent in Britain.

Such discrimination in favour of the South would seem hard
to defend, but a defence is not lacking. A Conservative member
of Parliament, representing a constituency not too far from
London, is reported to have said: 'The only part of the railway
system which is absolutely essential is the London commuter
service, extending about sixty miles around London'. Dr.
Beeching himself is reputed to have said that most commuter
services, though uneconomic, were being retained because they
were socially necessary.

The preference thus nakedly expressed may well be fatal to
Scotland; but who dies, if London live?

Dr. Beeching's report of 1963 merely proposed to carry out
with greater speed and ruthlessness the narrow and rigid
railway policy which had been followed all along so far as
Scotland was concerned. In accordance with his instructions he
made no attempt to survey the transport system as a whole,
let alone the economic conditions of different regions, but based
his decisions on railway statistics by themselves. After we have
cut out whatever fails to make a profit, we shall doubtless be in
in a better position to estimate how much damage has been
done to the national economy. But by then the damage may be
irreparable.

Besides ignoring present geographical and economic differences the report made no allowance for future possibilities. Even
from a general view it may seem less than wise to tear up
railways and pull down railway bridges at a time when motor

traffic on over-crowded roads looks as if it might be steadily grinding to a halt.

In Scotland the regions to be hit hardest were the very regions where the Government was struggling, however ineffectively, to reverse the course of depopulation and decline. The areas to suffer most were the Borders; the Southwest, which was to be deprived of its railway connexions with Stranraer and so with Ireland; and above all the Highlands, which were to be left without any railways north and west of Inverness. This meant that there would be places on the mainland (to say nothing of the Islands) as far as 150 miles away from any railhead. All of these regions, it may be claimed, present special problems unknown in the South. Certainly there is no part of England that is even remotely comparable with the Highlands.

Even as regards the past, Dr. Beeching's statistics are sometimes said to be based on false principles and ill-chosen samples, but it must be accepted that the railways in these areas, as in others, have been working at a heavy loss. It has also been said that any railways run so inefficiently would be bound to lose money; and even that this inefficiency is the result of deliberate policy. The last statement perhaps fails to do justice to the effects that can be produced by natural incompetence when combined with remote control.

Like any good administrator Dr. Beeching favoured speed of action, and Mr. Marples, the Minister of Transport, leapt at once to his support: 'I am absolutely at one with Dick Beeching on this'. Dr. Beeching himself magisterially dismissed Scottish arguments as 'unjustifiable', 'unreal', and 'unsound'. He could find nothing unique about the Highlands – all places presumably seem alike if you refuse to look beyond your account books. He brushed aside the view that industry and the tourist trade would be adversely affected. The absence of alternative transport was met by recommending the Highlanders to press for better roads – as if they had not been doing this in vain for years. If their roads (such as they are) were closed by snow for weeks in the winter, this could be met by the use of snowploughs and by better fences. It does not seem to have occurred to him that a succession of local buses can never be an adequate substitute for a through train on the journey of 140 miles or so between Inverness and Wick or Thurso. He may have regarded this as among the hardships which, on his view, were not a problem for the Railway Board. There was other machinery to deal with this – in particular the Transport Users' Consultative Committees. If he was correctly reported, it would be hard to find a more classical example of the indifference of John Bull to Scottish distress.

As we shall see later, those who objected to the projects of a successful institution like the North of Scotland Hydro-Electric Board were allowed every opportunity to press home their case. Those who objected to the closure of essential Scottish railway services were treated differently. The Transport Users' Consultative Committees, selected by the Ministry of Transport and responsible to it, chose on no clear principles which objectors they would hear; and they were said to have given inadequate notice and insufficient time for hearing them. In any case they could hear only objections on the narrow ground of hardship, and they could not allow objectors to cross-examine the representatives of the railways. Their strictly confidential reports on this limited topic were to go, it is true, to the Secretary of State for Scotland, and he would no doubt be anxious to press these, and perhaps other, objections on the Minister of Transport. But whatever promises or pledges the Secretary might give, Mr. Marples made it abundantly clear that it was the Minister of Transport who would be the sole and final judge. He alone, it would seem, had to consider unaided the wider economic and social issues which the Scots had not been allowed to raise. Yet the burden of proof was placed at once on 'his Scottish friends': it was for them to prove that a railway should not be closed. His attitude to Scottish delegations did not suggest that they would be likely to meet with much success even if they were allowed to state their case. We have no evidence that either he or his Ministry was qualified to deal with wider social and economic considerations in Scotland or anywhere else; and it was not easy to have confidence in any man who had so much confidence in himself.

At every stage of this bamboozling performance assurances were issued to check protests and damp down discussion. The relevant factors would be carefully examined at a later stage, and no railway would be closed until it could be replaced by adequate alternative means of transport. All this meant was that their fate would be determined, with the minimum of representations from Scotland, by one man who had already boasted of his lack of timidity and his eagerness for haste.

After violent agitation the two main Highland railways were in the end given a temporary reprieve, though not without the loss of many stations. Other Scottish railways, however essential for new developments, have been less fortunate.

5. *Ships*

Ships have long been the glory of Scotland and especially of the Clyde. Before the 1914 War one third of the world's total merchant shipping was built on that river – a truly amazing achievement. I have no figures for warships, but without the Clyde it seems probable that the War at sea would have been lost. Fifty years later shipyard workers from the Clyde were being recruited for Denmark and Holland, and this scheme received hundreds of enquiries on the ground that 'There is no future here'. Why should this be? The answer cannot be merely that ship-building is hard hit everywhere.

It is easy enough to say that this process is the result of inevitable economic trends, or even to put the whole blame on Scottish employers or Scottish workmen. But the policy of the British government bears at least some part of the responsibility, both by what it does and by what it fails to do. British shipowners were taxed in such a way that they found it difficult to replace old ships in a period of steady inflation; and by now Liberia has a larger merchant fleet than Great Britain. The Government seemed powerless to counteract the heavy subsidies given by other countries, including our own Dominions, to the yards with which British shipbuilders had to compete. Large foreign orders were lost by difficulties about credit, and the Minister of Transport told us at one stage that the Government could not subsidise shipbuilding by means of loans. As a result the famous firm of Denny on the Clyde went into voluntary liquidation, and the hopes of a new hovercraft industry in Scotland were destroyed. Soon afterwards, when the North-East of England was in trouble in 1963, the policy was reversed, and modest loans were given to shipowners to finance the building of ships. Continual changes in Government policy were by themselves bound to hamper any industry, but it is impossible to follow all their vagaries here.

Whatever may be the excuse for such policies, it is hard not to contrast them with the treatment of the aircraft industry, whose activities are centred in the South of England. According to official statements it received £300,000,000 of the tax-payers' money every year. Even so, it seems to be in almost continuous difficulty.

Great ships could be built on the Clyde, but they could not be repaired there – only after years of agitation did the Government concede the necessary graving dock. Fewer and fewer ships sail from there to foreign parts, and even the local Clyde steamers, so long a source of pride and profit, offer difficulties to London management. Pier after pier is closed down throughout the Highlands and Islands to the detriment, if not the destruction, of some once flourishing community. Fewer things can be more depressing than to find that services which used to make for profit and for pleasure are steadily becoming worse than they were fifty or even a hundred years ago.

The system of remote control makes for managerial inefficiency as well as for economic loss. At one time it was discovered that the Clyde ferries were much better than those to the Isle of Wight. Somebody in London decided it would be a good idea to switch the two – presumably on the principle that Scotland must always have the second best. As a result Scottish passengers had to face discomforts and perils in ferries wholly unsuited to the local conditions. Only after the fiercest outcries was the original position restored.

Fortunately in this case there was no tragedy, but this was not always so. When in January, 1953, the *Princess Victoria* sank with a heavy loss of life on her passage from Stranraer to

Ireland, the disaster was at least partly caused by inefficient control from London which had failed to take the necessary precautions for safety.

6. *Air transport*

There is also the question of air transport. It may be that airmen are accustomed to wider horizons, and there is gratitude for what they have done for the Highlands and Islands. Nevertheless the complaints about the London bureaucracy are of the usual kind. It is claimed, for example, that the Highlands and Islands had a better and cheaper and more profitable service when this was still in Scottish hands. The emergency ambulance services, so necessary for the more isolated regions, were drastically reduced because of a refusal to use the small planes and small runways which were suited to the country and had been so efficient in the past. The Toothill report (to which we shall come later) recognised that the air services in Scotland were inadequate, that tourism had been favoured at the expense of business, and that disruption of business traffic had done serious harm to the economy. But the main complaint is that Prestwick, an airport which is unique in Europe by its freedom from fog, has been starved in the supposed interests of London. By deliberate government policy it has been denied feeder services and direct Continental links: even its use by Scandinavian and Icelandic and Dutch lines on their way to and from America has been jealously watched and severely restricted. If, as Mr. Thomas Johnston proposed in 1943, it had been made the responsibility of a Scottish public utility corporation, it could have become a first-class gateway to Europe, and the gain to Scotland would have been immense.

This is not the opinion merely of Scotsmen. A dispassionate American expert speaks of 'the shabby aviation treatment of the Scots'. 'Stultification, restrictions, and bureaucratic manoeuvering by London, may hold down Prestwick by arbitrary means, but the real loser is Britain herself.'

The British Government may be willing, and even anxious, to hand over to local authorities airports that are losing money; but Prestwick, as we were euphemistically told, must be associated with others of international status in Britain. This means presumably that Prestwick must be subordinated to its London rivals, and London must continue to be the main gateway from Scotland into Europe, no matter how much it may be cluttered up with an excess of traffic. After all, this is only a mirror of the whole political situation.

Already in 1966 there were ominous signs of Prestwick's probable destiny. A big new airport at Abbotsinch – nearer to Glasgow but without Prestwick's natural advantages – has been built at vast expense and is already spoken of as a great international airport of the future; and the first bright thought of the new administrators at Prestwick was apparently to charge the American Air Force fees so high that it would be encouraged to move somewhere else. The Ministry of Aviation also showed its attitude, rather meanly, by throwing cold water on a proposal to put up a memorial plaque at Prestwick to Group Captain McIntyre – one of the leading pioneers in aviation and a founder of the airport, which without his foresight might never have developed into an invaluable transatlantic terminal during the War.

It should be added as a postscript that the official figures used to discredit Scottish claims are not always above suspicion. At one time we were told that British European Airways would have made a profit but for the loss on services to Scotland and must therefore be given a special subsidy if these services were to continue. Later it emerged that there was a loss, in some cases a greater loss, on nearly every local service in Britain.

7. *Electricity and water-power*

There is one field where Scotland enjoys a natural economic advantage over England: she is better able to produce from water-power the electricity so much resented by our friend from the Home Counties. The North of Scotland Hydro-Electric Board, set up in 1943 through the influence of Mr. Thomas Johnston in a coalition Government, was not placed under London control; and its aim from the first was to benefit the Highlands by bringing cheap light and power even to remote parts. It is acknowledged to have been one of the few institutions which have succeeded in helping this neglected area, though it still has much to do.

This does not mean that it has escaped unsympathetic sniping in Parliament and tiresome interference from the South. In 1962, for example, the Board was compelled to raise its charges, although it had made a profit of one and three quarter million pounds in the previous year. Even more serious is what looks like an attempt to restrict or prevent its further development and to destroy its independence.

The usual way of pursuing such an end is to appoint a committee – in this case the Mackenzie Committee – and to hold up further activity till a report has been produced and accepted. At the end of 1962 the committee duly reported that the overwhelming majority of witnesses had expressed satisfaction with the achievements of the Board. Yet in spite of 'the affection and esteem' the Board had won, especially in the Highlands, the committee recommended that it should be amalgamated with the South of Scotland Electricity Board, which had no experience of producing electricity from waterpower. The argument for this amalgamation was in the main the general one that the bigger the organisation, the more efficiently it can be run. The same argument could be used at a later stage for putting all generation and distribution of electricity in Scotland under the direct control of London.

The newly appointed English chairman of the South of Scotland Electricity Board welcomed the proposal with enthusiasm; but almost everywhere else such a fury of opposition was aroused in Scotland that the Government rejected this main recommendation of its own committee. But the proposed new projects of the Hydro-Electric Board were still held up until local enquiries could examine objections; and the local enquiries themselves seemed to be unnecessarily delayed. Between 1956 and 1963 the labour force was reduced from 8,500 men to 2,000. There is a fear, let us hope mistaken, that there will not be the skilled technical and labour force available to carry on the work. All this at a time when Scotland was suffering from unemployment.

Such enquiries nowadays are no longer held in London, but

local landowners can hire expensive lawyers, not only to defend their own sporting and fishing rights, but also, in their zeal for Highland welfare, to argue at great length about the technical and economic and even aesthetic aspects of hydro-electric power in general. What is even more remarkable, the Secretary of State insisted that one local enquiry should also examine these aspects of a project to which there had been no objections at all. He did so on the ground that the Mackenzie Committee had failed to consider the question of capital costs. This omission on the part of the Mackenzie Committee, and the even stranger ignorance of the Scottish Office after so many years of experience, could surely have been made good more cheaply and more effectively by consulting a couple of experts than by all the expensive legal paraphernalia of a protracted local enquiry.

The Report on the two proposed Hydro-Electric Schemes – the Fada/Fionn project and the Laidon project – was published in 1965. As was to be expected from its two distinguished authors, it is a formidable document full of facts and figures which no one who is not an expert can be competent to criticise. It condemned both schemes on economic grounds, and its conclusions may be right. Nevertheless I may perhaps be forgiven if I express some uneasiness about its general background.

The supposed advantage of hydro-electric generating stations is that although their original construction is costly, they last very much longer than other kinds of generating stations and their upkeep is much cheaper. Their fuel, so to speak, comes from Heaven and so does not increase in price and is not affected by inflation. These advantages, if I understand the Report aright, are set aside, whether on Government instructions or on other grounds. Inflation, for example, is not to be considered, because the authors understood that it was the policy of Her Majesty's Government 'to secure economic growth without inflation' – as if other Governments had not pursued this policy for years without success. So too it could not be assumed that fuel would rise in price 'in the relevant years' – although the Coal Board immediately afterwards proceeded to impose further discriminatory charges against Scottish coal in addition to those already existing. We might have imagined that while the rain, which is the fuel of a hydro-electric station, keeps on coming down, its price neither goes down nor up. And if the phrase 'in the relevant years' means that a hydro-electric scheme must be supposed in our calculations to have a life no longer than that of schemes based on coal or oil, are we not ruling out its greatest economic advantage?

These may be simple-minded misunderstandings to which there is an obvious answer, but one statement in the Report remains a source of uneasiness: 'We accept, according to your direction, 8 per cent as the "right" rate of "interest" for the purpose of this Report'. If the words 'right' and 'interest' have to be put in inverted commas because they are being used in some special sense, could this mean that the direction from the Government was intended to bias the calculations from the start?

These may be unworthy suspicions, but it is difficult not to remember how Mr. Johnston 'upset the astrologers on the London money market' when by enlisting the help of the Scottish banks he floated a loan of £5,000,000 for the Hydro-Electric Board in July, 1947, with an offer of $2\frac{1}{2}$ per cent at par. Its success showed what the people of Scotland were willing to do for a Scottish public purpose. Why should they not be allowed other opportunities of the same kind?

So far as generating stations are concerned, it appears to be commonly assumed – for example, in the Labour Plan for Scotland – that on the strength of this Report no further projects from the Hydro-Electric Board need be considered. If it is uneconomic to produce electricity from water-power in Scotland (though apparently not elsewhere), we should be told so directly and explicitly. Otherwise it may be suspected that obscure forces – or perhaps even jealousy of independent Scottish activities – are endeavouring to destroy by administrative action a Board which has done outstandingly useful work in the Highlands. Perhaps experts from Norway could explain to us why the abundance of cheap electric power at the service of Norwegian workmen makes the comparable figures for Britain seem almost ludicrous – 52,800 units as against 6,200 according to a report in 1963. What a breath of fresh air it would be if these matters could be discussed freely in a Scottish Parliament with power to make its own decisions!

8. *Coal*

Coal has been the foundation of Scotland's industrial prosperity, and it might have been expected that she would gain from the nationalisation of the coal mines in 1947. At that time the Scottish owners received £34,000,000 in compensation. Since then the National Coal Board has poured out some £100,000,000 or more for maintenance and development. What has been the result?

In spite of this vast outlay about £120,000,000 had been lost in Scotland between 1949 and 1962 in day-to-day operations; and in 1961 the annual operating loss rocketed to £20,000,000. Since nationalisation the total cumulative loss of the National Coal Board throughout Britain – some £80,000,000 – was alleged to be entirely due to the failure of the Scottish mines. If no coal at all had been mined in Scotland, the Board, it was claimed, would have made a total cumulative profit of £20,000,000.

If these figures are correct, no wonder the Board was compelled, however reluctantly, to close down one Scottish pit after another with sickening acceleration. The case was supposed to be so clear that repeated demands for an enquiry into the management, planning, and financial transactions of the Board in Scotland have been firmly and even resentfully refused. Government departments and similar institutions cannot admit mistakes. It is enough if they can say that in spite of the estimated 10,000,000,000 tons of Scottish coal reserves, mining in Scotland is uneconomic. It has even been suggested that Scottish managers at the pithead need an infusion of new blood, presumably from England.

The strange thing is that before nationalisation the Scottish mining industry was a good going concern. The average output for a day's work in Scotland had for years been above the British average. In the first year of nationalisation, when the

National Coal Board made a loss of £6,000,000, the profit from Scotland was £2,000,000. Even in the second year the Scottish mines gave a profit of £3,400,000. It was only when the Board got fully into its stride that the story of Scottish mining became one of steady and ever accelerating decline.

This astonishing failure clearly did not spring from any lack of good will. Millions of money were poured into show mines in Fife which, after a brief period of production, were condemned to die under a load of debt. Charges of incompetence and lack of foresight were indignantly rejected – the highest experts were consulted, and the devilry of nature was wholly unpredictable. In the absence of a public enquiry the true state of affairs must remain obscure; but it is not surprising if the bland assurances with which the Board meets all criticism are received in Scotland with some suspicion. In any case the economic results are only too sadly clear.

The two great aims of nationalisation were to secure better conditions of employment for the miners and to maintain equality of coal prices throughout the country.

It was inevitable that a number of miners would have to move at some inconvenience from older and less profitable pits to newer and more profitable ones. What came as a shock was that so many were thrown out of work altogether with all that this means in human misery. In the middle of 1962 it was alleged that the Coal Board's axe was poised to chop off more than two thirds of the country's remaining 106 collieries. Attempts have been made, whether successfully or not, to provide alternative employment; but the Board naturally declines to be made responsible for Scotland's unemployment problem – this is 'some one else's job'. At one time it even objected to the introduction of new industries into Fife. It has, however, tried to induce Scottish miners to emigrate to the more successful coal fields in England – another example of the way in which English take-over bids lead to the emigration of Scotland's best men. We need not here enquire into the truth of the charges that the promises made to encourage this emigration were often broken.

The principle that coal prices should be the same throughout the whole country has been abandoned. At the very moment when the productivity of the Scottish mines began to show a marked increase it was decided that coal was to cost ten shillings more a ton in Scotland than it did in the South. It might seem obvious that this must lay a further heavy burden on her struggling industry. It is, however, easy to bear with equanimity the sufferings of others, and we were given the usual official assurances that the burden was only a little one. We were even informed that since the Scottish mines are close to the manufacturing area, the higher pit-head charges need not mean that the cost of coal 'under the boiler' will be greater, and this is what matters. Here we have the usual failure to look at Scotland as a whole, much of which is remote from the industrial belt; but even apart from this the assurance is unconvincing. One big Scottish steel firm alone was said at the time to pay annually at least half a million pounds more for its fuel. What is quite certain is that charges for gas and electricity had to be increased immediately, with all that this implies for the industrial as well as the private consumer. Even the charges for electricity from water-power were obliged by Government request to follow suit. Assurances that higher charges for fuel and power do not discourage the new factories which the Government hopes to see set up in Scotland strain human credulity to the utmost.

The official pronouncements took a startlingly different tone when they turned to the South. The discrimination against Scotland was defended by a contrast with the coalfields of Yorkshire and the Midlands. These, we were told, supply the most vulnerable part of the country where competitition is at its keenest, and any increase in price in these areas would mean loss of business. Apparently increased prices and loss of business do not matter in Scotland, but they must be avoided in the richest parts of England even if this means the abandonment of the most fundamental principle of nationalisation. This strange argument was justified on the further ground that only so could the less lucrative mining operations elsewhere be subsidised. The argument, if it can be called an argument, became all the more strange when accompanied by an assurance that within a short time the Scottish mining industry would no longer be in need of subsidies.

If this is a sample of the mentality by which a great Scottish industry is now controlled, it is hardly surprising if Scotsmen think they could manage their own affairs better by themselves.

9. *Industry in general*

The complaint of Scotland is not confined to the outstanding examples so far mentioned; it extends to the Government's industrial policy as a whole. It has been maintained, for example, that during the two Wars Scotland got its first set-back because new factories were established in the South while Scotland was used mainly as a place for storage. Instead of bringing the jobs to the men, the Government preferred to conscribe Scotsmen – and Scotswomen – to factories in England. Mr. Bevin's innocent reply to Scottish protests was simply that the Government had every right to move British subjects to any part of Britain during a war. Questions are asked about the reasons for distributing strip mills, with all their further industrial benefits, in a proportion of three to Wales and one to Scotland – and that one only after a strenuous fight. The fundamental complaint is that modern 'growth industries', which attract other job-spinning industries, have in most cases been built up in England on the strength of Government grants and research and development projects. Scotland had to depend on her older industries and did not get enough growth industry to start the process of expansion. Belated attempts to remedy the situation have had only a moderate success, especially as expansion in Scotland has to be checked whenever there is too much expansion in the South. Those who swim against the stream may have to swim their hardest not to be carried farther down.

Trivial though it may sound, an unnatural dependence upon England seems to impinge on every walk of life. There is a widespread belief that the best of everything in Scotland is taken away to London – this is the answer one gets when one asks why it is so difficult to get characteristically Scottish products in their country of origin. The basis for this would seem to be bulk buying by the richer parts of the South. But it is frustrating to find that so many goods can be obtained only from England, and that even the simplest things have so often to be repaired South of the Border – with resultant delays which are effectively increased by the devious methods of British Railways. All this is connected, at least partly, with the commercial take-over bids which remove the control of Scottish enterprises to England (and sometimes the enterprises themselves); but it does look as if, under the present system, Scotland is tending towards the 'industrial helotry' which Mr. Harold Wilson, in his speech to the Council of Europe in 1967, deplored as a danger, not indeed for Scotland, but for British industry in its relation to the United States of America.

10. *White papers and reports*

In setting out the complaints of Scotland it is easy to give an impression of unrelieved gloom. In comparison with the South of England the prospect has long been gloomy enough, and it can be improved only by fundamental reforms. But in spite of difficulties Scotland does make progress and does share in the benefits of the Welfare State. Her level of wages, though lower than that in England, is going up, and the number of her unemployed, though far too large, is nothing like what it was between the Wars. The more cheerful aspects of the situation should not be forgotten although here we have to take them for granted. Whatever may be said on this subject, the fact remains that the present system of government and administration continues to drain away the wealth and skill of Scotland to more affluent regions in the South.

Similarly it remains true that government policies are determined by conditions in England and are too often applied to Scotland with little regard to her special needs and problems. But it would be misleading to give the impression that these needs and problems were given no consideration at all. From time to time we have reports and white papers to enlighten and guide us. We may think them inadequate, but at least they are there, and some of their recommendations may sometimes, after long delays, be translated into action.

It would be ungracious to ignore these efforts, but it is impossible to discuss them here with the thoroughness they deserve. All that can be done is to give some very summary impressions.

In 1961 we had the Toothill Report, which developed further a still earlier report by Professor Cairncross. The Toothill Committee was set up, not by the Government, but by the Scottish Council (Development and Industry). In order to secure strict impartiality the Toothill Committee had on it a majority of Englishmen, and in its report it made as many as eighty-one recommendations. Some of these perhaps showed too firm a grip on the obvious: the Scottish people ought to show initiative and enterprise, and managers should develop London connexions. The more detailed, and more useful, recommendations cannot be discussed here, but two important principles were put forward. The first, which had been advocated by Professor Cairncross ten years earlier, was that instead of aiming as in the past at the immediate relief of unemployment the Government ought to foster economic growth. This suggestion was promptly turned down. The second, not too elegantly expressed, was that where a 'region' suffered from the general financial measures of the Government there ought to be, where practicable, regional differentiation if uniformity resulted in a regional sacrifice out of proportion to the national gain. This reasonable proposal is almost bound to remain a pious hope unless we have a revolutionary change in the system under which Scotland is governed; but the Committee would have no truck with the idea that the functions of London departments should be transferred to Scotland or that Scotland should be allowed a Minister of Commerce like the one permitted in Northern Ireland. Although the need to co-ordinate 'regional development measures' was recognised, no serious attempt was made to suggest how this could be done.

In 1963 we were given a White Paper on Central Scotland similar to the one already produced for North-East England. This leaned heavily on the Toothill Report and renewed the proposal that the Government should seek to foster economic growth instead of concentrating on the relief of unemployment;

and this time the proposal was accepted. The White Paper, like the Toothill Report, was concerned only with the narrow industrial belt of Scotland, and even here there were strange omissions. Yet without a view of Scotland as a whole the best we can hope for is to set up a minor magnetic field in Central Scotland which may do something to counteract the pull of London and the Midlands, but unless watched carefully may itself draw skill and wealth away from the other regions of Scotland.

In January 1966 we were given a new White Paper on Scotland. This purports to set out plans for the expansion of the Scottish economy, within the framework of the National Plan, in the period up to 1970. It professes to deal for the first time with Scotland as a whole, and so may be thought to dispose at long last of the charge that this is what can never be done under the present system. It contains a lot of useful information; and it is to be welcomed as recognising in principle that Scotland's main problems should be studied in relation to one another. The whole of Scotland, except Edinburgh, is to be a 'development area' entitled to new special incentives for industrial investment.

Although it is natural that a White Paper should be based on previous Reports, a whole plan cannot be made by enclosing a lot of little plans within one cover or even by specifying a large number of desirable goals. To judge it one way or the other, we should have to see how it works in practice.

On the whole its prescription seems to be very much 'the mixture as before'. If the Scottish economy is to be 'revitalised', the Government must do this, that, and the other thing: the Government will even organise representative groups for consultation: the Government will increase what it calls 'public investment' in Scotland (mainly for housing and roads) to the impressive sum of nearly £2,000,000,000 during the period in question.

In the end everything must depend on the way in which the Plan is carried out; and, at least according to the Conservative Party, the Plan is already a wreck. The Budget which followed shortly afterwards did not inspire high hopes that it would be carried out effectively. This imposed a novel 'selective employment tax' which seems likely to deal a body blow to the Highlands, about whose welfare the White Paper had been so solicitous. The aim of this tax was to force employees out of service industries into manufacturing industries (which were supposed to be already hoarding labour). Its method was to impose an extra tax on all industries, but to return the tax to the manufacturing industries along with a bonus.

How far the method was fitted to further the aim is not here our concern. What is clear is that these new devices were directed, like so many others, to the rich manufacturing regions of England. The Highlands depend for their prosperity on providing services, and their manufacturing industries are relatively few. Hence these regions – and at least some others in Scotland – will pay the tax in full, but will receive hardly any of the bonus. Many workers will be thrown out of jobs, but will not find manufacturing industries able to offer them employment. They will, in short, be forced to emigrate. This already makes nonsense of the Plan for the Highlands.

Plan or no Plan, it looks as if Scotland will still have to stomach remedies – squeezes and freezes – devised for ailments other than her own. She begins to look like a hospital patient who has strayed into the wrong ward and is confined to bed by kindly doctors and nurses who seek to cure – or 'revitalise' – her by injections and drugs unsuited to her condition. The one thing they will not do is to let her get out of bed and walk.

White Papers must deal with the Scottish economy on broad lines and so cannot bring out the petty details in which London has to take a hand. It may be possible (if not very plausible) to argue that Scotland will gain if some authority in the South can decide, within a 'national' plan, which Scottish ports should be developed and which should be neglected; but it is not easy to see why, for example, Cairnryan, the port which used to handle the export of Scottish coal to Ulster, should be left to be dismantled by scrap merchants, while Maryport in Cumberland should be equipped to export coal from Durham to the same destination. If we turn to minor matters, it is not easy to see why the Minister of Works should be responsible for ancient monuments in Scotland rather than the nation to which they belong; or even why he should decide the speed limit in the Royal Parks of Edinburgh. If traffic lights are to be put up in Dundee, their exact position must be determined by the Ministry of Transport. If they are later moved to a more convenient position without his express sanction, it will be no offence for a motorist to ignore them. If the Highland Fund should seek a loan from the Board of Trade to further one of its projects which have done so much for the Highlands, they will find it easier to draw blood from a stone; and if exceptionally their request is considered, this will be accompanied by impossible conditions – such as that two of the directors of the project must resign and be replaced by two nominees of the Board. Such continuous petty interference is not well suited to encourage Scottish initiative or to 'revitalise' her energies; but it would be tedious to examine it in detail. We have had to consider primarily the larger policies of the chief administrative organs which exercise control in Scotland; and it is hardly an exaggeration to say of them that, so far as Scotland is concerned, they touch nothing which they do not deform.

11. *The case for Scotland*

It will be said that this account is over-simplified, one-sided, and unfair.

There is no reason to deny that it is over-simplified: every topic discussed in it could profitably have a whole book to itself. In mapping so large a territory there must be over-simplification: without this there could be no map.

The account is also one-sided in the sense that it is a summary outline of the Scottish case – the plea of an advocate rather than the decision of a judge. In England the Scottish case is almost unheard and unknown. The present attempt to state it, however imperfect, is necessary to challenge the far more one-sided assumptions under which Scotland is misgoverned. The case, I suggest, is very strong; if not unanswerable, it is at least unanswered.

The main contention of this chapter is that economic progress in Scotland is hampered and hindered by centralised control from London and by policies devised primarily in the interests of the South of England. Whatever qualifications should be added, this contention cannot simply be swept aside as unfair. Indeed it may claim to state the inevitable consequences of a system of government under which the power of making policies and of taking decisions, both on the public, and even to a considerable extent on the private, side of industry, is being steadily reduced in Scotland. This cannot but have adverse economic effects: its psychological effects may be even worse.

CHAPTER IX

THE HIGHLANDS AND ISLANDS

They make a desert and they call it peace
Galgacus

1. *Differences of attitude*

The Highlands and Islands (that is, the Western Isles) make up about half the total land surface of Scotland. They are, or were, inhabited by the Gaels, a Keltic (or Celtic) people akin to the Gaels of Ireland in blood and language, but also connected, if less closely, with Britons, that is, with the Kelts of Wales. The whole area may be described shortly as 'the Highlands', and its inhabitants are known as 'Highlanders'.

No sensitive Scotsman can view the fate of this region without a tinge of melancholy. Here is half of his country being steadily depopulated with ever increasing acceleration: a language and a way of life which goes back far beyond the Christian era is in danger of being wiped out. Even if he is an unrepentant low-lander, the Highlands are for him part of his own history, and the Gaelic language was once spoken by many of his own ancestors. Why should this land of a fine race be an under-developed country? Why should it become a playground for rich Englishmen and Americans? Why can nothing be done that would stop its decay?

This attitude, it must be feared, is to many Englishmen merly a piece of romantic rubbish. Even the most sympathetic of them have been known to congratulate themselves on the way the Highlanders, ever since the Rising of 1745, have been forced to abandon the country and the language that they love in order to settle in the Colonies or America or in Lowland cities (where so many of them died of tuberculosis). Some Englishmen, and even some Anglicised Scots, go so far as to express an open desire that the old language and the old traditions should disappear for ever. An advanced thinker has even propounded the idea that the best use for the Outer Hebrides would be to turn them into a penal colony.

How is it possible to account for such differences in attitude or to explain the unconcern with which the fate of so large an area of Britain can be viewed in the South?

2. *The English legend*

Part of this unconcern may spring from ignorance of the facts, but such ignorance in turn springs from the lack of concern. It is not usually recognised that in area Scotland is more than half the size of England, even with Wales thrown in. The fate of the Highlands is the fate of at least a sixth part of the total area of Britain and might appear to deserve some consideration; but geography, like history, takes on a special perspective when it is popularly expounded in London – as in the belief that England is an island, and that Britain has no inhabited islands except the Isle of Wight and the Isle of Man.

The main source of the differences between the English and the Scottish attitude appears to be found in the different legends accepted on the two sides of the Border. Popular speakers on the B.B.C. seem to confuse the temporal order with the order of distance from London. We have been told, even by the B.B.C. in Scotland, that the British character is made up of Saxon love of liberty and Norman efficiency. Usually, however, the prevailing view is more liberal. The Angles and the Saxons and the Normans, and even on occasion the Danes, are spoken of as if they were the original inhabitants of these islands. At the tail end of the list there may be a mention of the Britons as if they were late arrivals. When the benefits derived from the Roman occupation of Britain are extolled, it seems to be forgotten that if these benefits reached the Anglo-Saxons at all, it must have been through the Britons whom they are supposed to have massacred. The Gaels are still more dimly descried, if they are descried at all – they are too far North. Their disappearance would leave the average Englishman unconscious of any loss, though it is he who ultimately decides their fate. The rush of a few thousand Highlanders to Derby is known to have caused something like a panic in London in 1745, but otherwise they form no part of 'British' history. So far as they English legend is dimly aware of their existence, they appear as primitive barbarians without a past as they are without a future. Even in the North of England, which ought to know better, a gentleman on the radio who politely compares them with Bantus can meet with hilarious approval. One of the 'indubitable facts' of British history is that St. Augustine of Canterbury was the first to introduce culture and religion into a land of savages.

It should be unnecessary to mention, or to criticise, this English legend were it not for its effect on present attitudes towards the Highlands. No one acquainted with these dignified and courteous people can regard them as mere barbarians. Even in their decay they have their magic songs and proud dances, which are among the best indications of racial character. Many of them still show a command of language, even in English, and a liveliness of imagination which mark them out from other people. There should in any case be no need to delve into past history in order to claim for the earliest inhabitants of these islands the ordinary rights of human beings to continue their own way of life in their own country. In view of past injustices they would seem entitled to all the help and sympathy they can be given.

Such at least is the view widely held in Scotland. Why should it seem alien or unreasonable to our English brothers?

3. *The Scottish legend*

Only a detailed historical account could dispose of the English legend. Here it can merely be noted that history, like geography, appears very different when viewed from different sides of the Border.

According to the Scottish legend the Gaels belong to the Keltic peoples who dominated northern Europe for centuries before the Christian era and penetrated even as far as Asia Minor in the East and Spain in the West. Whatever civilisation there was in Europe outside the Greco-Roman world belonged to them. Something of their pride and chivalry peers out occasionally even in the dry pages of Julius Caesar. It would not be too difficult to trace similar qualities in their kinsmen who settled in the British Islands, qualities which have persisted down to the present day.

It is only too easy to find savagery in others and to ignore it in ourselves. There was plenty of savagery in the tribal warfare of the Gael; but was it any worse than the savagery found in the Anglo-Saxon Chronicle, not to mention that of later times? Even to-day civilised nations sink easily into barbarism in time of war, as can be seen in the cruelties of the German Nazis and more recently in the ruthlessness of some Frenchmen in Algeria. In time of peace and in a supremely civilised society like Eighteenth-Century France, ladies and gentlemen crowded to see criminals, real or alleged, being broken on the wheel or torn apart by wild horses. It is impossible to estimate a nation or race solely on the grounds of its deviations into savagery. Any one who knows the Gaels to-day will be struck, not by their brutality, but by a curious kind of gentleness.

As to the origin of culture and religion, the English legend again seems to fall into confusion about the temporal order of events. It is apt to forget that three British bishops attended the Council of Arles in A.D.324 – long before the Angles and Saxons had arrived in Britain. Places remote from London, like Ireland and Scotland, had become Christian years before the coming of Augustine, and their Gaelic missionaries had already converted the Angles of the North, not to mention considerable parts of Germany.

Even after Augustine came, many of these Angles still looked to Ireland and Scotland for their culture and religion. His mission was primarily to the heathen Anglo-Saxons in the neighbourhood of London at a time when there already existed a flourishing British Church. By a display of the pride for which he was notorious he succeeded in alienating the British clergy in spite of their humility and willingness to learn – in their simplicity they had imagined that pride was incompatible with Christianity. If he did not actually encourage his heathen friends to massacre them, his threats and prophecies were not calculated to act as a restraint.

A comparison of ancient legends is not very profitable even if their influence persists to the present day; but the Scottish legend at least calls attention to possible gaps in the English one. Let us turn to more recent events in which may be found the origin of the present unhappy situation.

4. *Culloden*

Although it is undesirable to dwell on past wrongs, yet in face of the complacent assumption that the Treaty of Union proved an unmixed blessing to Scotland and to the Highlands, it may not be out of place to refer briefly to Culloden. A recent book on this subject by Mr. John Prebble, an Englishman brought up in Canada, should be consulted by any one who wishes to know what happened. According to this detached historian it was here that there began the sickness from which Scotland, and the Highlands in particular, have never recovered.

In the year 1745, it will be remembered, some five thousand Highlanders got as far south as Derby in a misguided attempt to regain the crown for the Stuart dynasty. After defeating the few Hanoverian troops in Scotland they had rather unwillingly crossed the Border in the hope of English support, of which they got very little except for a few hundred men from Manchester. On the other hand, there was very little fighting in England, and the conduct of these barbarians seems, at the least, to have been no worse than that of other armies in this relatively civilised century. They were finally driven back to the North and were heavily defeated at Culloden by a Hanoverian army under the Duke of Cumberland.

The deliberate butchery of the wounded, both during the battle and after it, was bad enough in itself. What was far worse was the Hanoverian brutality which went on and on in a way that sickened the whole of Scotland. Houses were burned down with little regard to the distinction between friend and foe; the china and silver and wine of the barbarians were looted; the corn was destroyed; the cattle were driven off and sold; the women and children were left to starve where they were not raped and killed. It may be doubted whether the Highlands in all their long history had seen so much savagery practised with such cold-blooded determination and efficiency.

The army which committed these outrages was not an undisciplined one: it suffered rather from an excess of discipline. Up to 1500 lashes could be inflicted as a punishment – a soldier might have as many as 500 in one day. The women of the army came under the same orders, the same lash and drumbeat, as the men. By the orders of Cumberland, soldiers' wives were whipped for giving or selling food to starving Highlanders, even to women.

The prisoners taken were treated with great severity, especially by the officers, some of whom, it may be noted, were Scotsmen. Those who were gaoled were allowed no fires or candles in the depth of winter. In order that they might be judged by English law in English courts they were taken south in transports where cruelty and torture prevailed, as if the natural hardships were not severe enough in themselves. Even after they reached London the conditions under which they were held improved little, if at all. A few noblemen were taken to Westminster Hall to be bullied and insulted and in the end beheaded; but the common punishment for the remainder was the usual obscene hanging and drawing and quartering. The lucky ones were those who were transported to plantations in America, where they were treated more or less as slaves.

It was the citizens of London, to their credit be it said, who gave to Cumberland the name of 'Butcher', when they became at least dimly aware of what was happening.

Apart from the organised savagery used against the rebels, Cumberland and other English generals like the Earl of Albemarle displayed an· extraordinary attitude even to the loyal clans and indeed to Scotland as a whole. In breach of the Treaty of Union they overrode Scots Law even in the Lowlands and treated the whole of Scotland as a rebellious and conquered country. They seem to have regarded all Scotsmen as rogues, even those most loyal to King Geoge II. When Duncan Forbes, the Lord President of the College of Justice, suggested to Cumberland that the laws of the country should be tempered with princely mercy, he was given the polite reply: 'Laws! I'll make a brigade give the laws.' Cumberland even said of this wise and reasonable man that he was as 'arrant Highland mad' as certain other Scottish noblemen, who presumably had made similar remonstrances. This conforms to the traditional practice whereby the most modest and reasonable of Scottish criticisms are swept aside as a mark of insanity.

Culloden is no longer among the battle honours of any British regiment, but the subsidiary title 'Baron Culloden' can still be given to a Royal Prince – so little consideration for Scottish sentiment, Highland and Lowland alike, is to be found among the English advisers of the Crown.

5. *The aftermath*

The oppression of the Highlanders did not end with the massacres immediately after the battle. Six years later General Wolfe tells us that he deliberately sent out a weak detachment of soldiers to take a political prisoner, in the hope that it might be destroyed in an attempt at rescue, 'thus providing an excuse to extirpate the local population *"sans miséricorde"*'. He had described the Highlanders as 'the secret enemy' and apparently considered that even at this late date the most infamous methods of repression were completely justified.

How little foundation there was for his suspicions was shown by the actions of the exiled Highlanders who were trying to build up a new life for themselves in the plantations of Carolina. In the American War of Independence they were unwise enough to take up arms on behalf of George the Third, having been urged to this course by no less a person than Flora Macdonald, the heroine who had done so much to help Charles Stuart in his escape. For their misguided loyalty they suffered what may almost be described as a second Culloden, and once again had their property confiscated and their language proscribed.

Perhaps even more revealing is the observation of General Wolfe about the Highland soldiers serving later under his own command: 'They are hardy, intrepid . . . and no great mischief if they fall.'

From a government which shared anything of this spirit no

justice could be expected, let alone generosity. All the Highland clans, loyal and rebellious alike, were subjected to the same harsh and humiliating laws. The wearing of the Highland dress, and even of the tartan, was everywhere prohibited – the penalty for a first offence was six months in gaol, and for a second offence transportation for life. The poor clansmen who had no other clothes were forced to ludicrous makeshifts which could only make them figures of fun. Nothing could have been devised more galling to their Highland pride. Even the bagpipe was suppressed as 'an instrument of war'. It could be wished that modern instruments of war were no more lethal.

6. *The Highland Clearances*

According to Mr. Prebble it was by merciless brutality that the Highlands were subdued, the glens emptied, and the clans destroyed. Yet such is the resilience of human nature that the Highlanders were able to rally after this time of oppression. The subsequent decay was gradual and was caused mainly by measures which, even if not unreasonable in themselves, failed to take into account the economic effects of an abrupt change from the old patriarchal system to one entirely different.

Thus it seems reasonable that the chiefs should be deprived of their hereditary right to administer justice, a right not always exercised without corruption and even brutality. Unfortunately the new system of law altered their status from that of a semi-military chief managing the estates of a ramified family to that of an ordinary landed proprietor. As the chief was subtly transformed into a laird, his clansmen became mere tenants holding their crofts on disadvantageous terms and without security of tenure.

The result was the tragedy of the Highland Clearances. The new lairds, and still more those to whom they sold their land, too often became absentee landlords, if this term may be applied even to gentlemen who have offices in London; but whatever their location they discovered that sheep were more profitable than men. In order to convert their estates into sheep runs they proceeded to turn thousands of their tenants out of their crofts.

This new policy of evictions was far more devastating than the occasional oppression of a hereditary chief, and it was followed with increasing ruthlessness well into the Nineteenth Century.

It is impossible to find reliable figures, but it has been claimed that hundreds of thousands of men and women and children were driven from their homes, hundreds of hamlets were destroyed, and thousands of acres were thrown out of cultivation. The process began on a really large scale about 1762 and reached its climax in the thirties and forties of the following century with the great clearances in Ross and Sutherland. Without regard to age or health men and women had their cottages burned over their heads and had to lie in the open fields during the worst of a Highland winter. They were allowed to squat in wretched huts on the sea-shore or to sail for Canada in ships where many of them died of cholera. On the top of this followed the famine of 1846 when over 300,000 people were on the verge of starvation and entirely dependent on charity from Edinburgh and Glasgow. As late as 1851 some 450 crofter families were induced by false promises to sail from South Uist for Canada. Those who refused to go, even shrieking adolescent girls, were dragged on board by brute force.

The astonishing thing is that all this was endured with so little resistance by a fierce and proud race. Perhaps they had been cowed by Culloden and its aftermath, but some writers suggest that many of their fighting men were abroad serving as soldiers in the British army. If so, they received a poor reward.

It is commonly believed that the Highlands were cleared to make room for deer forests, but this was a later development, which began in the 1870's after sheep-rearing became less profitable as a result of Australian competition. In a land where hunting, shooting, and fishing had been almost free for all there were nearly two million acres of deer forest by 1883. In 1912 the total had grown to over three and a half million acres, of which a million and a half had been scheduled by a Royal Commission as fit for agriculture. It was not till the end of the Nineteenth Century that the British Government began to show some concern for the damage done by all this wastage and injustice. But when decay has gone far enough, it becomes difficult, if not impossible, to arrest it.

These extraordinary happenings have not been without apologists. Harriet Beecher Stowe, the humane authoress of *Uncle Tom's Cabin*, was induced by her aristocratic friends to defend the worst proceedings in Sutherland. Even to-day we hear voices innocently proclaiming that the landlords were moved by purely humanitarian motives: they sought to rescue their tenants from a life of poverty, and it was only a fortunate coincidence that the profits to be obtained from sheep happened to become known at the same time. But however noble their motives, the methods employed were outrageous and the results devastating. It is bad enough that so much land has been lost which once produced food and could do so again, as recent experiments have shown. It is far worse that so many of the oldest and finest stock in our country should have been forced to leave their native land for ever.

It would be tedious to recount the minor disadvantages under which the Highlands and Islands have suffered, and indeed still suffer in spite of all attempts at amelioration. If too simple a generalisation may be forgiven, the traditional crofter depended for his livelihood, not only on farming his tiny plot and keeping a few livestock, but also on inshore fishing and on weaving. This simple, yet varied life, if it was far from luxurious, may seem to some of us to be in some ways more rounded and satisfying than the nervous specialisation of modern cities. But how could this be understood by London politicians and officials? The crofters have at last been made more secure in the tenure of their land, but they cannot live on this alone. Their inshore fishing was made unprofitable even during the present century by a policy which, unlike that followed by Norway and Iceland, has allowed foreign trawlers to denude some of the richest fishing grounds in the world. More recently the market for their famous tweeds was damaged by imposing a purchase tax on so-called luxury goods. The lack of adequate roads and railways and shipping, the neglect and abandonment of the old piers, and the ever increasing cost of transport, have made the sale of local products more and more difficult and raised all prices for people already living near to the bone. It is even claimed – though this may be more doubtful – that in spite of paying the usual taxes they are deprived of benefits from the Welfare State because southern officials are accustomed to deal only with workers confined to a single job.

All of these charges, and many others like them, may be subject to some qualification. What remains certain is that, in spite of efforts to check it, the process of depopulation goes on and on.

7. *The rocket range in South Uist*

Even to-day the Highland way of life is exposed to new assaults from an uncomprehending British Government. The main centres of Gaelic culture are now to be found in the Outer Hebrides. South Uist in particular has, or had, a strong Highland community, where Gaelic is still the main language and might be expected to survive for some generations. Furthermore it enjoyed, what is not too common in the Highlands, considerable stretches of good arable land, known as the 'machair'. This was one of the few places never fully penetrated by the Reformation, and many of the crofters there are Roman Catholics, a living relic of the mediaeval Scottish Church and perhaps even of the earlier Keltic Church itself.

As infallibly as the needle to the pole, it was to this region that the Government turned when it decided that it must have a rocket range at home instead of overseas. This was the only possible site – all other sites having been rejected after careful consideration, no details of which were ever given. What was more, even within the island the only place where the range could be built was the *machair* land, on which the prosperity of the inhabitants depended. The crofters would of course be compensated, and the immense sum of £20,000,000 to be spent could not fail to benefit the islanders. The customary bland assurances were given that invasion by large numbers of purely English-speaking workers and service men would in no way affect the traditions and language of the original inhabitants. In any case the defence of Britain would be hopelessly crippled unless we had rockets 'Breaking the silence of the seas among the farthest Hebrides'.

There was the usual outcry from the islanders and from other Scotsmen convinced that the last remnants of their age-long tradition were to be destroyed. In spite of able support from prominent Roman Catholics the outcry fell on deaf ears. The earliest inhabitants of these islands were lectured on the nature of British patriotism, even by gentlemen whose names suggested they were recent arrivals determined to be more English than the English. We all had to make sacrifices, and Scotland could be no exception. What never emerged was the slightest understanding of how great this particular sacrifice was.

Meanwhile the scheme, in spite of becoming ever more modest, seemed to require more and more of the fertile land. The £20,000,000 was soon reduced to £5,000,000. It was even doubted whether the whole project might not speedily become superfluous since the improved rockets of the future may require testing grounds measured, not in hundreds, but in thousands of miles. If the whole scheme is to be abandoned after a few years, the mischief will already have been done. If, as some hold, the crofters who have lost their land and sold their stock will have to emigrate, the chances are that they will never return. The community is most unlikely to recover its former prosperity and certain to lose its ancient innocence.

The School of Scottish Studies in Edinburgh urged that at least some attempt should be made to record the speech and songs and traditions of the island before they had been corrupted by the new invasion. Their appeal for a small grant to help them in this endeavour was rejected by the Secretary of State: he was simple enough to think that this upheaval would not have any marked effect on the local traditions. Fortunately a Norwegian professor of Keltic Languages regarded this reply as irresponsible and condemned the whole policy as an act of barbarism. He came to the rescue by persuading the University of Oslo to give him a grant so that he might carry out some studies before it was too late. The charity of a foreign university had to supply the sympathy and help refused by the British Government.

8. *The need for change*

It would give a false impression not to recognise that during the last sixty years or so something has been done to ameliorate the position of the crofters throughout the Highlands as a whole. Their tenure has been improved, and there is a Land Court to which they may appeal. There is a special Crofters Commission; and indeed there has been a superabundance of commissions and committees and panels to enquire and advise and recommend. The North of Scotland Hydro-Electric Board, in spite of jealous suspicion from the South, has brought electricity to many parts, and the Forestry Commission has also done something to help. But, in spite of all this, depopulation and unemployment continue, and the problem remains unsolved.

A problem like this cannot be tackled by a conglomeration of Government Departments, some of which are in Edinburgh and some in London, so that co-operation between them becomes even more difficult than it would be otherwise. Always we find the same reluctance of Whitehall to recognise that Scotland has special problems to be met and overcome; and this is made all the more difficult because English Members of Parliament find it difficult to understand how principles and regulations admirably suited to the Home Counties can be devastating when applied to a wholly different situation in the North. It may – to give only one example – seem reasonable in England that the Government grant to support the rating system should vary with the population; but where there is a vast county with a small and declining population, the result may be catastrophic. The grant to Inverness-shire was savagely cut when the population fell below an arbitrary figure. The effect of this can be only worse services, higher rates, and further depopulation, which will lead in turn to further reductions in the grant, and so on indefinitely. What good the Government does with one hand it may easily undo with the other.

The obvious need to deal with the problem as a whole is so great that heroic measures may be required. Instead of the present chaotic system there should be a single authority with wide powers and with adequate finance which could be used without continual reference to London. It has been claimed that the Highland and Islands Development Board set up in 1965 will meet these requirements. It has some good men on it, and we must wish it well; but the omens are not too favourable, and we have still to see how it will work out in practice. The so-called Highland Fund, a small private organisation hampered by interference from the Board of Trade, has already shown how much can be done, even with grossly inadequate funds, by men who know the country. But what can be achieved against the rigid policies of Government departments working in the opposite direction? If, for example, the children of the glens are directed at a tender age to pursue higher education far away in the hostels or lodgings of strange towns, their parents will inevitably follow and no parents of young children will come to take their place. Even the green and happy isle of Arran seems destined in the long run to become a home for the aged and childless.

9. *'Why are you sleep?'*

The usual answer to all this is that the land is too poor to be developed. Something like half the total extent of Scotland is now devoted to grouse moors. It seems rather a lot, but we are sometimes told we must be content to leave this vast area as an undeveloped country and – during a few months of the year – a paradise for affluent sportsmen, who come mainly from the South of England or even from America and Western Germany.

Such a contention must be received with some scepticism. Large sporting estates in the Highlands may change hands at colossal prices – one of these was sold in 1961 for £420,000 – but this does little to help the local inhabitants. In spite of some outstanding exceptions both Scottish and English, there are many landlords, whether absentee or otherwise, who do not want the country to be fully developed – some of them, it is said, congratulate those who have no crofters on their land. English politicians whose only knowledge of Scotland is acquired during their annual visit to the grouse moors in August may receive a somewhat one-sided view of the situation.

It is true that the Highlands in many places are not well adapted to the growing of grain, and land which has been long neglected is bound to deteriorate. Yet the glens used to support a much larger population when methods of agriculture were more primitive than they are to-day. They also used to rear many cattle, and recent experiments show that they could do so again, to the great advantage of Scotland and of Britain as a whole. Modern science is developing methods for making peatland into pastures, and the modest application of these methods in the Highlands has already met with some success. The area as a whole is said to be the best in Europe for the growing of conifers, and with the necessary pulp-mills it could save the heavy cost of British imports from Scandinavia. Here in the modern jargon we have a region of 'unrealised potential'. The situation might be transformed with more research and with an adequate system of transport; but the Highlands are at present too poor to provide all this for themselves.

All this may be dismissed as wishful thinking. Those who accept such a view ought to study what has happened, and is happening, in Norway. With a population much less than that of Scotland, with far fewer natural resources and with a much more rugged climate, the Norwegians have succeeded in bringing prosperity to regions of their own country much more difficult than anything to be found in the Highlands and Islands. They have done this – through their government – by research and technology, by providing cheap and adequate transport, by granting loans to enterprising individuals on the security of their character alone, and by excluding foreign trawlers from their fiords in the teeth of obstinate British opposition. Much of the land is owned and farmed successfully by small peasants to the great advantage of the country as a whole. They are amazed to find that the very opposite policy has been followed in the Highlands – a policy, as it seems to them, of madness. Their amazement has been well expressed by a simple Norwegian skipper: 'Scottish people I do not understand. If my country owned these islands, we should all be rich, everybody, fishermen, farmers, shopkeepers, everybody. Why are you sleep? Such a terrible waste!'

Why indeed are you sleep? The obvious answer might seem to be that, unlike Norway, Scotland has no real control over her own affairs. She is hampered and thwarted at every turn by a lopsided and top-heavy system of administration which is not adapted to her needs. The complacency of the English in these matters is sometimes hard to bear. On their view they have benevolently brought the advantages of English civilisation to untutored barbarians. If anything is wrong, this must be ascribed to the inhabitants or to the climate or to the nature of the soil – never to more than two hundred years of neglect and misgovernment.

It is becoming common form to say, in irritation or in pity, that Scotsmen are always asking for help, when all they are asking for is the power to use some of their own money to make good the damage inflicted on them in the past. But the problem here goes far deeper than the doling out of financial favours or distributing them in a juster way. Is it not a loss to the whole of Britain that a vast tract of territory should fall into ruin? The loss is spiritual as well as material; but even if the English care nothing for Highland traditions and Gaelic culture, can they still say with General Wolfe of some of the best sailors and soldiers in the world 'it is no great mischief if they fall'. Is it impossible for them to follow the Norwegian example and consider the interests of our country as a whole? Can we not hope that even at this late date they might open their eyes and look at the situation from a British, and not just a narrowly London, point of view?

The lost men and women will never return, and the Gaelic language and tradition may disappear for ever, but at least in terms of a modest economic prosperity it is hard to believe that Scotland, if given the power, could not do what Norway has already done.

CHAPTER X

MIGRATION AND UNEMPLOYMENT

*Scotland has a pool of labour which firms in the
South might envy*

A Cabinet Minister

1. *Emigration*

The Highlands and Islands have become depopulated through
a long process which began with savage suppression and has
been completed through greed and indifference and neglect. The
same tendency to decline in numbers is to be found elsewhere,
though in a lesser degree. The Border counties, in spite of the well-
known toughness of their inhabitants, suffer from this wasting
malady, as do also the Northern Isles – the Orkneys and Shetlands.
Even in the rich industrial Lowlands the population, if it does not
actually decrease, fails to increase in a normal way. The relative
stagnation of industry which has been described earlier means
more than a mere failure to increase material wealth. The result-
ing unemployment has caused many of the youngest and most
vigorous men and women to seek their fortunes elsewhere. In
economic decline Scotland could still survive; but a disproportionate drain on her resources of mind and character, great
as these are, must mean in the end that Scotland will cease to be
herself. It is fear of this that presses so heavily on those who care
about the fate of their country.

The number of Scottish-born men and women living outside
Scotland has been estimated at a million and a quarter – or
about a fourth of her present population. Well over 600,000 of
these are known to be settled in England. One authority has
said that if we take into account the descendants of previous
emigrants for three generations, the number of people with
Scottish blood who live overseas (apart altogether from those
living in England and Wales) must reach a total of twenty-five

170

million – or five times the present population of the home country.

Even if some of these figures are exaggerated – and the second one does not profess to be more than a rough estimate – it cannot be denied that the number of exiles is disproportionate to the total present population. Nothing like this could be said of the southern half of the United Kingdom.

We can look at the situation in another way. In 1801 the population in Scotland was getting on for one-fifth of the population of England and Wales. In 1901 it was not very far short of one-seventh. By 1964 it had become less than one-ninth, and the process of decline is still going on. The rate at which the population increases in England and Wales is almost double the rate in Scotland. If the South of England is taken by itself, the rate of increase is said to be five times the rate of all the rest of Britain.

It may be replied that all this happens through the working of economic processes and is part of the inevitable price to be paid for the benefits gained from the Union with England. The price may seem rather heavy; but we shall be told in a politely jocular way that since the natural place for Scotsmen is at the top, they must necessarily gravitate to the centre of power and wealth. Perhaps we shall not even be spared the unprovoked rudeness of Dr. Johnson about the noblest prospect which a Scotsman ever sees – so often quoted as a gem of English wit. But Scotsmen do not complain that their compatriots may be led by the spirit of adventure to seek their fortune all over the world. What they resent is being forced to emigrate because they can find no work in their own country. This has been happening too long, and is happening now.

Like a human being, a country can give some of its blood with advantage to others and without serious loss to itself. But if this process is continued too far, it must result in anaemia, and ultimately in death.

2. *Unemployment*

The outstanding feature of the economic landscape in Scotland during the last fifty years has been the high rate of unemployment.

We need not go back to the nightmare period between the two Wars, though it is certainly not forgotten and has left a permanent scar. There is no comparison between what happened then and what is happening now, but the dreary fact remains that even in the Affluent Society and the Welfare State the rate of unemployment in Scotland has been consistently double that in the United Kingdom as a whole.

This way of describing the situation conceals the real disparity; for the United Kingdom as a whole includes Scotland and other regions of high unemployment like Wales and Northern Ireland. If comparison were made with England by itself, or – better still – with the favoured regions of the South, the rate of unemployment in Scotland must be at least three or four times as great. The character of Scottish unemployment seems also to be more oppressive: in November 1962, for example, it was stated without contradiction in the House of Commons that six out of every ten people unemployed in Scotland had been out of work for more than two months. This could not be said of the relatively few unemployed in the South of England.

Part of this unemployment may be caused by the way in which private English firms in times of difficulty close their Scottish branches or 'subsidiaries', whether these have been established by the firms themselves or are originally Scottish firms which have been taken over. But the modern system of centralised government and national corporations cannot be absolved of responsibility, direct as well as indirect. It may be mere coincidence, but the number of workers dismissed from the railways and the mines, together with the workers in the Shale Oil industry, which has been taxed out of existence, is not very far short of the total number of unemployed.

These body blows make the heart less sick than what may be described as a continual succession of jolts and jabs from which there appears to be no respite. Naval bases in Scotland are busy enough in time of war, but when the war is over they are dismantled and the ships are transferred to more agreeable quarters in the South of England. This is said to be necessary in the interests of economy; and we are told, no doubt in jest, that if Scotland had a permanent naval depot, some ships in the Royal

Navy would be manned entirely by Scotsmen, and even the British Navy cannot afford to have all its best men in a few ships. Royal Ordnance factories were closed at Dalmuir, Bishopton, and Irvine; naval establishments at Greenock, Dalbeattie, Invergordon, Rothesay, and elsewhere. British European Airways transferred maintenance work from Renfrew to the South; and so on and so on. The need for economy seems almost always to work to the disadvantage of the North.

Even apart from such large-scale economies the complaints about administrative action are many and various, as we have seen in earlier chapters. Here we must be content to give a typical, if very minor, example of the sort of thing that happens. Scottish buildings have traditionally been of stone, while the English practice is to use bricks. But Government buildings in Scotland have to be brick-built – on the alleged ground that bricks are cheaper: this may be true in England, but was not always true in Scotland. Even when stone is permitted, the type of stone is chosen on the basis of English experience; and then it is discovered, not surprisingly, that this type of stone has to be imported from England. Furthermore, by some curious coincidence, the ordinary rate per ton charged for moving Scottish stone on British Railways was, at least at one time, 25 per cent more than the rate charged for carrying Northumberland stone for similar distances. If this sort of practice prevails, it is no wonder that the trade of mason in Scotland should be in danger of extinction.

Complaints of this kind may, some of them, appear to be concerned with small matters, but it is no small matter if centralised administration always works in the same direction, not from any ill will, but from the inevitable tendency of English officials to base their decisions on English experience and on what is suitable for English conditions. Such decisions have indirect effects as well as direct ones. They set up chain reactions since the loss of income caused in Scotland acts unfavourably on other trades and so throws other people out of work besides those who are immediately affected.

This does not mean that a British Government will do nothing to counteract the damage done by its own sins of omission and commission. On the contrary, it is prepared to make some attempt at stopping the leaks, especially when there is a General Election in the offing. The Local Employment Act of 1960 set aside large grants in order to bring industries to the regions which suffered most from unemployment. Of these special grants Scotland received more than the lion's share. This is sometimes used to show that Scotland is favoured at the expense of England and so has no ground for complaint. Welcome although these grants are, they are attempts to make good some of the losses suffered in the past. If you let a ship run on the rocks, it is no great favour to spend money in repairing the damage – especially when the money comes in the end from the unfortunate owners themselves. Without this help things would admittedly be even worse than they are, but new leaks are sprung as quickly as the old ones are stopped, and the population of Scotland has begun to decrease, not merely relatively, but absolutely. A policy with these results cannot properly be described as a success.

Some of these 'grants' may look more generous than they are. Many of them may be loans which have to be repaid at a high rate of interest. The amount freely given was said at one time to be about £200 for each new job created – less than would have to be paid for unemployment benefit.

3. The 'brain drain'

The unemployment figures for Scotland, serious as they are, conceal the true picture in another way. By the nature of the case they can take no account of the large numbers who have been forced to emigrate in order to find employment elsewhere. Without this enforced emigration the unemployment figures would be very much worse than they are.

Some of this emigration is unorganised – there are sad stories of isolated Scotsmen tramping the roads to the South in search of work. Some of it is organised by governmental action; some of it by private firms.

The village of Corby in Northamptonshire is a striking example. The majority of its inhabitants are now Scottish because in the depressed Thirties a large steel firm moved many of its workers from the neighbourhood of Glasgow to the South. In this case the move was made in order to be near to some specially rich sources of iron ore, but it was none the less a blow to Scotland. Similar actions on a lesser scale and for less good reasons have the same unfortunate effect.

It is far more serious when emigration is organised by the Government itself. The uncontradicted allegation that the Forestry Commission refuses to let its Scottish graduates serve it in Scotland has already been noted; similar policies are said to be followed, if in a lesser degree, by various national 'corporations'; and a whole vista is opened up when a complacent Englishman proudly informs us that half the employees in a factory working for a public Board in Scotland are English. A better authenticated example of Government action in the strict sense is the case of the Royal Ordnance Factory at Dalmuir. When this was closed in 1958 skilled employees were transferred to the South. They had accepted 'the responsibility to transfer' under an agreement negotiated ten years before with trade union representatives, who were presumably mainly English. An example already mentioned is the organised transfer of Scottish miners to southern coalfields. At least in some cases redundancy pay was cut when an unemployed miner refused to move to England.

These transfers of skilled workers are a loss to Scotland far beyond the mere numbers involved. If under the present system the population of Scotland decreases steadily in relation to that of England, this is bad enough; but what is devastating is the decrease in quality. It is the best men who are taken away – the young men with their families, not the old; the skilled men, not the unskilled. This must in time produce an ageing population and an unbalanced economy.

On the higher levels of intelligence Government policy works even more disastrously in the same direction, though here its methods may be less obvious. A minor factor is the prevailing tendency to pay smaller salaries in Scotland than are paid in England. It is hard to see, for example, why a Scottish dentist should be paid so much less than an English one that he is unable to pay dental technicians, who in consequence have to migrate to England; or again why Scottish teachers, even if better qualified, should be paid less than English ones. Scottish librarians are also grossly underpaid, partly, it is said, because there has been no time to pass a Library Act for Scotland such as has been enjoyed by England for some years. All such practices work against the interests of Scotland, but the greatest source of complaint is the unfair treatment of research. Nearly all government research departments – some say as much as 97 per cent – are located in England, especially in the South. Scotland may still produce far more than its share of graduates in science and technology, but it is said that nine out of ten can find no work in Scotland – they are compelled to leave if they wish to earn a living. The millions of tax-payers' money spent on the evolution of aircraft, radar, tanks, atomic weapons, guided missiles, torpedoes and so on go to establishments in the South. So too with less immediately practical institutes of research. Where there is money for these, the British Government appears to think first of placing them in Oxford and Cambridge and London, and perhaps in Manchester. Apart from a very few exceptions, almost always the result of violent agitation, Scotland comes last in the queue. When proposals were made in the World Health Organisation to establish an international centre of medical research in Edinburgh, these were met with a chorus of protests from the South of England.

We may hope that some of these charges are overstated. Even so, it is clear enough that through no fault of her own Scotland suffers from a 'brain-drain' far more serious than any drains of her material wealth and almost inconceivable anywhere else. This phrase has been used by English newspapers complaining that since the War some of our ablest scientists are tempted to work in America because of higher salaries and greater opportunities; but this loss is trifling in comparison with the loss suffered by Scotland through many years.

Englishmen can recognise clearly enough that it may be bad for England to lose her ablest sons, no matter what success they may achieve in exile; but they are strangely reluctant to accept the same principle for Scotland. When the Scots, in Parliament or elsewhere, complain of forced emigration, this is commonly received with indifference or even irritation. If a Minister of the Crown expresses sympathy with Scotsmen who dislike being compelled to work in England, he is greeted with shouts of 'Why?' A vigorous Member of Parliament can loudly proclaim that the cure for unemployment in Scotland is to bring the Scots to England. Even in the House of Lords, where one might expect better manners, a noble peer can sneer at those who wish to remain in Scotland and suggest that this is because they prefer to enjoy the high rate of unemployment benefit.

So long as such attitudes are found in an all-powerful and predominantly English Parliament the prospect for Scotland is dismal indeed.

4. *The Irish Invasion*

The real extent of Scottish depopulation is concealed in other ways. So far the complaint has been merely that Scotland is denied her normal rate of increase: her population grows much more slowly than that of England and Wales. But this modest increase would have turned into a devastating decrease – there was for the first time an actual decrease in 1965 – were it not for one factor of which most Englishmen are blissfully unaware. The native stock has been steadily replaced by immigrants from Ireland.

The invasion of the Irish has been going on for a long time. Ireland too has suffered from misgovernment, far more seriously than Scotland, and has been unable to support her native population. In the Nineteenth Century when Scotland was pioneering the new industries, Scottish firms were able to import cheap manual labour from Ireland. As the Highlanders sailed out, the Irish sailed in. This first invasion is now a matter of past history. The second invasion is in some ways perhaps more serious. It occurred especially between the Two World Wars – during the very period when Scotland suffered so tragically from unemployment. It is still going on, although it has diminished in recent years and may diminish still more in the future. In Eire the Irish now control their own destiny and can do something to staunch the outflow of Irish blood from which they have suffered to long.

The first invasion, although caused mainly by British misgovernment in Ireland, can be put down to the working of economic forces during a period of *laissez-faire*; but the second invasion has been furthered, if unconsciously, by the action and inaction of British Government, in Scotland itself.

It is hard to write on this topic without laying oneself open to the customary jibes at Scottish narrowness and intolerance; but this is no reason why the broad facts of the situation should be ignored. In Glasgow a third of the inhabitants are said to be Irish or of Irish descent; and any one who visits almost any Scottish town can confirm that they have spread over the whole country. The fear or hope is sometimes expressed that further immigration, coupled with a high birthrate, will in time reduce the Scots to being a minority in their own country.

Although these fears and hopes may be exaggerated, few reasonable men, and certainly few reasonable Scotsmen, will regard it as an unmixed blessing that an unusually homogeneous country should be split up into two nations. Yet if the native stock is doomed to decline, Scotland may be considered fortunate in so far as the Irish invaders belong to a race not wholly alien to her own. Provided their numbers were not too great, there would be some hope of their becoming assimilated in the course of time – there are already signs of their being affected by some of the traditional Scottish ideals. Some of them have shown themselves men of ability, and they have strengthened Scotland in the field of sport.

Whatever may be hoped for in the future, the mass immigration of men and women with a lower standard of living was not an unmixed blessing to Scotland – especially at a time when she was already crippled by unemployment. At least in the early stages the Irish sometimes failed to display the more sober virtues cherished by the Scots: law-abidingness, for example, has not always been their most outstanding characteristic. In the course of time they tend, some of them, to become rootless, especially if they abandon their religion. Even if they remain citizens of the Republic of Ireland and owe no allegiance to this country, they are given voting rights which – notably on questions of marriage, divorce, termination of pregnancy, and so on – enable them to influence legislation for Scotland, and to some extent for Britain as a whole. They do not love the English, but it is doubtful how far they identify themselves with Scotland; the supporters of one of their great football teams are said to wave the flag of Eire with what looks like defiance at the playing of 'God save the Queen'. When they succeed in joining the Establishment, it is not unknown for them to proclaim that Scotland has all the self-government she requires. This is a little hard to bear, though not so hard as the taunt from Ireland itself 'You poor Scotch, you will never be free.'

The problem has not been made easier by the fact that there were two kinds of Irish invader – the Orange and the Green. The Orangemen came in far fewer numbers and were assimilated without difficulty – many of them were of Scottish descent. Nevertheless the double invasion meant that the more robust Irish methods of religious controversy were introduced as substitutes for the traditional Scottish practice of theological argument. The clash between the two kinds of invader sometimes led to disorder at the beginning of the century, and the effects of this bad tradition continue even to-day. Violence is always infectious, and it could not be claimed that native Scotsmen were immune. Troubles of this kind do not diminish when they are complicated by economic competition and racial differences, but on the whole there has been relatively little intolerance: there seems to be more in Liverpool, where there is a similar problem. In the poorer quarters the two races have had to live side by side, and such rowdiness as there is is now displayed mainly on the football field; it seems to spring more from traditional hooliganism than from religious conviction, and it is deplored alike by Scottish ministers and Irish priests. A distinguished Glasgow Irishman, Sir Patrick Dollan, testified, shortly before his death, to the absence of hostility between the two races. He spoke movingly of his boyhood when his strictly Protestant neighbours regularly prepared breakfast for his family who went to Mass, and his own family returned the compliment by getting ready the midday meal for the Protestant family who had been attending Church.

This gentler spirit has not always prevailed, but it shines 'like a jewel for its own sake' in an intolerant world.

In spite of profound differences in temperament the Scots have shown sympathy for the fate of Ireland, which suffered so much more than their own country. As has already been said, they were willing to subordinate their own claims for Home Rule to the more pressing claims of the Irish. Yet the departure of Irish representatives from the Parliament at Westminster has been a serious loss to Scotland. The Irish never made the mistake of appealing to reason in the Scottish way which makes so little impression in the South. So long as they were in Parliament, they were able to sting the English out of the illusion that these islands are inhabited solely by Englishmen.

5. *The immigration muddle*

It may be said that all this has nothing to do with the policies of successive British governments.

This claim unfortunately is not wholly true, as would be obvious if we pushed our enquiries back into the Nineteenth Century. We forget too easily that in the Irish potato famine of 1845–49 nearly a million British subjects died of starvation in a country that was not short of food; and about the same number were forced to emigrate under conditions not far removed from those of a modern concentration camp. These disasters were accepted in London with the customary equanimity – 'Dependence on charity is not to be made an agreeable mode of life'. The whole tragedy sprang in the last resort from the system of land occupation in Ireland. This system, for which the British Government was ultimately responsible, was not reformed till the beginning of the present century, and it certainly played its part in forcing the Irish to abandon their own country and seek a livelihood elsewhere. But this is now past history. Let us be content to look at the last fifty years.

It is admirable to keep an open door for citizens of the Commonwealth and indeed of the world; but it is less admirable to entice masses of them through this door by artificial inducements. On reflexion it may seem unwise so to arrange your Welfare State that immigrants after a very brief period should be paid more for doing nothing than they can earn by hard work in their own country: this is what may be called an artificial inducement. It may seem even more unwise to forbid the deportation even of those among them who devote themselves to a life of crime. Such measures, so far as I know, have not been adopted by any other country, whether in the Commonwealth or outside it.

To say this is not to reflect on the character of the immigrants, many of whom may be most worthy. It is merely to suggest that a government ought not to provide temptations which the imperfect human nature common to us all may not always be able to withstand.

One curious exception to this practice may be noted in passing. Immigrants who become dependent on public assistance or who turn to crime cannot be deported; but under the Criminal Justice Act of 1948 English magistrates were empowered to deport Scottish criminals and send them back to Scotland on probation. This they have done at times without even warning the probation officers. On one occasion three Scottish criminals were told 'go back to Glasgow where you belong'. All of them, it may be added, had Irish names. Whether this way of singling Scotland out for special treatment has now been abandoned, I am unable to say. It may be contrasted with the immunity from deportation of an Irish youth who appeared before the Scottish courts. He had been able for a considerable time to enjoy a comfortable life in Scotland by dint of inventing a wife and five children in need of public assistance. Apparently he had been born in 1933, married in 1935, and blessed with his first child in 1937. Apart from this achievement he was a good simple boy who sent the bulk of his weekly gains back to his old mother in Ireland.

There is a belief held in Scotland that Irish immigration in search of public assistance was not unorganised. In the terrible period of unemployment between the Wars the Irish were already well established. Ireland also was suffering from unemployment, and Irishmen, it is alleged, were brought over in batches to fill jobs under Irish foremen long enough to qualify for the 'dole', as it was then called. When they were qualified, they abandoned the jobs, and a new batch of Irishmen was brought in to take their place. This process could be continued indefinitely.

These and similar legends may be exaggerated, though it is true that Irish immigrants still come in surprisingly well informed of their rights in the Welfare State, including those to sick pay. It seems fair enough to say that the untrammelled benefits provided by the Welfare State have played some part in bringing into this country too many of the less valuable elements in the Irish invasion. These results were unintended and unforeseen. They belong to the policy of muddling through.

One muddle leads to another one; and similar, though more difficult, problems which affected England have been met by restrictions on immigration which are bound to seem unfair and discriminatory. If the first muddle had been avoided, the second need never have arisen. But since the Irish are exempt from these restrictions, this question does not concern us here.

It must be emphasised that arguments of the type I have used depend on the relative numbers involved. Few political thinkers would maintain that we were morally bound to admit into this country millions of Russians and Chinese bent on obtaining the vote in order to destroy our democratic system and replace it with communism.

6. *Segregation in schools*

The immigration policy adopted by Parliament applies to the whole of the United Kingdom, but it has had special effects in Scotland because of another factor which is too often overlooked.

The bulk of the Irish invaders are Roman Catholics. As such they insist that their children must be educated in separate Roman Catholic schools. In other countries they have to follow this principle at a financial loss to themselves, and this they regard as unfair. In Scotland after the First War they were given educational privileges unknown outside predominantly Roman Catholic countries. They enjoy full control over their own schools, which are built and financed and maintained by the State (including the local authorities).

There is much to be said for this generous system although it means that the Church of a racial minority is the only one to be subsidised by the State. The Scots have accepted it without question in accordance with their traditional demand of justice for all men. It sets an example of religious toleration which in these milder days we may hope will in time be followed elsewhere. But it has had two effects that are unfortunate for Scotland.

The first effect is an inevitable one in the circumstances. Since the religious division is also a racial one, the segregation imposed in the schools perpetuates and hardens the division of Scotland into two nations. The rift between them would be complete were it not for the fact that the Irish for the most part go to the Scottish universities for their higher education. It is only at this stage that the youth of the two nations begin to meet in a common effort and to enjoy the opportunity of achieving some sort of mutual understanding.

The second effect is less defensible. It arises because the Westminster Parliament, which was willing enough to pass this humane legislation for Scotland, is adamant in its refusal to give the same rights to Roman Catholics in England. This is one reason why so large a part of the Irish immigration has been siphoned off into Scotland. It helps to explain why a general muddle about immigration has hit Scotland so hard.

In order to avoid the usual misunderstanding it must be emphasised that the demand for complete segregation in the schools – even where, as in one case, the children are compelled by circumstances to use the same building and the same dining hall – comes solely from the Catholics, and not from Scottish Presbyterians. On the other hand, there has recently been some talk in liberal Catholic circles in favour of integration. This would be a great benefit to Scotland as a whole.

7. Hopes and fears

Of the two evils by which Scotland has been beset, an excess of immigration and an excess of emigration, the second is at present far and away the worse.

A flow of immigrants may enrich a country. The flow becomes an evil only when it is excessive in quantity; and what is, or is not, excessive may be hard to determine. Yet an inflow may be considered excessive when it becomes too great to be assimilated so that where we had one homogeneous nation we find ourselves with two that are very different. Something like this is what has happened in Scotland. On the other hand, Scotland was fortunate so far as her peaceful invaders were of a gifted stock akin to her own. If we peer into the remote future, it may seem not unreasonable to hope that in the course of time a new and perhaps richer nationality might emerge; it might combine Irish imagination with Scottish logic. This would be more likely to happen if the two races were able to meet openly in an Edinburgh Parliament and to co-operate, even if not without friction, in trying to settle the affairs of Scotland at present so mishandled from outside.

It is the excess of emigration which is apt to produce hope-lessness and even despair. No country, not even Scotland, can suffer without permanent loss so great an outflow of her best blood and her best brains; and no amount of tinkering by amiable or indifferent strangers is likely to put matters right. The Scots, who have contributed so much to the welfare of Britain and the world, are being told, with kindly patronage or ill-concealed irritation, that their distresses spring from their own lack of vigour and initiative. It is hard to believe that initiative can be fostered by turning Scotland – and so many of her institutions – into a branch office of a London firm. If the remaining Scots are reduced to a race of mediocrities trained to await benefits and receive instructions from elsewhere, this would be a terrible condemnation of the present system. It is a gross exaggeration to speak as if they have wholly lost their ancient virtues; but if they are to recover their full vigour and initiative, this can come only by giving back to them some real control over their own fate.

These are long-term problems, and nothing is so uncertain as the future; but it is well at times to look forward to the distant goals that we may desire, or even hope, to attain.

One other observation – a more painful one – must be added.

Perhaps I spoke too hurriedly in saying that an excess of emigration is far and away the worse of the two evils by which Scotland is threatened.

In the South there is what is called an exploding population, and it is sometimes said that by the end of the century England will have an excess of twenty million inhabitants. As a result the envious eyes of some 'national' planners are set on the open spaces of the North. There is talk, for example, of a Solway barrage, which to some minds appears to mean that large stretches of South-west Scotland should be annexed to England. It has been suggested that the valley of the Tay and the fertile Carse of Gowrie could be turned into a series of conurbations for the benefit of English immigrants. Even in the Highlands the regions proposed for the new invaders include the Moray Firth and the country round Stornoway. Always, be it noted, it is the most favoured parts of agricultural Scotland that are singled out to become occupied territories. In comparison with this the unhappy efforts of Cromwell to establish settlements in Ulster would seem almost trivial.

Such schemes, if taken seriously, would mean the death of Scotland as a nation. If this is to be the final outcome of the Treaty of Union and of Scotland's loyal partnership through so many years, it would surely be time for the Scots to fight for independence before it is too late.

CHAPTER XI

IMAGES AND STEREOTYPES

Green fields of England! whereso'er
Across this watery waste we fare,
Your image at our hearts we bear,
Green fields of England, everywhere.
                              A. H. Clough

1. *Images and stereotypes*

During the Second World War some of us may have encoun-
tered an occasional refugee who – if it is not too unkind to say
this – was unable to escape from the rooted conviction that
Englishmen were trying to be Germans and were doing it very
badly. This naturally aroused his pity and at times his exaspera-
tion. He did his best to spread enlightenment, which was not
always too well received. Fortunately he was not in a position
to do anything more.

We may think that this is a caricature, but in fact nothing is
easier than to slip into attitudes of this kind: we are all tempted
to do it in some degree. We have only to suppose that our
national ideals are ideals, not merely for ourselves, but for all
mankind. Up to a point the assumption may be justifiable; for
to suppose others incapable of sharing our ideals would be even
more arrogant – we should be regarding them as 'lesser breeds
without the law'. But we should not apply our ideals too
rigidly to others or suppose that there can be no genuine ideals
except our own.

The trouble becomes acute when we are too pleased, not
merely with our ideals, but with our achievements. We then
have what may be called an image or stereotype of ourselves as
the ideal nation, and of others as trying, more or less ineffectively, to be like us. We become, as it were, the standard to

which others ought to conform and, if possible, should be made to conform.

In some ways the word 'image' is better than the word 'stereotype': it sounds slightly more flexible. A stereotype is an image that has become rigid. Both words are akin to the word 'legend', as this was used in an earlier chapter; but a legend at least professes to describe the past, while an image or stereotype is directed mainly to the present.

Every nation has images or stereotypes of itself and of its neighbours. These determine to a great extent both what it sees and how it acts or reacts. We must here try to understand them as psychological factors affecting the relations between England and Scotland. This they do in every sphere; but we shall from now on be concerned mainly, not so much with the way in which Scotland has suffered from their political and economic effects, as with the way in which she is impeded in the development of her own traditions and ideals. This is a more difficult and ultimately more important problem, which must here be treated in far too crude a way. After the last sombre chapters we are in need of relaxation, and perhaps some measure of caricature may be forgiven.

This being understood, we may proceed to state boldly and baldly the main contention of this chapter. It is this. The troubles of Scotland arise partly from the rooted English conviction that Scotsmen are trying to be Englishmen and are not doing it very well. The English by their sheer numbers are in a position to put this right, and this they are only too willing to do. What is more unfortunate is that by modern means of communication they are enabled to spread their English stereotype in Scotland itself at the expense of the native product. If only they would relax the rigidity of their stereotypes and conceive it possible that even in these islands other reasonable beings might have different ideals, many of our difficulties would be overcome.

In the sphere of law the English stereotype, as we have seen, has been formulated clearly by the highest authorities. Let us recall one outstanding example from Lord Cranworth: 'But if such be the law of England, on what ground can it be argued not to be the law of Scotland? The law as established in

England is founded on principles of universal application.' This was further generalised by Lord Campbell: 'The law must be the same in all countries where law has been considered as a science.'

The formula need not be confined to the law: it can – and does – conveniently cover other established English institutions as well.

2. *English and Scottish stereotypes*

The English stereotype of themselves is based on national self-admiration. All national stereotypes are; but the English, it has been thought, carry this practice to extremes. The characteristic is of long standing. Even the mediaeval Arab historians, who knew nothing else about the English, knew that they held all other nations in contempt. One jolly Englishman, so the phrase goes, is a match for at least three foreigners – or is it seven? – especially if they happen to be French.

The stereotype the Scots have of themselves is more limited. They too are certainly not without self-admiration, but they have more sense of the equality of man and take a respectful interest in other nations and their ways. Yet they have – or had – one rooted conviction: namely, that one Scotsman is a match for at least three Englishmen.

The Scottish stereotype, besides being more limited, is perhaps also more kindly. This can be illustrated by a phrase used by Sir James Barrie and still heard occasionally in Scotland. In reply to the question, 'Is so and so a Scotsman too?', you may get the answer, 'No, he is just English'. This recognises that the English are at least on the lower rungs of the ladder that leads to the full height of perfection appropriate to the inhabitants of these islands.

For ethnological equations of this type the evidence has to be selected with the utmost care. If, as seems probable, they were originally concerned with prowess in war, the English can look back to Crécy and Agincourt, the Scots to Bannockburn: defeats must be discreetly overlooked. But national stereotypes are extended to every walk of life and can become ever more remote from the truth. The boldest freebooters who ever sailed the sea succeeded in persuading themselves that the British Empire was a fulfilment of the promise 'The meek shall inherit the earth'. Some Englishmen even cherish a firm conviction that the English have always left the Scots to settle their own affairs in their own way.

It is absurd to take national stereotypes seriously, except perhaps as the expression of ideals. If you try to apply them to actual individuals you know, it will often become obvious that they do not fit at all. If you imagine that they are based on supposed racial differences, you may find that you have built up your stereotypes on somebody who doesn't belong to the race in question. I was astounded when the late Sir Richard Livingstone, an old friend whom I had always regarded as among the flower of Englishmen, insisted that he was a mixture of Scots and Irish and added with great vehemence: 'As to the English, their mental processes are entirely beyond my comprehension'.

If we were asked to name a typical Victorian Englishman, we might be tempted to choose Mr. Gladstone. Yet, though born and educated in England, he was a pure-bred Scot. Once this is realised he may begin to show some characteristics supposed to be Scottish – his devotion to theology; his tendency to go on arguing at greater length than might seem necessary; his readiness to flout public opinion in his zeal for good causes, as in his practice, even when Prime Minister, of talking to prostitutes in the streets and bringing them home to Mrs. Gladstone in order to save them from the error of their ways. That eagle head and eye, and even the collar, seem almost to demand as their setting a pulpit and a Geneva gown, complete with bands. Yet he was so conditioned by his English upbringing that he would walk for miles to a conventicle of his own rather than accompany his sovereign to a service in the Church of Scotland; and he took an active part in introducing the English public school system into Scotland in order to win young Scotsmen away from the faith of their fathers and so to accentuate social distinctions by the aid of religious differences.

The fact is that national stereotypes are based more on a traditional way of life than on racial differences. Yet Scotsmen may be tempted to imagine that some of the most magnificently English among our more recent politicians inherit from their Scottish forefathers a tendency to be more liberal and less inflexible than is common among undiluted Englishmen. Mr. Harold Macmillan with his 'wind of change' might be a case in point.

Another characteristic of national stereotypes is that they obscure similarities, much in the same way as family resemblances obvious to strangers are often concealed from members of the family themselves. In one of Frank O'Connor's short stories two Irish priests pursue a delinquent girl on board a French ship lying in harbour. The skipper, being a Frenchman, takes the lowest possible view of their motives and incidentally addresses them as 'English'. When they protest that they are Irish, he says: 'I know all that: you call yourselves Irish, and the others call themselves Scotch, but you are all English. There is no difference. It is always the same; always women, always hypocrisy, always the plaster saint'.

Perhaps if we could become less obsessed by our own stereotypes, we might comfort ourselves with the thought that the British nations may be more alike than we imagine, sharing not merely some common vices, but even some common virtues.

Rigid stereotypes, national and otherwise, besides being partly false and partly silly, can be really harmful in so far as they prevent us from seeing every man as a unique individual. If we proceed to play about with them here, it is because they may have serious consequences.

3. *The English stereotype of England*

If we sought to do justice to the stereotype the English have of themselves, this would be a lengthy business. It would consist mainly in a eulogy of English virtues, a eulogy often richly deserved. It would be a pleasure to attempt such a eulogy here, but this would be irrelevant to our present purpose; and in any case the English image of themselves is widely known. We are concerned only with the way in which it affects the English attitude to those who are not English. In this ungracious task we hope we may be forgiven if we elaborate a little further the thesis already put forward: namely, that the English stereotype of themselves tends to foster a lack of sympathy with other points of view. This is what is known as their insularity. It has led even a friendly European to write a book entitled *The English – are they human?*

Inability to allow for other points of view may be illustrated by the story of the English lady on a Rhine steamer who couldn't understand why she and her party were being stared at. When told 'It is because you are foreigners', she said indignantly: 'Tell them we are not foreigners. We are English'.

The point was put in another way by Bernard Shaw, when he said: 'The English, if they think at all, think about the English'. This does not mean that in thinking about themselves they compare themselves with others. Far from it. Standard weights and measures are not compared with others – they are the standard of comparison. Nothing bores Englishmen more quickly than a comparison between them and other nationalities – unless it is designed to show where other nationalities have gone wrong.

The same tendency comes out in another way. Even English defects, so far as they are recognised at all, are treated as virtues. As another friendly European writer has said: the English give the irresistible and maddening impression of thinking it rather cute that their cooking and their laws and their pubs are so impossible, and rather gallant of them to bear all these afflictions so gaily and bravely. Their pride in 'muddling through' is a still more obvious example.

All this is part of the inflexibility which is at once their strength and their weakness.

As can be seen from the lady on the Rhine steamer, the English maintain their inflexibility even outside their own country. A distinguished French politician went so far as to say: 'The defect of many English people is that they cart England around with them to the point of insanity'. The word 'insanity' ought to be reserved for Scottish protests against English interference, but foreigners seldom display a due sense of linguistic propriety. Although badly expressed, what he meant is obvious enough.

If some Englishmen carry England around with them in foreign countries, they do so still more when they visit Scotland. Englishmen of the best type have always been welcome in Scotland. But there are others, not always so gifted, who can never understand how the inhabitants of this English province should deviate from the stereotype the English have of themselves. Their indifference, or even hostility, to all things Scottish, and to all signs of Scottish patriotism, does a great deal of harm, especially if they hold official positions; and their condescension does almost more. But here we begin to pass to the English stereotype of Scotland, and this is our main concern.

4. *The English stereotype of Scotland*

National stereotypes, however self-laudatory, do relatively little harm within the borders of the country itself: they may even inspire the natives to efforts that would not otherwise be forthcoming. Their harmfulness arises mainly when they develop into derogatory stereotypes of other nations. It becomes serious, as Sir Isaiah Berlin has pointed out, when they are exported and to some extent imposed on others who have national stereotypes of their own.

Even here a good deal depends on the nature of the stereotypes exported, and the English stereotype of Scotland is in fact very mixed. Sometimes it is too flattering. On television an English lady once said something like this: 'Aren't the Scots wonderful? A truly educated race!' The others taking part in the discussion were too polite to contradict her; but so favourable a judgement, however welcome, must bring a blush of shame to the cheeks of Scotsmen familiar with the real situation. More remarkable still, Scotsmen have in the past been sometimes regarded as an exception to iron English rules. The fact, for example, that they did not speak with an English public school accent was sometimes excused as an amiable eccentricity which did not necessarily put them beyond the pale. It might not be untrue to say that they are generally considered to possess some of the less spectacular virtues – to be competent and hard-working and honest and even intelligent. Their military prowess also has been generously recognised.

So far as the Scots are supposed to share in the virtues which the English attribute to themselves, the English stereotype of Scotland is highly favourable. In some moods the English are even prepared to lump Englishmen and Scots together and to be unconscious of the difference. In a radio quiz, when Sir Walter Scott was described as an Englishman by one participant, there was some demur from the Scottish side, and the English speaker asked in manifest astonishment: 'Aren't Scotsmen English?' This was received with amusement, but it seemed almost ungracious not to accept so high a compliment.

The English stereotype of Scotland becomes more interesting when it begins to emphasise differences, and it may be worth while attempting to pursue some of these differences, if they are not taken too solemnly.

The one thing every Englishman knows is that Scotsmen are 'dour'. This word (generally mispronounced) is not altogether clear in its English meaning. Certainly Scotsmen are dour (or hard): they could never have survived otherwise alongside a really tough people like the English. But they can also be 'douce' (or gentle). They can on occasion be 'cantie' and even 'crouse'; but this lies far beyond the English horizon. Furthermore they can be 'kindly'; and it is no use telling me that 'a kindly Scot' means merely one who is Scottish by birth. But if the English stereotype appears to be somewhat restricted, it must be remembered that stereotypes by their very nature must be over-simplified.

Another feature in the English stereotype is that the Scots are parsimonious. Here too there is a basis of fact: poor men have to be sparing, and many Scottish stories, especially those made up in Aberdeen, make fun of the trouble taken to save money. In the English version this is sometimes twisted into vices alien to the tradition of Scotland, such as greed and extortion and even sponging. So far from being extortionate, an Aberdonian is as anxious to save money for others as for himself: he disapproves of extravagance as such, but in fact he is most generous. As to sponging on others, this is in flat contradiction with Scottish pride and independence. Unfortunately it is

193

now easy to spread such distortions in Scotland itself and throughout the world. Even a long-suffering Scot may feel irritation when a foreigner plays up gleefully to the English by repeating charges which he might more profitably apply to his own people.

Yet another English conviction is that the Scots are without humour. This view is ludicrous to any one acquainted with the Scottish people or even with their literature and songs. Perhaps we have here the usual tendency to disparage one's nearest neighbours or rivals. The Americans, for example, believe the English to be 'dumb' or humourless; and indeed, like Continental Europeans, they have been known to ask why it is that Scotsmen have so much humour and Englishmen so little. There are different kinds of humour, and all of them are precious. Perhaps the English are here again supposing that their own variety is the standard for all others. This would suggest rather that their sense of humour is limited, as would also their habit of insisting on how humorous they are. 'We English', they say, 'have the great gift of laughing at ourselves'. Yet the evidence for this is strangely lacking. When asked for instances of such salutary behaviour, they are apt to mention *The Diary of a Nobody*; but what this book does is to make rather cruel fun, not of the English as such, but of the English lower middle class. This is a very different thing, and I know nothing comparable to the many stories in which the Scots poke fun at themselves as Scotsmen.

Although so many Englishmen stiffen and freeze at any jest against themselves, they have no hesitation in directing their humour against others. A standard music-hall device is to address a Scotsman with a list of words, if possible mispronounced, like 'kilt', 'haggis', 'bagpipes', 'parritch', and ending with 'hoots, mon'. This, like other stock gambits, is a good example of the primitive humour which finds everything outside the tribe to be excruciatingly funny. What is extraordinary is that sometimes even civilised Englishmen, not only use the same technique, but expect their Scottish friends to join in their shrieks of laughter. Perhaps the lack of enthusiasm with which these sallies are received is the source of the conviction that

Scotsmen are without humour. It might be possible to suggest a simpler explanation.

On a different level is the fixed belief that in Scotland it is always raining except when it snows. This is indeed one of the stock jokes, though it is taken very seriously. Here, as in other cases, those who are mesmerised by a stereotype have a curious knack of finding what they expect to find. An example of this used to be connected with the Russo-German frontier before 1914. Although it ran through the middle of a flat plain stretching for hundreds of miles, the Germans who visited it would stretch their hands out towards the East and exclaim, with a shiver, 'Ach! Wie kalt!' The English stereotype ignores the fact that Scotland is an area with almost as many different climatic regions as England itself. In a long cold spell like the freeze-up of 1963 the greater part of Scotland may have consistently better weather than England, but nothing would induce an Englishman to believe this. He spreads his dismal picture to the ends of the earth, and it is something of a miracle that the Scottish tourist trade is able to survive.

Samples of this kind may seem small beer, as indeed they would be if they were confined to England. The real trouble arises when Scottish ideals and traditions are depicted in Scotland itself as ridiculous and irrational so far as they differ from English ones. This is particularly depressing when the Scots are following a wider European tradition from which the English have departed and of which they are unaware.

5. *The Scottish stereotype of Scotland*

Scotsmen have – or at least had – a stereotype of themselves as flattering as national stereotypes usually are. They are sometimes charged with self-praise, but this is no more true of them than it is of the English – to mention no other nations. At times they may have to emphasise their achievements in protest against the distorted pictures that have been spread abroad. An example of this can be found as early as 1320, when in the Declaration of Arbroath they had to refute English misrepresentations in order to secure the attention of the Pope. Generally speaking, they may take their own merits less for granted and as more open to discussion; but this might be a sign of modesty.

The Scots certainly ascribe to themselves the more sober virtues – like honesty, competence, thoroughness, and reliability; and in these they are apt to consider themselves superior to the English – slower to promise and readier to perform. But the main qualities in which they have claimed to be outstanding are their zeal for freedom and equality and their capacity for rational thought.

When exaggerated such claims become laughable, especially if ideals are confused with achievements; but they are not wholly without historical support. From the Latin verses commended to William Wallace as a boy and John Barbour's well-known eulogy of freedom, the passion for liberty runs right through Scottish literature and political thinking. The liberties of the realm, the liberties of the Church, the liberties of the Parliament, the liberties of the people have been the aim of endeavours throughout the centuries. It is no accident that Adam Smith was the first to propound the doctrine of free trade. One foreign historian has even maintained that the liberal tradition in British politics has sprung mainly from Scotland. From pre-Reformation times onwards Scottish political thinkers have exercised influence also on the continent of Europe. It would be foolish to lay too much emphasis on this; but it would be a still greater mistake to ignore it, and it would be a pity if it were forgotten – as it almost is – even in Scotland itself.

It may be replied that it was only their own liberty that was pursued by Scotsmen. This charge would come strangely from liberty-loving Englishmen, who have imposed on their neighbours – not to mention remoter regions – so many struggles for freedom. Enthusiasts for liberty usually begin by defending their own, and only later extend their range to include the liberty of others and ultimately of all men. The Scots need be no exception.

As to equality, the passion for this is bound up with the passion for the liberty of the people. This too runs through Scottish literature. It is to be found, for example, in Sir David Lindsay's *Ane Satyre of the Three Estaits*. It comes out everywhere in Robert Burns and receives its popular expression in 'A man's a man for a' that'. It also comes out in political thought and action.

It would be absurd to maintain that Scotland is without class differences and class snobbishness. No nation, not even the American, is wholly free from this. None the less there are differences of degree; and it would not be untrue to say that the Scots have been more democratic, and the English more hierarchical, in their outlook. At times the English tell us frankly that 'we British' – they mean 'we English' – are bound by class distinctions to an extent unknown elsewhere. More recently they have shown a tendency, very marked on television and radio, to explain to each other at great length that class distinctions no longer matter. It never seems to occur to them that if this were really true, it would be unnecessary to talk so much about it.

We come to more difficult ground with the Scottish claim to greater rationality in thought and action. This would be ludicrous if it were a pretension to general intellectual superiority. What is true is that until the present century education in Scotland was more widespread among the people than it was in England. The claim to greater rationality must be interpreted as a claim to a different intellectual approach. It may seem arrogant to say that the Scottish approach is more philosophical; but it can be described as a habit of seeking for principles manifested in experience and of applying these principles to fresh cases. This Scottish ideal comes out in their law and their theology and, I am told, even in their heraldry; but it is of much wider scope. In this respect the Scots resemble the French rather than the English. These differences are never so sharp as they appear, but it seems fair to say that there is a genuine contrast between the Scottish approach and the English distrust of abstract thinking, their preference for rule of thumb, their dependence on precedents, and – if we may mention this again – their glorification of 'muddling through'.

In philosophy itself the Scots can claim to have produced two of the greatest figures in both the mediaeval and the modern period – Duns Scotus and David Hume. Even apart from these giants, Scottish philosophy, though this is forgotten to-day even in Scotland, had a wide international reputation and exercised a powerful influence on European philosophy, particularly in France.

It is not good enough to dismiss the national stereotype of Scotland as mere bragging. The Scots may claim with some reason that for a small nation they have in thought and action contributed much to the civilisation of Europe and the world. If they sometimes exaggerate this, it is unfair to demand that they should be free from a human weakness which is common to all nations without exception.

6. *Alien stereotypes of England*

Nothing need be said here about Scottish stereotypes of England. Like the English stereotypes of Scotland, they might not be flattering or even just; but the English are sublimely unconscious of them, and are in no danger of being induced to accept them in place of their own.

We have already alluded to some continental stereotypes of the English – doubts about their humanity, convictions that they are all hypocrites and all mad. It was widely believed at one time that all Englishmen had tails, and this may serve to remind us how false and twisted alien stereotypes can become. But the best parallel to the English stereotype of Scotland is the American stereotype of England; for of this the English are becoming at least dimly aware. At times, as a result of invasion by American cinema and television, they have even been known to say that they prefer their own traditions, however inferior, simply because they are their own. Scotsmen too may have such a preference without being unreasonable.

The American stereotype is mixed, but it tends to regard Englishmen as 'dumb' or humourless; as 'stuffed shirts' or social snobs; as 'snooty' or showing condescension or contempt for men of other nations; and as pursuing English interests inflexibly under a cloak of outward amiability. There would be no point in taking this stereotype seriously; but Englishmen who resent it may be better able to understand resentment against similar English stereotypes of Scotland.

Even in these days Scotsmen are sometimes exempted from American criticism of the English. At a party in California a lovely and learned American lady, whom I hardly knew, called out to me suddenly: 'Mr. Paton, you are the only nice Englishman I have ever met. All the others were Scotsmen'. I was so taken aback that I blurted out the melancholy truth. It has been a life-long regret to me that I missed the opportunity of making some slight return, by keeping silence, for all the benefits that I owe to England and to Englishmen.

7. *English policy in Scotland*

The national stereotypes outlined here in a crude way are trivial enough in themselves and may be dismissed as unkind family jokes. In any case our concern here is not with family bickering for its own sake, but with the effect of national stereotypes on English policy and Scottish reactions.

Once it is assumed that the English take England to be the only standard of excellence, it becomes easy to understand why they treat Scotland as a province rather than a partner; why they endeavour to extend their control over every sphere of Scottish activity; why they use every encroachment as a precedent for fresh encroachments; why they consider the adoption of English models to be the sole method of reform; why they despise what they describe as 'local cultures' and seek to turn real Scotsmen into imitation Englishmen; why they resent any exhibition of Scottish patriotism; why they insist that Scotsmen shall have no powers to legislate for their own affairs, and not even an opportunity to say whether they want such powers or not; why in short they refuse to regard Scotland as a nation entitled to such rights as are freely accorded to all other nations, even the most primitive and insignificant; and why in so doing they continue to regard themselves as models of sweet reasonableness and justice and generosity.

These are matters of high policy, and we should walk warily: other factors enter in – notably the instinct of the powerful to increase their power and the passion of administrators to flatten out for their own convenience differences among those whom they control. On a humbler level we must glance for a moment at the way in which ordinary citizens are affected by national stereotypes, especially when an alien stereotype is imposed in place of their own.

8. *English propaganda*

A national stereotype affects not only what men do, but also what they say, and even what they see. This is true of any fixed idea, whether national or not. If you expect blemishes in your fellow men, it is blemishes that you will find. If you hold it a blemish to depart from the English norm, you will see many blemishes in Scotland. Even in the earlier centuries English visitors gave a much less favourable account of Scotland than was given by the French.

Nowadays some English residents in Scotland talk down to Scotsmen in ways that are hard to credit. They think nothing of lecturing a Scottish audience on the inferiority of their law, their industries, their architecture, their science, their education, their traditions, their religion, and their 'local culture'. The whole intellectual and cultural life of Scotland, if recognised at all, is said to have decayed in the last 130 years. One of the most depressing of charges is that a nation of pioneers is utterly deficient in initiative. This is like tying a man up and then taunting him with an inability to move.

It never occurs to these gentlemen that perhaps an unsuitable system of government may have something to do with these appalling results. On the contrary, they hold that of all the bad things in Scotland nationalism is the worst. The typical clichés are trotted out without a trace of sympathy or understanding, or even of common sense and ordinary respect.

It is to be hoped that this sort of propaganda is misreported in the press, but uncorrected reports have to be taken at their face value, and it is as uncorrected that they affect public opinion. Needless to say, there are also Englishmen who show sympathy and understanding when they come to Scotland, and even when they are subjected, as they sometimes are, to a barely concealed distrust. Some – to borrow a phrase from one of them – may become 'honorary Scotsmen'. The wisest of them, whatever they may feel, refrain from lecturing Scotsmen in a way that would be unbecoming to an old-time district commissioner addressing a primitive Bantu tribe.

9. *The effect in Scotland*

Unfortunately the English stereotype of Scotland is so widely spread by means of modern mass communication that it may be undermining the traditional spirit of independence and self-respect in Scotland itself.

Some Scotsmen, it is to be feared, have abandoned their Scottish patriotism – or parochialism – altogether, or almost altogether, and are only too anxious to further the cause of anglicisation. They echo English clichés about Scottish traditions and ideals and practices. Some of them – though this, I am sorry to say, is found more often in women – become almost venomous in their contempt for Scotland's past and present.

Much more serious is the effect on the plain people of Scotland, who have not ceased to be patriotic, but are bewildered by the suggestions of their inferiority and by the continued assumptions that most of what they used to think right is really wrong. Some, it is to be feared, become bitter and aggressive in their feeling of being left defenceless. Others may become timid and unsure of themselves – everything in fact that their ancestors were not.

Attitudes of this kind may be revealed in little things. A Scots girl, when asked on television whether she thought the Scots were fit for self-government, said something like this: 'Well, perhaps not yet; but with a little training they might soon become so'. She meant, presumably, training by the English. She also said the Scots were not a 'cultural people like the English'. No Scot could conceivably have said anything like this fifty years ago, so perhaps the English propaganda is beginning to take effect.

A new bitterness appears to have arisen even in the attitude to old jokes. The chestnuts once swallowed with relish seem now to cause acute indigestion. The old tale of the Scottish visitor to London who had learned nothing of the English because he had dealt only with heads of departments is received with cold disgust – perhaps because it suggests that Scotsmen may be well content to hold minor positions in English business. Younger men seem to squirm even at a harmless speech made by Sir Harry Lauder after the first World War. He said we ought to express our gratitude to our Allies – the French, the Americans, the Italians, and of course the English – for helping Scotland to beat Germany. This was funny at the time because it was not too wildly remote from the way some Scotsmen actually felt; and it belonged to the old Scottish game of poking fun at themselves. To-day it appears to be seen as a sycophantic effort to obscure the utter insignificance of Scotland in world affairs, and the humour has gone sour.

Neither Scotland nor Britain will be enriched if an inferiority complex is to take the place of the old sense of humour and the unruffled assurance which used to go with a proper pride.

CHAPTER XII

BROADCASTING

What is he buzzing in my ears?
Robert Browning

1. *The invasion of the mind*

If a nation is to be reduced to a province, it is not enough to limit and control its exercise of political and economic power: it is necessary also to provincialise the mind.

Even without government action it is not difficult to provincialise the mind when a smaller partner is linked with a larger and richer one. The relative size of the book-markets is bound of itself to work in this direction. English books will be read in Scotland, no matter how false an image they give of that country; but Scottish books, at least those about Scottish history, will be little read in England because of the indifference of the English people. Scottish authors in general must write for an English public in order to earn their bread. If they depict the Scottish scene at all, they must simplify it for readers who cannot appreciate its subtleties. Too often they indulge in caricatures which play up to English preconceptions. The Scottish image of Scotland is at a disadvantage from the start.

A similar result is produced even more obviously by the developments of modern journalism. The London press invades Scotland with so-called Scottish editions. These give some Scottish news, especially about sport; but in the main they spread purely English stereotypes and images. In days when a newspaper with a circulation of a million copies pays its way with difficulty, Scottish newspapers are bound to have a hard struggle. It is surprising that they succeed so well. Without them Scottish opinion would find almost no expression at all.

The means of mass communication invented during the present century supply the richer and more powerful partner with a psychological weapon far more formidable than that of mere print. Nothing need be said here of the cinema: it is obvious enough that Hollywood, for example, has influenced, not merely modern English speech, but even the morals and manners of this country as a whole. With the invention of radio and television there comes an almost irresistible invasion, however benign, into the homes of the people.

Broadcasting – if this term may be used to cover both radio and television – has an influence almost impossible to exaggerate. If many people believe everything they see in print, how much more will they believe speakers whom they see and hear daily in their own homes? No government and no Church has ever before had such a power to sway the minds of men.

In the future what may be called the ethos of every nation – its traditions and legends, its images and stereotypes, its attitudes and ideals, its morals and its religion – will be dominated, and even formed, by broadcasting. If Scotland is to be treated as a nation, as was recommended even by the Royal Commission, she ought to have a broadcasting system which is not controlled by London. Otherwise her distinctive ethos is bound in the long run to disappear.

2. *The British Broadcasting Corporation*

Under the Charter of June 1952 the British Broadcasting Corporation is composed of nine governors appointed by the Crown and subject to removal by the Crown. They exercise supreme control over every side of broadcasting, and in particular over finance. No breath of democracy can disturb their calm. They are supported by a General Advisory Council, but this is appointed by themselves, as is also the vast array of officials in London, who, both as bureaucrats and as Englishmen, are bound to resent and resist any diminution of their powers.

Scotland, like Wales, is allowed to have, not a Corporation, but a National Broadcasting Council of its own. This sounds well, but the nine members of the Scottish Broadcasting Council have to be selected in London: they are appointed, and can be removed, by the Corporation. Even so, they are apparently considered unworthy of trust: their every activity is hedged around in a document bristling with suspicion. They are subject to such reservations and directions as may appear to the Corporation to be necessary for certain specific purposes; and these purposes include, not only party political broadcasts, but even broadcasts intended for reception in schools – is it supposed that Scotsmen if unsupervised might corrupt their own children? As if this were not enough, the Corporation is given *carte blanche* to impose further directions for reasons of finance or in the interest of due co-ordination and coherent administration. On the top of all this the Postmaster General is given the power to suspend any or all of the functions of the Council, if he opines that an emergency has arisen in which it is in the public interest to do so. All these directions the Scottish Broadcasting Council is bound to obey. Even the employees appointed by the Council may be rejected or dismissed if the Corporation and the Chairman of the General Advisory Council think their employment detrimental to the administration of the Corporation.

The document here summarised should be studied as a clear expression in black and white of the English attitude to Scotland. In this sphere at least the determination to dominate is unconcealed, and the proffered autonomy is bogus.

Control at the centre is not merely for ornament but for use. The National Broadcasting Councils of Scotland and Wales have always held that at a general election their national Home Rule parties should be given an opportunity to plead their cause on the air. So eminently reasonable a demand must be rejected. At the General Election of 1955 the Welsh Broadcasting Council proposed to grant it, and it was discovered that the British Broadcasting Corporation even with its wide powers had no authority to impose a veto. What happened? Without consulting Parliament the Government and the official Opposition, by no means disinterested parties, went into cahoots with one another. As a result of their deliberations the Postmaster General opined that an emergency had arisen and issued a direction confining political broadcasts to parties which put forward more than a hundred candidates at a general election. As there are not a hundred constituencies in Scotland, let alone Wales, the Scottish and Welsh parties were effectively gagged, so far as broadcasting was concerned. Are they so dangerous that the chance of their being allowed to broadcast an election manifesto can be regarded in London as a national emergency?

It should be added that, as a result of protests, the restrictions have recently become less severe.

In matters of finance also the control granted to the British Broadcasting Corporation is absolute, and this alone would be enough to give them powers that are irresistible. It is hard to see why the Scottish Broadcasting Council should not be allowed to disburse in its own way whatever modest sums are set aside for broadcasting in Scotland. Here too, as so often, the figures published about the relation between the revenues contributed by Scotland and the expenditure in Scotland are unsatisfactory; and it is alleged that details readily given in Oslo and Stockholm are resolutely refused in London. Does Scotland receive fair treatment in this respect or not? Is it, for example, true that the fees paid in London, as I have been told by a Scottish singer, are double those paid in Glasgow to the same broadcaster for the same work?

There are large areas in Scotland where reception is inadequate and some where it is non-existent. There are geographical difficulties, but difficulties are made to be overcome; and the desire to overcome them would be stronger in Edinburgh or Glasgow than it appears to be in London. It would seem to require some explanation why the only programme received in parts of the Highlands is one that comes from as far away as Moscow. The really powerful transmitters in this country appear to be confined to the South of England, and Scotland has to put up with the second best. Although the most recent advances, like B.B.C. 2 and coloured television, may come to her years later than to England, she has to pay the same licensing fees as her more favoured neighbours in the South. Even in extreme cases complaints are met with little sympathy. The inhabitants of North and South Uist, for example, who can receive little or no British radio, let alone television, asked for a license to operate their own local transmitter. The license was refused.

If we set aside these details, the fact remains that the British Broadcasting Corporation is a monopoly under the absolute control of London. This is a thoroughly bad arrangement even apart from the special interests of Scotland. If you fall foul of any part of this vast institution, you are off the air for ever, so far as the B.B.C. is concerned. Winston Churchill himself was prevented from broadcasting at the very time when the country was most in need of his counsel. The disadvantages of such a monopoly are sometimes recognised, but it continues undiluted so far as radio is concerned. In television we are allowed to have as an alternative a system which depends on advertisements proclaimed by voices whose manifest insincerity is calculated to corrupt the young. Even this commercial system has some real advantages; but the proper alternative, or rather substitute, is to have a genuinely federal system of broadcasting in which Scotland and Wales, and also the English regions, might play their own independent part.

3. *Brainwashing*

Although the Scottish Broadcasting Council is hedged around on every side and has no real control over its own finances, it is supposed – except at general elections – to determine 'the policy and content' of the radio service provided by the Corporation 'primarily' for reception in Scotland. Very late in the day it was given somewhat similar rights in television. What does all this amount to in practice?

The restricted powers granted to the Scottish Broadcasting Council are confined to the hours allotted to Scotland in the so-called Home Service (Scottish) (Radio 4). These amount perhaps to a quarter of its total time on the air. The rest of the Home Service in Scotland is controlled by London, as is the whole of the Light Programme (Radio 2) and the whole of the Third Programme (Radio 3). Apart from a fraction of a fraction Scotland has no say on the character of the material pumped daily into Scottish homes.

It is often said that Scottish programmes may be unsuitable for export South of the Border; but it never seems to occur to any one that London programmes may be unsuitable for export to the North. If the alleged unsuitability arises from differences in language, it holds equally in both directions; but this question will be dealt with later. The main ground of complaint is that in the vast bulk of broadcasting in Scotland a purely English, and mainly London, point of view is taken for granted. 'The Church', for example, is the Church of England. 'The Law' – this must cause great confusion – is the Law of England. 'Education' is English education. Even 'the British character' is merely English; and if the Scots regard themselves as British, which in fact they do, they find ascribed to themselves characteristics utterly alien to their own traditions. The images and stereotypes and legends dinned daily into Scottish ears are purely English. If Scotland is recognised at all, the image projected is that of an insignificant and perhaps eccentric English province, a topic for occasional jocularity, but unworthy of serious consideration or respect.

All this is usually done in innocence and without any awareness of its unfortunate effects. The British Broadcasting Corporation, like so many so-called British institutions, seem to have little or no notion of a Britain enriched by its multinational character. Some provincial Englishmen maintain, not without justice, that it is barely conscious of the fact that England is not merely London.

Although this London attitude is unfair to Scotland, there would be less complaint if it were confined to an English broadcasting system, and Scotland were able to control her own. As things stand, Scotsmen have an alien image and stereotype unremittingly insinuated into their minds day after day – an image and stereotype which ignores and misunderstands or even condemns their whole history and tradition. I do not wish to use harsh terms with false associations, but if brainwashing is understood to be a method of influencing minds by continual suggestions and assumptions without any pretence at argument, it would be hard to deny that Scotland is subject to a brainwashing which may in the end be fatal.

Sometimes, it must be noted with regret, even the frail defences by which Scotsmen are supposed to have some control over broadcasting in their own country can be forgotten. In April, 1966, without consulting the B.B.C. Controller in Scotland, there was displayed on Scottish screens what purported to be an interview with a group of Glasgow gangsters. These gave a lurid description of the utter lawlessness prevalent in the city and in effect charged the Glasgow police with inefficiency and even cowardice. Later on it emerged that the so-called gangsters were not gangsters at all, but some rather attractive young people who were performing this masquerade for what they called a 'giggle'.

Such methods blacken the image of Scotland, but although they reveal the danger of London control, they are not to be regarded as typical. The normal procedure may be illustrated by a more innocent example.

Scotland has always been proud of her education, and interest in her ancient universities extended into the humblest homes. Time was when a bus-conductor in Aberdeen could astonish the English visitor by replying, when asked whether anything of importance had happened recently in the town, 'Well, the University has just appointed a new Professor of Systematic Theology'. More recently a Glasgow working man, forced to earn his livelihood in England, was asked what he missed most in his environment: he replied without hesitation: 'The University'. Yet to-day, so far as broadcasting is concerned, there might almost be no Scottish universities: if mentioned at all, they are commonly lumped together with the new 'redbrick' universities of England. The fact that their weathered stones and granite should be so misdescribed may seem of little importance. What is devastating is that, both by what is said and even by what is left unsaid, the image of the Scottish Universities projected into Scotland is that they are of no importance and never have been. Why should so false a picture be imposed by London on a nation which has cherished its universities for over five hundred years?

This manifestly just complaint should not be misinterpreted as a desire on the part of Scotsmen to cut themselves off from England and even from the rest of the world. The Scots, like the English, would want to take material from every part of the world (and not least from England); but there is a vast difference between taking what you want and having to put up with whatever you are given. London borrows a great deal – some might say too much – from America; but it is hard to imagine that any Englishman would wish to have his broadcasts controlled from New York or even – if this were not unthinkable – from Edinburgh.

4. *Scottish programmes*

Even if London projects a sadly distorted picture of Scotland, this, it may be said, can be corrected in the hours assigned to Scottish programmes in the Home Service (Radio 4). But why should such correction be necessary?

The Scottish National Council, in spite of the restrictions under which it works, does its best, and we should be grateful to it; but the sheer bulk of English importations makes its task difficult, if not impossible. Since the Council is concerned only with the programmes which the Corporation provides 'primarily' for Scotland, it seems from the start to be confined to narrowly Scottish interests. The limitation of the hours almost forces it to confirm the English picture, both by what it has to provide and by what it must fail to provide.

Some hours, for example, must be set aside for programmes in Gaelic – a language which pitifully few Scotsmen can now understand. In a sensible system the Gaels should have their own transmitters even at some expense to the rest of the country. The Scottish people must be allowed to hear their own traditional songs and stories, to see their own dances, to listen to their own bagpipes. Time must also be given up to sport in Scotland since sport is the main preoccupation of modern man. Because the general news must come from London, the Scottish news is merely an appendix which can have no concern with world affairs nor even with Britain as a whole: it must be confined to parochial events – an occasional fire, the launching of a ship, the opening of a small factory, the closing of a local mine, and so on. When needs of this kind have been satisfied, what time remains for the wider interests which Scotland, from her own point of view, shares with the rest of the world? The

'distinctive culture, interests and tastes' for which the Scottish
Broadcasting Council is supposed to cater, must inevitably
seem to be confined within the narrow limits of their own
country. The higher culture has to be imported from the South.
All of this serves to confirm the resident Englishman in his
stereotype of Scotsmen as clinging pathetically to the remaining
rags of a primitive peasant culture; and this stereotype may
gradually come to be accepted by Scotsmen themselves. It may
even come to be true.

No wonder there is a wide-spread feeling, as was recognised
in the Pilkington report, that the programmes do not meet the
essential needs of Scotland. It is commonly said that they
portray the Scot as a being with none but the most parochial
and shallow of interests. It has even been said that they depict
him as 'clottish' (whatever this may mean); and that what is
offered is 'a music-hall picture of Scotland'.

Some of these complaints may be exaggerated, but they spring
from a genuine feeling of injustice. The Scots have explored
and battled and traded and ruled and taught in every quarter
of the globe. They have a traditional interest in Europe and in
other continents greater than that of the average Englishman.
They have explored too the world of the mind and been pioneers not only in material inventions and scientific discoveries,
but in philosophy and economics and history and literature and
the wider achievements of the human spirit. Yet so far as broadcasting is concerned, it would seem as if they hardly ever looked
beyond their own kail-yard.

5. *Imitation and creation*

It would be absurd to blame the Scottish Broadcasting Council
for the unhappy results of broadcasting in Scotland. Here, as
usual, it is the system which is at fault rather than the men who
run it. The defects of the system are more far-reaching than has
been suggested. Creative enterprises are not to be expected from
administrators without full responsibility and real control. It is
the Yes-men who are encouraged by the present arrangements,
and this must mean the reign of mediocrity. On the whole we
should be thankful that things are no worse.

If we try to look briefly at some of the main tendencies, it must be remembered that a random sampling may easily give a false impression. It must also be remembered that if our concern is mainly with faults and flaws, this does not mean that there are not also merits, which may display themselves even under difficult conditions.

Under the present circumstances it is almost inevitable that there should be much imitation of English methods and models, and it is hardly surprising if the imitations are not so good as the originals. All of this confirms the stereotype that the Scots are imitation Englishmen and rather second-rate ones at that.

The tendency to imitation is to be found especially among what may be called official broadcasters – the men who introduce programmes, edit magazines, conduct interviews, and direct discussions – though it is also present in many of those chosen to play a more modest part. It becomes painful in attempts to be funny light-heartedly about nothing in particular after the English fashion. The English have a genius for what may be called intellectual or verbal play, as in debates at the Oxford Union, though even there the weaker brethren sometimes work at it rather too hard. When Scots attempt to play about in a similar fashion, they are apt to become elephantine: of all peoples they are the least suited to be Smart Alecs. Scottish humour, if I may be dogmatic, is at its best when it is brought to bear on something definite and does not strain to be funny without relief. The native article is not excluded from Scottish programmes – this would be impossible; but we get far too much of the imitative kind.

If we turn to more serious matters, it would be false to suggest that traditional Scottish attitudes are given no chance to find expression. After a struggle the Scots were allowed to have a short programme of their own on more general topics. Discussions are occasionally permitted even on such questions as Home Rule and on proposals to introduce bishops into the Church of Scotland. Yet it looks at times as if the speakers were chosen to give the preponderance to one side. The supposedly neutral chairman may make little attempt to conceal his prejudices; and if he is an Englishman, as for some reason he often is, he is probably unaware that he has any. If this came out in the give and take of argument, there would be less cause for complaint. It is more unsatisfactory when he exudes the customary clichés and assumes without argument that what he regards as a narrowly Scottish view is too irrational for serious consideration.

The same lack of respect and understanding is shown on comparatively neutral subjects. In questioning the headmaster of a famous Scottish school the interviewer may hardly bother to conceal his amazement at the idea that it is able to compete with the English Public Schools; he may even suggest, with what looks rather like a sneer, that by the lowness of its fees it is offering a first-class education at a cut rate. Another may persist in trying to make Highland villagers say that their refusal to attend dances or cinemas is imposed upon them by their minister; and only their strongest protests can induce him to admit that he and they seem to be at cross purposes.

Even when there is no active hostility, there is too often complete ignorance of Scottish practices and traditions. There is already enough misunderstanding of Scotland in the programmes imported from London, and it seems unnecessary to add more in what purports to be a Scottish programme. It is hard to believe that anything like this could happen in any other country.

Let no one imagine that this is a plea for Scottish broadcasting to be more consciously Scottish. English broadcasting is not consciously English: it just is English. American broadcasting is not consciously American: it just is American. Scottish broadcasting ought to be in the same position. The traditional Scottish practice has been to express the truth as one sees it without fear or favour – without considering whether one is being Scottish, and without looking over one's shoulder to see its effect on alien critics. When this practice is abandoned, Scotland will be down and out. What has been suggested here is that in broadcasting Scotsmen should not try to imitate anybody – not even themselves.

To sum up. The voice of Scotland finds no adequate expression in the present broadcasting system: once so clear and decisive it is narrowly restricted and is swamped by a multitude of alien voices. Even when it is heard, it is too often checked and corrected and misinterpreted by unsympathetic voices from the South so that it appears hesitant and confused or else strident and aggressive. It is almost forced to become self-centred and self-conscious, precisely what a truly national voice ought not to be. In a satisfactory broadcasting system it would be able to take its traditions and ideals for granted – not to mention the elementary facts of the Scottish scene – and to look calmly at the wide world from its own point of view instead of having to shout in the tones of a recalcitrant province in order to make itself heard at all.

CHAPTER XIII

BROADCASTING AND LANGUAGE

I am always sorry when any language is lost,
because languages are the pedigree of nations
Dr. Johnson

1. *The voice of Scotland*

What has been said of the voice of Scotland, taken metaphoric-
ally, applies also in a more literal sense. The traditional speech
of Scotland is subject to the same distorting influences, and the
average Scotsman is deprived of his traditional standards
without acquiring any others. To those who care nothing about
language, this will seem a small matter, and complaints about
it will be merely silly. To those who recognise that speech, as
the expression of thought and emotion, at once reveals and to
some extent determines the character of men and of nations, it
will seem that the treatment of Scotland in this respect also
leaves much to be desired. If we may adopt the view of Dr.
Johnson, Scotland is being deprived of her pedigree, as of so
much else.

This is a topic of special difficulty to our English brothers, as I
know from sad experience. Since to them English is just
Standard Southern English, they find it difficult or impossible
to understand even the terms on which any discussion must
proceed. A summary attempt to clarify these terms is unlikely
to be successful, but it cannot be omitted here. Readers
allergic to philology may be advised to go straight on to the
next Chapter.

The distinctive speech of Scotland has a centuries-old tradition and history of its own which has nothing to do with Southern
English. It is derived from the speech of the invading Angles
who occupied the Lothians as well as what is now Northumberland. As is sometimes said rather smugly in Scotland, the acute

Angles went North, and the obtuse Angles went South. I like to add that the right Angles went to Yorkshire.

Southern English, on the other hand, is a development of Mercian and has been dominated by London, which has suffered from a kind of verbal instability since the time of Chaucer. Most of the traditional vowel sounds have changed, as is still happening in Cockney to-day. This has produced some of the peculiarities of English spelling: the written vowels, for example, are pronounced in a way which to any Continental speaker sounds perverse. The trilled 'r', universal elsewhere, has faded and has further affected the English vowel sounds, many of which have become diphthongs and even polyphthongs. In this, as in other matters, it is the English who have deviated from the European tradition.

In this deviation the traditional Scottish pronunciation of English had no part: it retained the pure vowels and trilled 'r' of Europe and the rest of the world. This is why it is still easier for Scotsmen to learn the pronunciation of foreign languages.

The Scottish speech is thus a form – in some ways an older form – of English or Anglish: it has nothing to do with Gaelic or any Keltic language. It may be called a dialect of English (or if you prefer it, of Insular West Teutonic); but it is not, and never has been, a dialect of Southern English. To make this clear, let us describe its original form as 'Inglis', which is its old name. It is now often called 'Scots' and also 'Lallans', that is, the language of the Scottish Lowlands.

Until the Union of the Crowns in 1603, Inglis was the language of the Court, the Law, the Church, and the Universities. It was a language of great richness and had its own literature and its own poets, too often misdescribed as Chaucerians.

After the Court moved to London in 1603 the old Inglis inevitably declined, but it survived – as Lallans – in the dialect of the people. This has found literary expression in prose writers like Walter Scott and Robert Louis Stevenson, but above all in poets from Robert Burns to Hugh MacDiarmid. The English may regard it as the speech of yokels or even of scullions, but there is no dialect of England that can be compared with it.

It still trails its clouds of glory and, except where contaminated by bad English or American, is a perfect instrument for humour and for tenderness. Even to-day its distinctive vocabulary is amazingly rich.

There is no subject in which Scotland receives less understanding from South of the Border. Some of the things said are almost incredible in their fatuity. A reputable critic can dismiss modern writing in the Scottish dialect as a kind of Jingoism and can treat it with what look like efforts to be funny: apparently ignorant that words have different senses and association in different contexts, he takes to task a modern Scottish poet, Mr. Sydney Goodsir Smith, for writing 'Lowse we the bands' – a phrase intelligible to every Scottish ploughman. 'Come now, Mr. Smith', remarks this sensitive judge of language – 'How *lowse* can you get?' If we could get rid of lousy criticism, we might get as far as 'Laus Deo'.

What we are mainly concerned with here is not Lallans but something different. Partly through the influence of the Authorised Version of the Bible there grew up in Scotland a new form of speech. This became the language of the pulpit, the law-courts, and the universities; and because these institutions retained a measure of independence, it continued to be the speech of educated Scotsmen. I will call it Educated Scottish English – as opposed to Standard Southern English. Apart from occasional Scottish idioms and expressions it uses the vocabulary and grammar of standard English: it is in fact simply the Scottish way of pronouncing English. The essential point is that in many respects it is continuous in its pronunciation – but only in its pronunciation – with the older language which I have called 'Inglis'. To treat it as an unsuccessful attempt to imitate the accents of the South is ridiculous.

Why should this be so difficult to understand? We can all recognise American English, Canadian English, Australian English, even Irish English. None of these countries has the slightest wish to abandon its own pronunciation in an effort to imitate the sounds of Standard Southern English. Educated Scottish English is no less honourable than they. With even less plausibility can it be regarded as merely a degeneration from the speech of Southern England; for unlike them it has an age-long independent tradition of its own.

Of all these varieties of English, Standard Southern English may well be the richest and the best. At least to my own ear it is at its best one of the loveliest and most flexible forms of human speech. But this does not mean that other forms are without their own excellence and their own standards. There may be, I believe there are, general linguistic and aesthetic standards by which different languages may be judged, if only with the utmost caution; but it would be arbitrary and parochial to identify these general standards with the conventional standards of Southern English or to suppose that Southern English is the sole norm by which all languages, or even all varieties of English, must be judged.

2. *Its treatment in broadcasting*

So far as Scotland is concerned, the sad thing about British broadcasting is that it ignores traditional Scottish standards of speech and puts nothing adequate in their place.

This is true to some extent even of 'Inglis' or 'Scots' or 'Lallans' in the Scottish programmes. Some speakers and singers are perfect in their pronunciation and are a joy to hear. Others make the uncouth noises with which unfortunately we are only too familiar. Worst of all are those who make the language 'refained' by introducing a mixture of sounds from the South, or who pronounce almost every syllable as if it were Southern English. There seems to be no standard recognised at all, and a great opportunity has been missed.

The main trouble, however, is concerned with what I have called Educated Scottish English. This we are allowed to hear occasionally, with varying degrees of excellence, from lawyers or teachers or ministers of religion, and, on a rather lower level, from commentators on sport; but the standards, such as they are, must inevitably be set by the regular official broadcasters. In its English regions the policy of the B.B.C. apparently is to select these from individuals who speak Southern English with some trace of a local accent. If Scotland is an English province it has to be treated on the same principle. Hence too many official broadcasters in Scotland – there are some notable exceptions – appear to be Scottish speakers who have learnt to mispronounce Southern English in a way supposed in London to be characteristically Scottish. Whether they are specially trained for this purpose or discovered by research remains a mystery.

This means that the average Scotsman is offered a hybrid standard which is alien and artificial and can be no use to him at all or indeed to anybody else.

The reasons given for this decision are even stranger than the decision itself. The first is that official broadcasters must be intelligible in every part of Scotland. The second is that they must be intelligible to foreigners (including presumably Englishmen). Both these reasons reveal an abyss of ignorance so great as to make the head reel.

What we are talking about is not a revival of Gaelic or even of 'Lallans', but merely the intelligent use of Educated Scottish English. This, although it may give some indication of where the speaker comes from – the Highlands or Lowlands, the East or the West – is intelligible to any Scotsman, educated or less educated, from any part of the land. It is incomparably more intelligible to the vast mass of the Scottish people than any variety of Southern English even when mispronounced in a way regarded as suitable for Scottish ears. To foreigners it is usually more intelligible than Southern English because it keeps its pure vowels and trilled 'r's and at its best pronounces every syllable slowly and distinctly instead of running them together. It is, in fact, how foreigners expect English to be spoken. To argue that Scotsmen should be deprived of their own standard speech on the ground that this would be unintelligible to foreigners is not only unconvincing in itself: it is directly contrary to the facts.

What is more, good educated Scottish speech is perfectly intelligible even to Englishmen. It offers no more difficulty than educated American speech – perhaps less. No doubt if you have never before heard a different way of talking good English, you may find some slight difficulty at first. Some modern Englishmen may be for a moment puzzled to hear the word 'extraordinary' pronounced with all its six syllables instead of the two to which it is so often reduced; but this is an obstacle not impossible to overcome.

The alleged reasons for ignoring Scottish standards are all the more startling when it is remembered what vast quantities of the most vulgar English speech are imposed daily on the Scots in their own country. No one asks whether this is intelligible to them or not.

It is hard to see why Scotland should be deprived of her traditional standards even if these seem uncouth to Englishmen judging by conventional standards of their own. To Americans of the Middle West the English accent, as they call it, seems a curious patois which is not only affected, but almost unintelligible. The English would rightly be the first to resent it if their standards of speech had to be defended against such alien criticisms.

In the past Englishmen have treated the Scottish pronunciation with more respect. Wordsworth could say of it,

'Choice word and measured phrase, above the reach of ordinary men; a stately speech.'

Matthew Arnold could complain that it made Scotsmen sound much more impressive than was warranted by what they said. More recently a typical product of Eton and Balliol has written: 'A Scottish accent can be so easy on the ear that the speaker actually endears himself by that alone.'

Such judgements may serve to remind us that the music and dignity of Scottish speech can be admired by lovers of the English language; but the right of Scotsmen to develop their own standards in their own way should not be made to depend on testimonials from the South.

3. *The effects of London policy*

What in brief are the effects of the arbitrary linguistic policy which Scotland has to endure?

In the first place it projects a false picture of Scottish speech as if it were an uncouth deviation from Southern English. This comes out even in historical plays, where proud old Scottish ladies are made to talk in the mincing accents of an Edinburgh Miss recently returned from a six months finishing course in

London. Worse still are the professedly Scottish serials where half the cast seem to imagine they can conceal their Cockney vowels by sporadic attempts at a trilled 'r' or even by saying 'I ken' at the beginning of a sentence. This is not only an offence to lovers of language: it puts the supposedly Scottish scene completely out of focus.

What is more serious is that this false image tends, so to speak, to make itself true: it sets standards which people begin to follow. The artificial and second-rate language of Scottish broadcasting is being imitated, however unsuccessfully, as in the case of the young lady who said proudly, 'Ai cen't tock Scatch'. In the course of time Scottish speakers may conform to the stereotype of themselves as feeble imitations of Englishmen, and very poor imitations at that.

Scottish English, like Southern English, has many uncouth varieties and needs standards at least as badly. Many Englishmen seem unable to distinguish good Scottish English from its most degenerate forms, and British broadcasting appears to share this disability. The English of the less educated sort can get their standards from their own official broadcasters with their golden voices – sometimes perhaps slightly off the gold standard. Scotsmen are given instead a sort of hybrid artificial language as their model – one which has no tradition or history behind it. If they cannot have their own standards, it would be far better to offer them good Southern English as their model. Why should they be fobbed off with an imitation which doesn't even pretend to be other than second rate?

Curiously enough, these distortions are extended even to place-names in Scotland. There are, to take one example, many place-names with a hammer stroke on the last syllable – like Dunbar, Dunblane, Dunkeld, Dundee. For some unknown reason many Englishmen insist on putting the emphasis on the first syllable, even when surrounded by Scotsmen using the correct pronunciation. Sometimes, it is true, they reverse this process and put the accent perversely on the last syllable when it is really on the first, as in names like Oban and Forfar. It is amazing that such mispronunciations should be taken over even in Scottish broadcasting by men whom one would expect to know better. It is as if they wanted to wipe Scotland off the map!

A friend of mine, a fierce upholder of the English language, tells me that the broadcasting authorities seem to have issued a decree that wherever there is a vulgar pronunciation of English words, this is the pronunciation to be used. Perhaps there is some exaggeration in this; but by parity of reasoning it would seem that some tame Englishman is assigned to headquarters in Scotland with orders that his pronunciation of Scottish place-names (and also of family names) is always to be followed, especially if he has never heard them before. This seems to be thought more genteel.

One beauty of Scottish speech (and I am not talking of a slum language adulterated with ungrammatical English or American) is that it is clear, decisive, confident, every syllable pronounced like the stroke of a hammer – the expression and mirror of the Scottish character. It is pitiful to-day to hear Scottish children who have been given no clear standard to follow: all they know is that it is wrong to trill their 'r's. This is specially evident when they talk to some amiable Englishman speaking in what to them is an alien patois hard to understand. A Scots boy from a humble home where some dialect of Lallans is spoken can without much difficulty adjust his speech to Educated Scottish English because this retains the vowel-sounds and trilled 'r's to which he is accustomed. Indeed there is a long tradition of being bilingual in this respect – of speaking the language of Burns for some purposes and the language of the Bible for others. When this standard is taken away, he is left in a confusion and uncertainty which may lead to self-distrust, if not to neurosis. Perhaps this may help to explain why we are so often told that the youth of Scotland are lacking in the power of self-expression.

To deprive the children of Scotland of the standards that are their birth-right must seem to any lover of language to be wicked. Yet this can be done in all innocence by a few amiable and irresponsible English ladies and gentlemen. Surely if anything in the world should be decided by Scotsmen, it is their own standard of speech.

4. *What should be done?*

These contentions may still be open to misunderstanding, even perhaps to the absurd interpretation that a narrow patriotism should prevent Scotsmen from learning to speak, or even to understand, the noble language of Southern England to the best of their ability.

It is natural that Scotsmen educated or long resident in England should modify or abandon their own form of speech. Some retain their native accents undiluted, like the gentleman who remarked that even after twenty years in the South he had not succeeded in learning how to mispronounce the letter 'r' correctly. Others may be able to attain some degree of approximation to standard Southern English if they follow good models – what is pitiful are their unsuccessful attempts to imitate a kind of suburban English far inferior to their own. Yet others, sometimes able men who have no ear for language, invent a hybrid language of strange noises never heard on either side of the Border. All of this is obviously their own concern.

What we are concerned with here is only the public policy of broadcasting in Scotland. There are other influences making a dead set against Scottish speech – most obviously some teachers of elocution. But it is the power of broadcasting that is decisive, and what has been argued here is simply that Scotsmen ought to determine how that power is to be used.

This means that Scottish control of broadcasting should be real and not illusory. Such a claim is, one would have thought, obviously reasonable in itself, and, as we have seen, it goes far beyond the sphere of language, however important this may be from some points of view.

The obvious solution – if we may revert to the more general problem – is to have an independent Scottish Broadcasting Corporation which enjoys real control and is able to meet the special needs of Scotland. The best way of doing this would be to have some sort of British system in which genuinely independent regions could treat with one another, and could borrow material from one another, on a footing of equality; but this

223

ideal should not be used as a device for postponing all attempts to meet the urgent and immediate needs of Scotland herself.

We need not pause to expose the arguments which purport to prove that Scotland has neither the money nor the ability to do what is done by every nation of comparable wealth and size, and even by many which cannot be compared with her in either respect. If Scottish broadcasting could be freed from its Southern shackles, we might hope for a burst of creative energy. At the very least there would be a new centre where able young men would have some chance to develop their powers freely in their own country instead of having to seek their fortune in the South.

5. *The pattern*

The development of broadcasting in Britain displays in miniature a pattern of the treatment to which Scotland is increasingly subjected.

A new situation arises, and a new institution has to be created to meet it. The institution is at once centralised under the rigid domination of London. There is a pretence at devolution, but the powers devolved are restricted and controlled on every side, not least as regards finance. The central authority takes decisions, which may or may not be wise, about the English provinces. These decisions are unhesitatingly applied to Scotland without regard to Scottish opinion, which can do nothing but grumble and protest. When, in reply to protests, reasons are given for these decisions, they are manifestly not the real reasons: they would not deceive a child. If they were the real reasons, they would show that the authority was incompetent to take any rational decision at all. The authority remains blandly innocent of all the damage it may be doing, and the snarls of protest are put down complacently to the unreasonable nationalism for which the Scots are notorious. Yet there is no other possible means of redress.

The revealing thing in all this is that there seems to be no genuine English interest involved. If the broadcasting monopoly could be broken, this would be to the advantage of all Britain, and not least of England herself.

CHAPTER XIV

THE SCHOOLS

*The children of the poor must be supported and sustained on
the charge of the kirk, trial being taken whether the spirit of
docility be in them found or not. If they be found apt to
learning and letters, then may they not, – we mean, neither
the sons of the rich, nor yet of the poor, – be permitted to
reject learning, but must be charged to continue their study,
so that the commonwealth may have some comfort by them.*

First Book of Discipline (John Knox)

1. *Past and present*

At the beginning of the present century it could still be claimed,
with some show of plausibility, that Scotland enjoyed the best
system of public education in the world. All children, even
those from the poorest homes, were supposed to receive a
sound elementary schooling. From the Shorter Catechism they
learned that man's chief end is to glorify God and to enjoy Him
for ever; and with the aid of the multiplication table (which was
commonly bound up with it) they were able to deal with the
practical difficulties of the work-a-day world. Those of them who
possessed genuine talent and worked hard were able, if not
without sacrifice on their own part and on the part of their
parents, to become citizens (as they were called) of the ancient
Scottish Universities. In relation to her size Scotland was said
to have the largest number of schools in Europe and the highest
proportion of university students. The success attained in every
walk of life by the products of her educational system contributed
to her national pride and to the reputation she enjoyed throughout the world.

Such at least was the Scottish legend, and it certainly em-
bodies a great ideal – cherished at least since the Reformation,

and perhaps earlier – even if this ideal, like other human ideals, was imperfectly realised in a difficult world. Hence Scotsmen may be puzzled and confused when it is dinned into their ears, that 'we British' have always shamefully neglected education, and especially university education. But what is really disturbing to-day – not to say shattering – is to hear so many voices proclaiming loudly that education in Scotland is far inferior to that in England and that the only way of reform is to copy English models – often the very models which the English themselves begin to find more and more unsatisfactory.

There has never been a lack of voices from the South deploring what are regarded as deviations from the English norm. What is new is that these voices become ever more blaring with the aid of modern inventions. Can it be true that the ever-increasing centralisation of government has taken the heart out of Scottish education as out of so much else?

2. *Administration of the schools*

It may be replied that as Scotland already controls her system of education any complaints about the present position are irrelevant. If the Scots have allowed their education to degenerate, this is entirely their own fault.

Such a picture does not do justice to the real situation.

In Scotland as elsewhere the control of education was originally in the hands of the Church. After the Reformation the Church of Scotland, although hampered by poverty, had a strong interest in the education of the people, and by the democratic character of her courts the opinion of laymen could be expressed at every level from the parish to the nation. Most of the Scottish schools continued to be under her control till 1872, though there were also town grammar schools and private foundations. In that year she, together with the Free Church of Scotland, generously handed over her schools and school-buildings to the State without seeking or receiving any financial recompense.

The control of these schools was assigned locally to *ad hoc* authorities – for long known as School Boards – whose members were supposed to be elected because of their special interest in education. This method worked reasonably well, as it still does in America. Yet in 1928, as was pointed out in an earlier Chapter, the schools were suddenly transferred to the control of town and county councils elected for quite other purposes. This was done, not in the interests of education or in order to meet any Scottish need, but simply to fit in with English methods of derating agriculture and industry in what was supposed to be a temporary emergency.

Members of these local authorities are sometimes of outstanding ability, but on the whole they are ill-equipped to deal with education, which for most of them is a secondary interest. Educational policy has too often been subordinated to irrelevant political prejudice.

Whatever may be thought of this, a national system of education cannot be adequately controlled, let alone developed, by an agglomeration of local authorities. This can be done only by a national administration, and it will be remembered that in 1872 Scotland had no national administration except for the Lord Advocate. Hence the administration of Scottish schools was for a time brought directly under the tutelage of London officials as ignorant of Scottish ideals as they were complacent about their own. In spite of protests this continued even in form till the office of Secretary for Scotland was restored in 1885 – in actual practice it seems to have continued a good deal longer. The damage done cannot be calculated, but, according to one authority whom I knew and respected, 'the true aims of instruction were forgotten, and the formative value of education was sacrificed to the informative'.

The situation may be less unsatisfactory to-day, although some educationists, even in Scotland, talk and behave, however unconsciously, as if the aim of the schools should be to impart information rather than to develop, in the interests of the individual and of society, whatever capacities for thought and action a child may possess. The local authorities in Scotland, so far as they are concerned with schools, are now under a Scottish Education Department in Edinburgh. This is officered by educated men of good will, and the system (here inevitably over-simplified) might develop satisfactorily if these officials in turn were responsible to an elected national authority with a revenue of its own adequate for modern needs. Instead of this they are, like other civil servants in the Scottish Office, responsible only to an over-burdened Secretary of State appointed by the head of an English political party and supervised by a watchful Treasury. He in turn is responsible to a predominantly English Parliament reluctant to admit that Scotland should be treated differently from an English province. Like any other Cabinet minister he is bound to defend in public 'the policy of the Government as a whole' and so to subordinate the educational interests of Scotland to the dogmas of his own political party.

This, it may be said, is only what Scotland has to suffer in other spheres – except where she is in the still worse position of being directly controlled by government offices in London. But in the case of education the unfairness of the system is glaring since, at least so far as popular education is concerned, her traditions are so much better and older than those of England. In a matter which concerns not merely her economic, but her spiritual, life her people have no adequate power to control and develop the education of their children in accordance with their own ideals. What happens, it is not unfair to say, is that the Scottish officials have to wait and see what is done in England and then to follow suit. It is hardly surprising if Scottish education is now alleged to trail behind that of England. This is the result one would expect.

3. *The contrast with England*

Because of the fundamental differences of the two countries any attempt to base changes in Scottish schools on an English model is bound to be unsatisfactory from the start. Education is a living and growing thing, and, like other living things, it can grow healthy only if it does so in accordance with its own nature.

In Scotland education has been relatively homogeneous and democratic. Even in the village schools the children of the laird, the minister, the farmers and the ploughmen, might, at least in their earliest years, sit together on the same benches to the advantage of them all. In the towns also famous schools, some of them founded long before the Reformation and many of them of a respectable antiquity, carried on the same tradition, although in the last hundred years their status has been to some extent lowered by the fashion of sending Scottish boys to English Public Schools – a fashion which has gradually extended from the nobility and gentry to the professional classes and well-to-do business men. In spite of their small financial resources these old Scottish schools did marvellous work and produced, as they still do, many distinguished men for the service of Church and State. The astonishing lowness of their fees and a system of small bursaries meant that they were open to able children even from families who had little of the world's wealth. To say that they catered for only one social class is nonsense.

This ideal, however imperfectly realised, was in marked contrast with the system South of the Border. There it was thought dangerous to educate children above their station, whereas, in Scotland, if I may exaggerate a little, their education *was* their station. The famous Public Schools of England – in the main independent boarding schools reserved for the well-to-do – have become sharply distinguished from all other schools. They may have suited English conditions at one time, even if it is sometimes held that they do so no longer. They have many merits and some demerits, neither of which need be discussed here; but in the modern age it is not altogether an advantage to divide a country into two classes – the Public-School boy and the non-Public-School boy, the latter of whom has been regarded, and has even regarded himself, as socially inferior. Some modern Englishmen are so hostile to this tradition that they wish to do away with the Public Schools altogether. This would not only destroy something of value, but would also be an astonishing interference with private liberty.

Whatever may be the merits and demerits of the English Public School system it would be arrogant to assume that it provides the sole model which all other countries ought to follow and by which their education ought to be judged. The educational systems of France and Germany and many other

European countries have been far too successful to be swept aside as obviously inferior. It is with these European countries that Scotland should be compared; and in the light of their achievements, as well as her own, there would seem to be many reasons – if reasons must be given – why she should be free to develop her own homogeneous system in her own democratic way.

4. *The status of teachers*

If public education in Scotland must be adjusted to an English model, the model obviously cannot be the English Public Schools, which in the past monopolised whatever dignity was credited to education in the South. The model to be adopted must be the State Schools which are beginning to be developed in England but are still – to put it mildly – lacking in prestige. This means that Scottish schools, even the most famous, must be treated as if they corresponded to the less distinguished part of the English system. If this is what is done, the traditional status of Scottish teachers – not to mention the teachers themselves – must inevitably be depressed. The educational effects can only be bad.

In the days when Scotland could still be proud of her education the village dominie, and still more the headmaster or rector of the town grammar school, were important figures in their community, but a great deal of this prestige seems to have been lost. Teachers are generally excluded from the local education committee and feel themselves dominated by men, sometimes by self-important men, whose qualifications to control education are not conspicuous. The authority of the headmaster in particular has greatly declined. Since Directors of Education were introduced after the English example, the headmaster in some places may be allowed no say in the appointment of his own staff. In extreme cases he may arrive at school one morning to find that one of his teachers has been removed and replaced by another. Directors of Education may do good work: some of them may even sanction new experiments (so long as these are inexpensive). Yet we should not forget that a good headmaster makes a good school – a great headmaster has an almost miraculous effect – and he cannot do this unless he possesses genuine authority and considerable freedom. What is indisputable is that breaches of Scottish tradition are arbitrarily imposed from above; and arbitrary imposition from above is itself a breach of Scottish tradition.

On the financial side Scotland presumably receives her Goschen proportion of the amount assigned to the State schools in England. She is in no position to devote a larger share of her national revenue to education, however much she may wish to do so. The plans of the local authorities for expanding education can be cut down by the Secretary of State because of some Government policy determined by English conditions. As the system works out, Scottish teachers can never be paid more highly than teachers in English State schools, even when they have higher qualifications. Too often they are paid less. It has even been claimed that on the average they are paid as much as 8 per cent less. In practice they must wait for any increase in salary till after teachers in England have been awarded theirs; hence they must always lag behind and, if they are unlucky, they may be caught in a freeze. In any case their salaries are tied to the percentage increases awarded in England: if English salaries have gone up by, say, 12 per cent., Scottish salaries are not allowed to go up by more.

The supposed devolution allowed to Scotland is only a façade. This would become even more obvious if there were time to examine the complicated machinery of the Scottish Joint Council for Teachers' Salaries, the appointment of arbitrators, the final decision of the Secretary of State, and so on. Even the façade is being steadily nibbled away; there is, for example, a proposal to transfer the appointment of arbitrators from the Lord President of the Court of Session, who knows the Scottish situation, to the London Minister of Labour, who does not.

There are other ways in which the status of teachers can be lowered. At the beginning of the century in Scotland almost all male teachers were expected to be University graduates; and there still is a far higher proportion of graduates in Scottish Secondary schools than there is in English ones; but if the Government succeeds in its latest policies, men as well as

231

women will be admitted to the teaching profession without ever having breathed the liberal atmosphere of a university.

It is not surprising if the status of the Scottish teacher has declined; if the schools are grossly understaffed; and if the confidence of Scotsmen in their own system of education has been at least partially undermined. This in itself places obstacles in the way of progress. Nevertheless it would be false to suggest that Scottish education has declined absolutely in the last half-century. In some respects it has improved; and if it has improved less rapidly than English education during the same period, this is partly because English education (outside the Public Schools) started at a lower level.

It is generally admitted that even to-day Scottish primary schools compare favourably with those in England or America. The most serious criticisms are directed against the secondary schools, and here there is a danger of judging them by an inappropriate standard. They are continually being urged to introduce an equivalent to the English Sixth Form – that is, to keep their pupils longer at school and abandon a general education for a more specialised one. Whatever may be thought of this highly disputable proposition, it is stupid to condemn the products of Scottish schools because they are less specialised than older pupils in England. This criticism is in any case concerned with the best preparation for entrance to the Universities. The condemnation meted out to the work of secondary schools as a whole is more disquieting, especially when we are told that hard work and ability to learn are now discredited in Scotland. This attitude cannot but be encouraged by educationists who sneer at the 'lad o' pairts' and seem to believe that the schools should cater only for mediocrity. Nothing could be more disastrous to Scotland or to any other country.

These questions go beyond our present scope, but all this outside criticism does not make Scotsmen more contented with a system of government under which it is impossible for them to control their own destiny even in matters where their past success has been most conspicuous.

Perhaps we may be forgiven if this gloomy section is ended

on a less serious note. There is a light-hearted radio competition, known as 'Top of the Form', in which schools vie with one another in displays of general knowledge. The questions devised are naturally more suited to English conditions in spite of amiable but sometimes mistaken efforts to prevent this; and they are posed in accents which Scottish children sometimes find difficult to understand. In spite of this handicap, out of the first fifteen competitions Scotland won 8, Wales 4, and England 3. This seems to be not far from the proper proportion and may suggest that Scottish education is less degenerate than is commonly supposed. Even as late as 1966 supposedly tongue-tied pupils from the Scottish schools had won this competition three times in a row.

5. *Innovations from the South*

Every system of education has to adjust itself to a changing world. The need for adjustment becomes more pressing – and also more difficult to meet – at a time when science is developing with a rapidity hitherto unknown. The necessary changes should be thought out on first principles and with due regard to existing conditions: they should not be made by blindly imitating models hurriedly devised elsewhere.

The first effort to reform the State schools of England was admittedly not a success. The panacea proffered was what came to be known as the eleven-plus examination. Educationists confidently assured us that at this tender age children could be separated, even by one examination, into those fitted for academic courses which might lead through the grammar schools to the University and those who were not so fitted. The latter were consigned to other secondary schools, which – in spite of bold denials – came to be regarded as inferior and as less likely to equip pupils for remunerative positions in the outside world. So great had been the confidence in this strangely rigid reform that little or no provision was made for transferring children at a later age from one type of school to another. After some years the theory and its practice were widely discredited.

As a result a new panacea was offered with even greater confidence – the so-called 'comprehensive' school. As this new reform is still in its infancy, it is not easy to know exactly what is meant by this slogan. Sometimes it looks as if a comprehensive school must be a huge glass building in which hundreds of children can be assembled without regard to differences in ability. The analogy of a great factory with one assembly line, or even with several, is not a promising one. But if a comprehensive school is not this, the meaning of the phrase becomes vague and requires further elucidation. Both in theory and practice the new reforms are still in the stage of 'muddling through'.

In accordance with the policy of assimilation the eleven-plus examination (or something very like it) had to be imposed upon schools in Scotland. One wicked sequel to this was that for a time 80 per cent of the children in Scottish Secondary schools were unable to study any foreign language. There was fortunately a reaction later, and it became possible to study foreign languages even in the primary schools; but why should children have to suffer from such inconstancy?

When the eleven-plus examination fell into general disfavour, we were told that once more Scotland must follow the newest English model. For a time a very charming and highly intelligent English lady was even made responsible for Scottish education, although her knowledge of it was manifestly not from the inside. She informed us blithely that we must now go all comprehensive, and even – in a burst of egalitarian enthusiasm – that in comprehensive schools there must be no streamlining. This appeared to mean that in the modern educational factory the ablest and the stupidest children must all move at the same pace along the same assembly line. Any experienced teacher – if I may say so without disrespect – must be tempted to regard this as a lapse into the larger lunacy. One can only hope that she did not mean what she seemed to say.

It is not our business here to assess in general the merits of different types of school, nor do I wish to condemn comprehensive schools in particular: they may have their own merits, though these have yet to be proved in practice; but it is hardly possible to refrain from suggesting that some of the arguments put forward on their behalf are poverty-stricken in the

extreme. Some of their defenders seem to think that they can
further their case by charging their opponents with snobbishness
and dishonesty. Even a highly intelligent English Minister of
Education is reported to have said that the reasons for introducing comprehensive schools were not properly understood:
the reason was simply that it was wrong to assign children
irrevocably to different types of school at an early age. This
means, if I followed him, that because one foolish modern
experiment had failed, we were justified in scrapping the traditional schools which had done so much good work – not least in
Scotland – long before the eleven-plus examination was
invented.

What is more, too many of the arguments put forward are
not really concerned with education: they stress the need to
find a cure for English social snobbery. This disease I should
not myself have thought so widespread or so deadly – perhaps
because I have spent most of my life in a democratic university
like Oxford, where a man's brains are considered more
important than the social status of his father. But it must be
admitted that British Broadcasting encourages a more alarmist
diagnosis. From one point of view even grammar-school boys –
not to mention Public-School ones – seem to be enthroned as
Brahmins into whose shadow no man of lesser caste may step.
From another point of view – as when some good-looking young
men in uniform were shown sitting at ease in an officers' mess
'as if they were Public-School boys' – they appear to be looked
on almost as if they were monkeys dressed up. Nonsense of this
kind is a poor foundation for educational reform.

The ancient schools of Scotland have been happily free from
such absurdities. Most of them have always been comprehensive
in a liberal sense of that word: they have catered for children
of varying ability, of different social origins, and often of both
sexes. It is unreasonable that they should be suddenly destroyed
in order to find a cure for the alleged snobbery of the English.

This is another example of the way in which Scotland is
forced to swallow what are supposed, rightly or wrongly, to be
the best medicine for English ailments. It is not obvious that
big schools are *always* better than small ones: the 'wee schools'

235

of Scotland have done excellent work and still do so even to-day, though they too seem doomed for destruction. It is not obvious that what is suitable for Croydon must be equally suitable for Strathyre. Nor is it obvious to me – though it may be to some administrators – that money is better spent on vast new buildings than on the salaries of teachers: I would rather be taught by a man of genius in a hovel than by a mediocrity in a palace. But what I am arguing here is only that Scotland should have the power to develop her own educational system in her own way without regard to a mass of irrelevant considerations intruded from the South. She might make a mess of it, but at least the mess would be her own.

CHAPTER XV

THE UNIVERSITIES

Cameron (the ghillie): *'When my father has taken his degree in Aberdeen*
he will return and be a crofter again.'
Simon: *'In that case I don't see what he is getting out*
of it.'
Cameron: *'He iss getting the grandest thing in the world out*
of it, he iss getting education.'

Sir James Barrie

1. *The ancient universities*

Great as is the importance of the schools, it is the universities
which in the last resort determine the academic reputation of a
country. Of the four ancient universities of Scotland – St.
Andrews, Glasgow, Aberdeen, and Edinburgh – the first three
were founded by Papal Bulls in the Fifteenth Century; and
like Oxford and Cambridge they inherited from the Middle
Ages the twin ideals of a liberal education and academic
independence. Edinburgh was founded soon after the Reformation and carried on the same ideals. All four were established
before the Union of the Crowns in 1603; and like the Church of
Scotland, with which they were so closely connected, they
received guarantees under the Treaty of Union in 1707. Cynics
maintain that but for this good fortune Scotland would still
be waiting at the end of an English queue hoping that one day
she might be allowed a university of her own.

In the beginning, and indeed later, these universities had to
struggle against poverty, but the astonishing thing is how much
they did with how little money. Much of the teaching was
elementary, but they carried on the democratic tradition of
being open to able boys from all classes. Even in the earlier
centuries they produced outstanding scholars, such as George

237

Buchanan and John Mair, who influenced European political and religious thought. In the Eighteenth and Nineteenth Centuries they enjoyed a still higher reputation and exercised a still wider influence. Their graduates played a conspicuous part in the developing universities of the British Dominions and the United States. Their gates were open to English non-conformists, so long excluded from Oxford and Cambridge; and even English noblemen, like Lord Melbourne, after a period of dalliance at Oxford or Cambridge, sometimes came to Scotland in order to be educated. Without the Scottish universities it would not have been easy to develop modern science and medicine and industry or to administer the British Empire. It is in the face of such achievements that criticisms from South of the Border have to be judged.

It is hazardous, and perhaps foolish, to compare institutions whose character has varied during so many centuries, but it may be true that some of the education provided in Oxford and Cambridge was on a higher level than that in the Scottish universities. On the other hand, it was confined to a privileged few, not all of whom took full advantage of their opportunities. In more recent times English university education at the undergraduate level has become more and more specialised, whereas the Scottish tradition was that specialisation should be preceded by a wide general education, even if this had to be at a modest level. This difference can perhaps be exaggerated. It may be claimed – if gross over-simplification may be pardoned – that if Oxford gave the most thorough training in Classics, and Cambridge in Mathematics, the Scottish universities at the peak of their fame were pre-eminent in philosophy. It may even be argued, as Dr. G. E. Davie has done in his book *The Democratic Intellect*, that in Scotland the approach to every subject was philosophical. That is to say, it was an attempt to stimulate youthful minds, not so much to precise scholarship as to the habit of thinking about what they were doing.

So dangerous an ambition may have been regarded in England as grotesque, and perhaps from one point of view it was; but the ideal that every one before being admitted to courses on Theology, Law, or Medicine should study (1) *literature* (at that time mainly Latin and Greek), (2) *science* (mathematics and physics), and (3) *philosophy* is certainly not to be despised. It resembled in its modest way the Oxford ideal of Literae Humaniores before Classics and Mathematics had been divorced from one another; but Scotland may have been quicker to recognise that philosophy need not be confined to a close study of Aristotelian texts. In any case it might have been thought that variety in methods enriched British education. This view was not accepted south of the Border.

During the Nineteenth Century, British Governments endeavoured by a series of Royal Commissions to impose what they assumed to be better ideals on Scotland. Gentlemen like T. H. Huxley and J. A. Froude were sent from London to instruct the Scots on the best methods of popular education (then in its infancy in England) and to see – in the words of their Commission – that 'the local peculiarities' of Scottish higher education should disappear. At that time the Scottish Universities were still in a position to put up some resistance, and the result was a series of prolonged and embittered controversies not calculated to further the interests of education. In the end a kind of compromise was reached which has worked not too badly. The Scottish universities still retain fragments of their old tradition that philosophy should be encouraged and that specialisation should be preceded by some general education.

In spite of this partial success it seems a pity that the Scottish universities should not have been allowed to develop in their own way, as they could have under a Scottish Parliament. In many ways they were in advance of their time, and there was a strong movement to meet new needs – especially those of science – by introducing new post-graduate schools after the general degree in Arts had been attained. Such proposals for advanced teaching and research could be carried out only with Government help; and even if a Royal Commission might show some interest, the British Parliament was determined that no grants should be given to Scottish universities pursuing an independent policy of their own. Such modest grants as were given out of British taxation were confined to the English universities and their off-shoots in Ireland. Only the Scots considered this to be unjust.

Whatever be our view of differing educational ideals, there can be no doubt that the Scottish Universities were prevented from realising independent ideals of their own.

By the irony of fate a system of post-graduate education is now being developed in England, and Scotland in some ways is being left behind. In the very newest universities experiments are being made which are lauded as revolutionary. What are these revolutionary changes?

Curiously enough, at least some of them are attempts to impose a little general education before specialisation begins. There is even, at least in one case, an attempt to make philosophy compulsory. It is irritating when ill-informed critics, both in Scotland and outside, lament the failure of the Scottish universities to make revolutionary experiments of this kind. All the more so because the impetus towards these alleged revolutions was given by the late Lord Lindsay of Birker, who was applying to English conditions principles long familiar to him as a student and professor at the University of Glasgow – the very principles which the Scottish universities had been defending during so many years in the teeth of English opposition.

Here perhaps I may be allowed to register and repudiate the often inconsistent sneers sometimes directed, in the press and in broadcasting, against the Scottish universities and their students. 'The universities were far too academic'. 'The universities aimed only at a practical training for ministers, lawyers, and doctors'. 'The students sought learning only in the hope of future monetary gain.' 'The students never thought of entering the Civil Service or of pursuing a political career'.

Such unfounded aspersions are offensive, not so much when they come from a visiting Englishman like the late Dr. Joad, perhaps himself not the most obviously disinterested of philosophers, but from half-baked Scotsmen anxious to show how superior they are to the traditions of their own country. It would be easy to refute these charges in detail, both from the records and from personal experience, but they hardly deserve to be treated seriously. I have merely put at the head of this chapter a rather trite quotation from Sir James Barrie to remind us of an older legend. I follow this up, not too solemnly, with memories of a conversation I was lucky enough to have with Mr. Ramsay Macdonald long ago at Chequers.

In talking about Scottish education he spoke of his visit to India some years before and his discussion there with an Englishman perhaps not too tactful in his choice of audience. Let us call him 'Mr. Tactless'. The dialogue ran something like this.

Mr. Tactless: 'The Indian Civil Service should be confined to young men educated in the English Public Schools.'

Macdonald: 'Why?'

Mr. Tactless: 'Because they are the only chaps who know how to handle the natives.'

Macdonald: 'Is this an *a priori* truth or does it rest on empeerical evidence?'

Mr. Tactless: 'I should say it rests on empirical evidence.'

Macdonald: 'Then perhaps we might examine the empeerical evidence. Let us look at the Official Gazette.'

This may not be its correct name, but it was an official publication listing the Provinces and their Governors. Macdonald remembered the names of both in precise detail. I cannot do the same, but the list began something like this.

United Provinces. Governor: Sir Alexander MacPherson. Education: Gordon's College and the University of Aberdeen.

It may sound incredible, but according to Macdonald the first four governors on the list – or was it the first five? – not only had Scottish names, but they had all been educated at Gordon's College and the University of Aberdeen.

The dialogue ended like this.

Macdonald: 'If we are to go by the empeerical evidence, it looks as if entry into the Indian Civil Service should be confined to young men educated at Gordon's College and the University of Aberdeen.'

2. *The present prospects*

However much we may regret lost opportunities, what really matters is what is happening now. It is to be feared that the prospects are not rosy. The 'local peculiarities' which made Scotland famous are still in process of being ironed out.

Modern science demands an ever-increasing specialisation not always easy to reconcile with a general education. Above all it demands more and more money, especially for laboratories and apparatus, and this can be supplied only by the State. As a result even the two ancient universities of England had to surrender, however reluctantly, much of their traditional independence, although they have the immense advantage that their claims will always be represented in any British cabinet. He who holds the purse-strings is bound to have ever more control over policy. In the case of Scotland this means in present circumstances ever more control from the South.

It is true that government control has hitherto been cushioned by a University Grants Committee which was given the task of distributing most of the huge, even if still inadequate, sums that are now available. This Committee is composed of distinguished academic men, who are certainly not unsympathetic to Scotland or to the independence of universities in general. Even so, there has been an ever-growing tendency for them to exercise control over university policy and expenditure. More and more voices are now raised demanding that government money should be administered directly by the Government itself.

It is impossible to discuss here the incoherent changes endured, even under the University Grants Committee, by the ancient University of St. Andrews – presumably because of varying policies in London. It was pressed, for example, to increase its numbers far beyond the capacity of its own buildings and of a lovely university town of only 10,000 inhabitants. In 1953 it was amalgamated with the University College of Dundee, and years of labour were spent in dividing up subjects and faculties between the two institutions. Then at the very moment when the new Tay Road Bridge made co-operation between the two halves of the University much easier, it had to be divided into two independent universities both lopsided because of all the work that had been wasted. Such changes become all the more disturbing when the Government in its spasms of economy fails to find the funds necessary to finance them properly.

Complaints of this kind are now overshadowed by the revolutions recommended for Scotland in what is known as the Robbins Report on Higher Education. This was published in 1963 and accepted by the Government almost before the ink was dry. It is, as we might expect, an able document, clear, informed, full of good intentions, and anxious to be fair, though much of it seems to rest on the assumption that the esteem in which an institution is held depends not so much on its achievements as on the labels we attach to it. It would be out of place to criticise the Report here in detail, but some casual remarks may be hazarded about its general attitude.

The dominant point of view seems to be that of the London administrator anxious to get rid of 'anomalies' and to further the aim of 'co-ordination'. There is one illuminating sentence about Oxford and Cambridge – I quote it only in part. 'The number of times when it is necessary to except Oxford and Cambridge from general statements about British universities ... are not compatible with a situation in which they, like other universities, are largely dependent on public funds'. This appears to mean that universities in receipt of public funds ought to be made so alike that administrators can find it easier to generalise about them. In itself this already bodes ill for Scotland.

As its authors claim, the Robbins Report is unique inasmuch as it is the first to be concerned with higher education in Great Britain. In an elaborate explanation of what this means they fail even to notice that it is the first to lump together English and Scottish education: so revolutionary an innovation, it would seem, requires neither mention nor defence. As a result education in Scotland has to be looked at through predominantly English eyes on the basis of predominantly English assumptions: it has in fact to be considered mainly in what may be called footnotes and afterthoughts.

The general outlook is revealed by the statement that the way was paved for free and elementary education by the Forster Act of 1870 and a corresponding Scottish Act two years later;

and again that the foundation was laid for a system of secondary schools for all children by the Education Acts of 1944 and 1945. This already shows the London perspective we have noted earlier – what happens in Britain outside England doesn't happen at all. It ignores the Scottish belief that this paving the way and laying the foundation was already begun by John Knox three hundred years earlier, or even – if we remember the higher education in the ancient Scottish universities – half a millennium earlier.

The actual treatment of Scottish higher education follows the usual pattern. We have first of all the formal compliments. 'The Scottish universities are right to say that their standards and characteristics should be preserved'. Elsewhere we have the customary criticisms based on the acceptance of English norms. The Scots have not developed the English and Welsh practice of spending two or three years in the sixth form. The level of work in Scottish first year university classes tends to be less advanced in those subjects which are taught at school, in comparison with similar classes in England and Wales. Because of the wider spread of subjects in the early years, and the rather less specialised nature of many honours courses, the Scottish four-year honours degree is approximately the same as that of the three-year degree in England and Wales.

I do not know on what evidence these one-sided generalisations are based, but they seem to accept a purely English norm: they take early specialisation both in schools and universities as the sole standard of value. Early specialisation may, though again it may not, be the best way of producing professors; but as a way of producing graduates fitted for all walks of life it is highly questionable. Indeed the Report itself admits this elsewhere. A distinction of ideals should not be elevated into a standard of merit.

The distinctive character of the ancient Scottish universities, however little this may be recognised in England, was secured by the Act of 1889, which gave them special relations to each other and to the Privy Council. The Report, however, has no hesitation in recommending that the Act should be repealed. The arguments advanced in favour of this cannot be discussed here: my own experience suggests that they are grossly biased. Scotsmen may believe that the alleged 'possible' disadvantages of the present system could have been more easily met by amending the Act itself – and perhaps even by bringing the new Scottish universities under it. This possibility is not discussed. The 'anomaly' of the Scottish universities must be removed, and their distinctive rights must be swept away. They must fall into the ruck of so-called civic universities whose origins and traditions have been entirely different.

More menacing still is the proposal to extend the powers of the University Grants Committee and to make it – under a fresh name – subject to a London Ministry of Arts and Science concerned with all 'autonomous' institutions, including universities, and also with research. This may be better, as the Report itself argues, than putting the Scottish universities under an English Ministry of Education; but whatever concessions may be made to Scotland, the general principle appears to be that – as is said elsewhere in a more limited context – the arrangements proposed for England and Wales 'should, of course, also obtain in Scotland'. With enthusiastic approval from the 'overwhelming' majority of the Committee of Vice-Chancellors and Principals – presumably the English majority – the Scottish universities are to be deprived even of the frail protection offered by the Secretary of State for Scotland, though his views would be 'taken into account' by the English Minister – we know already how little this means in practice.

The actual results of the Report are already worse than the Report itself. Any new university in Scotland must be based on a separate Charter like the civic universities in England – so much so that in one case the Charter is said to have been drawn up in terms of English law, which has no place in Scotland. Apparently, we are all to have English 'statutes' instead of Scottish 'ordinances'. The ancient Scottish universities are threatened with dire consequences if they should wish to make the necessary reforms by using the powers given them under the Act of 1966 instead of starting afresh with a separate Charter for each. The common character and distinctive standards of the Scottish universities must be swept away. Furthermore, instead of being put under a Ministry of Arts and Science as proposed in the Robbins Report, they were made subject to a new London Ministry of Education and Science set up in 1964 and so are now geared to English schools instead of the Scottish schools with which they have been connected for so many centuries. The painful results of this outrage have already begun to make themselves felt. The high-handed action of Mr. Crosland in suddenly increasing the fees of overseas students (to which we refer later) is a case in point.

3. *Financial inequalities*

Under present conditions a great deal must turn on finance. Here, as usual, there are no easily intelligible principles governing the allocation of grants to Scotland; and there are many complaints, supported sometimes by detached observers, that she does not receive her fair share of the funds available.

Some of the money allotted to higher education in Scotland comes direct from the Government and is administered by the local authorities and the Scottish Education Department. This concerns only the grants allocated to universty students for their fees and subsistence. It is possible, though no one seems to know, that Scotland receives the Goschen proportion of the total amount allotted for this purpose; but for some inexplicable reason the grants to Scottish students were for years less than those given to students at the red-brick universities – less also than those given to English students at the Scottish universities, who were thus put, through no fault of their own, in a position where they could seem to be more lordly than their local contemporaries. What was worse, the grants given depended on a means test much more severe in Scotland than it was in England so that Scottish parents had to make greater sacrifices than their English counterparts of the same level of income. The old university bursaries, which were given mainly for merit, had become of little value because of inflation; and under the new system Scottish students, if their parents enjoyed an income above the severe means test, were deprived, no matter how able, of their traditional pride in paying for their own education. In Scotland this curious system was not mitigated, as it was in

England, by State Scholarships given for merit. All you had to do was to obtain the low minimum entrance qualifications, and after that the amount of your grant was determined solely by the relative impecuniousness of your parents. What a way to encourage mediocrity and idleness! After years of protest some of the worst inequalities were removed in 1963; but why should it be necessary to fight so long in order to obtain elementary justice?

If we turn to the revenue of the universities themselves, the great bulk of this now comes, not from fees or endowments, but from the University Grants Committee. Here there is no question of any Goschen formula for Scotland. The principle governing the distribution seems to be that of need.

As a result of past neglect the needs of England are proportionately greater than those of Scotland. During the Nineteenth Century several 'civic' or 'red-brick' universities – unhappily so described – were added to the two ancient English universities; but the luxuriant proliferation of new universities has taken place in the last forty years or so. England is now able to boast of twenty-nine universities in all. Scotland still has her original four, although four more are being added, mainly by the elevation of existing institutions and by dividing St. Andrews into two. The proportion of students attending the Scottish universities is still relatively high – it was estimated not very long ago as 33 per 10,000 of the population, while in England it was said to be only 19.

As a general rule no financial provision can be made for special needs in Scotland – or at least not without a bitter fight. The special needs of England must, on the other hand, be met from the taxation of which Scotland pays her share.

On this basis needs seem to be assessed on the assumption that the Scottish universities can have no needs beyond those of the red-brick universities – only Oxford, Cambridge, and London have special needs peculiar to themselves. Even if we accept this assumption – and why should we? – it still appears to be true that Manchester and Birmingham receive larger sums than do Edinburgh and Glasgow in relation to the number of their students. How can this be justified?

Whatever be the explanation of this particular anomaly, the general principle seems to be that subsidies should depend on promises rather than on achievement. Much of the available money must go to infant institutions which can promise to increase their intake in the future. Residences are built at great cost in budding English universities in order to house in comfort the students they have yet to acquire. The University of Glasgow where thousands of students already pant anxiously after truth, too often under conditions which make study difficult, is apparently expected to wait for full modern amenities until the future needs of England have been satisfied.

Let us hope that these financial inequalities are less than appears at first sight. But the point is that, whether they are or not, there is little that Scotsmen can do about them except make ineffectual protests which are apt to be dismissed without argument as another sample of Scottish parochialism and irrationality.

4ᵃ *Grumbles galore*

Other disadvantages from which Scotland suffers can be mentioned only in a summary way.

Where a university had endowments for its own chairs, its grant was reduced by the amount of income these provided. This looks as if Scottish endowments were swallowed in order to benefit the more needy universities of England. One result of this was that the higher professorial salaries which used to attract so many outstanding scholars to Scotland had to be brought down to the level fixed for the English universities – apart from London, which is specially favoured with allowances for travelling.

The low fees in Scotland had to be raised, if not quite to the English level, at least to a level at which the traditional difference is greatly reduced. It may be thought that this aim could have been attained with greater advantage by lowering the English charges, especially now that most fees are in effect paid through government grants. High fees press only on parents already suffering under the means test. But assimilation, it seems, has to work only in one direction even where the Scottish practice is obviously better.

It may be that some of these decisions could be defended separately on rational grounds. As a whole they have an effect not obviously advantageous to the Scottish universities, and the fact stands out that Scotland has no power to decide these matters for herself.

This complaint becomes all the more serious because something has gone wrong under the present régime. For the first time in all their long history Scottish universities are said to have refused admission to Scots who have duly qualified for entrance. The numbers affected may be subject to dispute, but even a few years ago such a position would have been inconceivable. It should surely be possible to provide extra places for the Scottish students who are now excluded.

The situation is not made easier by the fact that the coveted places are filled by students mainly from England. Any murmurings about this are greeted by prominent Englishmen with the customary homilies about the parochialism of Scotsmen and their failure to recognise that universities must be international. It seems even to be hinted that the presence of English students is necessary to make a university like St. Andrews truly 'chic' – that is, presumably, more like Oxford and Cambridge.

It is in the oldest, and in some ways the most attractive, of Scotland's universities that the trouble about places becomes acute. In the year 1965 56 per cent of the entrants to Queen's College, then a constituent college of St. Andrews University, though soon to become the independent University of Dundee, came from outside Scotland; for the University of St. Andrews as a whole the figure was 47 per cent. Is there any English university which can claim that half its students come from outside England? Nothing remotely like this is found, so far as I know, in great international universities like Harvard or Paris.

English critics display high moral enthusiasm for international universities, when by 'an international university' they mean a Scottish university in which the Scots are outnumbered by the English; but their zeal appears to cool when the word 'international' is taken in a more normal sense. The Scottish universities have always been international: they have always welcomed students not only from England but also from

Europe and America and the British Commonwealth. They still do. Such genuine internationalism was given short shrift by an English Minister of Education, when without consulting the universities he suddenly ordered the fees of overseas students in Scotland to be raised from £70 to the £250 he imposed elsewhere. So gross an offence against the comity of nations is alien to the whole academic tradition. Why should the Scottish universities have been subjected to such short-sighted and high-handed direction from the South? Is this an example of what they now have to expect?

Two of the ancient Scottish universities have already agreed to send to London all applications for admission, since Scotland lacks the necessary computer; and it looks as if the other Scottish universities may be pressed to follow suit. The unfortunate effects of these and other probable changes cannot be discussed here; but in general the homogeneous system of education enjoyed by Scotland for centuries can no longer be developed by Scotsmen in accordance with their own ideals. It must be twisted bit by bit to fit in with English norms and with a system of English education which, whatever its merits, has never really been a system at all.

One last point. The amount and quality of research in Scotland can no longer be determined in Scotland itself. When we remember that government research institutes, except on rare occasions and after bitter fights, are confined to the South, it becomes obvious that the reputation she enjoyed in the past can never under present conditions be restored. More and more money will naturally be allotted where most research has already been done, and Scottish men of genius, like Sir Alexander Fleming and Sir Robert Watson-Watt, will continue to make their discoveries in laboratories outside their native land.

5. *A reasonable claim*

In the field of education, as elsewhere, Scotland needs genuine autonomy if she is not to be unworthy of her past. It is important that so reasonable a claim should not be misunderstood.

No one suggests that in education Scotland is deliberately persecuted or oppressed. The days are past since Cromwell could impose his puppets on the Scottish universities with power to 'plant and dis-plant' the teachers. In the Nineteenth Century there was still far too much of the 'jealous, tenacious, wrangling, over-bearing humour' of which Sir Walter Scott complained, but this is now confined to occasional outbursts from a few distinguished English professors in Scotland. The methods employed to-day are more gentle – and for that reason all the more effective. What is so dangerous is the English benevolence which is determined to share its own – unachieved – ideals with other people whether they want to have them or not.

The argument does not turn on the alleged superiority of Scottish achievements. Still less is it a claim for sticking to old methods without change. On the contrary, it is a claim for freedom to choose new methods in the light of past experience and to learn from other civilised countries instead of having to imitate blindly the untested models imported from the South. This is the elementary right of any nation, but Scotland's claim is particularly strong in view of her achievements in the past.

What stands in the way of so reasonable a claim? Nothing, it would seem, but a centralising bureaucracy supported by the unconscious passion of the English for assimilation and their habit of treating Scotland as an English province. No genuine English interest is at stake, let alone a British one.

If some of the details here discussed seem relatively trivial, their cumulative effect may be great. It is not enough to see that Scotland suffers in general from a clumsy and creaking machinery of government which places her at a permanent disadvantage. It has also to be made clear that she suffers from frustration in the details of ordinary life and even – if I may use the term without pomposity – of spiritual life. What happens in education is sadly typical of what happens everywhere. There can be no cure unless the whole system is ended and something better put in its place.

CHAPTER XVI

AN APPEAL TO REASON

We've drunk to our English brother
(And we hope he'll understand)
Rudyard Kipling

1. *The claim for Scotland*

Perhaps in conclusion we may sum up our modest claim for Scotland in the light of the preceding arguments.

The claim is that under the Crown and within the framework of the United Kingdom Scotland should have her own Parliament with genuine legislative authority in Scottish affairs.

This reform, it has been contended, is necessary to secure good government in accordance with Scottish wishes and traditions and to promote the spiritual and economic welfare of the Scottish nation. It is also necessary in the interests of the United Kingdom, if the welfare of the whole depends upon the welfare of all its members.

Besides this major claim there is a minor or secondary one, which is consequential. Since Scotsmen have a special concern with the government of their own country, they should be given a clear opportunity to say what kind of government they prefer. This means that they should be allowed some sort of plebiscite or referendum – the name matters little – held in Scotland itself. It is contrary to common sense to assume that the fate of Scotland can best be settled by a predominantly English Parliament if it knows nothing about what Scotsmen want.

The argument is directed partly to Scotsmen themselves. Some Scotsmen have become apathetic and accept too readily the belief that they can have no power to change their present circumstances. Many remain vaguely uneasy, but do not see clearly what is happening to their native country. Others have been brainwashed and accept without question warped accounts of their own history, both ancient and modern. For all these I have tried to provide a rough map – it can only be rough – which may help them to explore for themselves the strange situation in which they now find themselves. Perhaps it may also be of help to those – an increasing number – who are acutely conscious of separate injustices, but have not been able to see them as a whole.

Yet the appeal I make, even if this is a too sanguine hope, is directed, not merely to Scotsmen, but to all men of good will, especially among citizens of the United Kingdom, and in particular to Englishmen, who form the majority of such citizens and therefore have the decisive power. It assumes that as reasonable men they are also citizens of the world – devoted in words and deed, not merely to the supposed interests of England, but to liberty and justice among all nations, not excluding their nearest neighbours. Nothing that I may have said, perhaps in irritation, about English attitudes to Scotland will, I trust, be allowed to obscure this more fundamental assumption.

What our English brother is invited to do is to think, as dispassionately as possible, about Scotland and her proper relation to the United Kingdom of which she is an honourable part. Thinking requires an effort; and most thoughtful Englishmen will agree that this is one of the topics about which they hardly think at all. Yet it is not unreasonable to ask what is their considered policy for Scotland – that is, if they have one – and what are the principles on which this policy should be based.

2. An appeal to reason

It will, I hope, be agreed that no one has a right to sweep aside all Scottish claims – or even our present plea – by saying that they are too irrational to be worth considering. This simply assumes – in an unnecessarily offensive way – what it has to prove. Nor does it become less fallacious when expressed in more emotive terms, as when the Scottish case is ruled out of court as sentimental and unrealistic and prejudiced and extreme and fanatical and rabid and insane. We may surely expect all reasonable Englishmen to accept the view that rational discussion of this or any other subject should be carried on within the bounds of ordinary courtesy.

To dismiss a claim as irrational is itself an appeal to reason. As such it must be supported – or at least be capable of being supported – by rational argument. The supporting argument, if there is one, can hardly rest on the principle that patriotism is always wrong – that no men have a right to love their country, to be proud of their traditions, or to seek to manage their own affairs. The English take a proper pride in their own patriotism and cannot reasonably deny a similar pride to others. By signing the Bill of Rights the British Government itself, as we have seen, is officially committed to the principles embodied in both our claims for Scotland: it is pledged 'to uphold the principle of self-determination of all peoples and nations and to facilitate this right through plebiscite or other recognised means'. It is commonly said, with some show of justice, that the British have taught and applied this principle throughout the world.

If it is held, as it appears to be, that Scotland is an exception to this otherwise universal principle, the burden of proof must rest on those who hold it; and manifestly it is a heavy burden. It is no answer to put Scotland on the defensive and to say she must prove, and prove to the satisfaction of Englishmen, that she too can reasonably claim the rights which are freely accorded to the rest of the human race. To any impartial observer, and surely also to any reasonable Englishman, the boot would seem to be on the other leg.

The problem before us is to find reasons – and not merely excuses – why Scotland should be treated as an exception to an otherwise accepted rule. It is not easy to see where such reasons can be found. Presumably they must rest on the exceptional character either of the Scots or of the English or of both together – a character so exceptional that it must over-ride ordinary human rights and obligations in the sphere of government.

3. *Exceptions and their grounds*

To fall back on the exceptional character of Scotsmen or Englishmen does not offer a very promising line of defence. Though it seems to lurk behind some of the arguments used, it is seldom brought out into the open. If it were brought out, it might be seen to work in a direction opposite to that intended.

It can hardly be said about the Scots, as it used to be said unfairly about the Irish, that they are unworthy, or incapable, of self-government. They have been far too successful in governing other people (including the English) for this to sound even plausible. Equally absurd would be the contention that Scotland is too poor and backward to enjoy the rights freely granted to other nations with strong English approval. Her claims to self-determination cannot be dismissed as weaker than those of such countries as Trinidad or Malta or Lesotho. Assumptions of this kind are not in need of refutation: to state them explicitly is to refute them.

No less preposterous would be the view that Scotland is not a nation, but merely a part of the English nation. She is, on the contrary, one of the oldest nations in Europe and has had too long a history, and too great a reputation in the world, to be dismissed so lightly. In any case, whatever be the characteristics necessary to constitute a nation, the most fundamental is consciousness of nationality, and this Scotland has never lost. An impartial observer would be hard put to it to find anywhere in the world a people without self-government whose right to be regarded as a nation is so strong.

If we abandon assumptions which mean in the end that the Scots are exceptionally unfitted for self-government, the argument can hardly be that it is the English who are so exceptional that they are entitled to deny to their immediate neighbour the rights which they, in common with other reasonable men, recognise as rights of the human race. It may be said that this is precisely the kind of privileged position that they claimed for themselves in the heyday of the British Empire; and an unfriendly critic might perhaps be tempted to say that they are now compelled to concentrate their colonial ambitions on their unfortunate partner. In relation to Scotland the English do sometimes behave as if they were the only disinterested and trustworthy persons in the universe; but this must be considered as a pardonable human weakness rather than as a rational ground for over-riding the claims of others. The essential characteristic of disinterested persons is that they claim no special privileges for themselves. A claim to special privileges is unreasonable, and indeed immoral, whether it is made by individuals or by nations.

4. *Political realism*

It may be objected that this talk about principles is all very well, but is unrealistic – high-falutin' and up in the air: what we have to deal with is an actual concrete situation.

There seems to be some confusion in this. Throughout the whole course of this discussion I have tried, whether successfully or not, to deal with the actual concrete situation. What I am trying to do at present is only to examine the practice of rejecting Scottish claims as irrational. This rejection, if it means anything, is, as I have said, an appeal to reason; and so, whether you like it or not, it is an appeal to principles. There is no other way to get rid of sheer prejudice and muddled thinking. What I have been trying to do in this chapter is to argue as politely as possible (and not merely to assert) that the habit of sweeping Scottish claims aside as more or less insane is itself a product of muddled thinking and sheer prejudice. It will not stand up to dispassionate examination.

The use of the word 'unrealistic' is itself suspicious. Does it mean that, whatever be the arguments used, the plain fact is that the Scots occupy little more than one third of a small island otherwise inhabited by Englishmen (and Welshmen), and that the English are determined to maintain their grip on Scotland (and Wales)? If this is so, let it be stated bluntly without any affectation of intellectual and moral superiority. No reasonable man and no reasonable Englishman could possibly defend such an attitude as rational. It seems rather to be the product of an aggressive, if unconscious, nationalism.

It might seem rather more plausible to urge that it is reasonable to appeal to precedents as well as to principles. But an appeal to precedents is merely a buttress for injustice unless we can show that these precedents are themselves in accordance with principles of justice. There are only too many precedents for attempts to bring Scottish affairs under the rigid control of London. This civil servant's ideal was already expressed by King James I and VI once he had established himself in his southern capital. 'This I must say for Scotland, and may truly vaunt it; here I sit and govern it with my pen; I write and it is done.' The process of administrative encoachment has continued since the Union of 1707 and has accelerated steadily during the present century. It is precisely this which rouses opposition and is in need of reform. If it is unjust in itself, it cannot become just merely because it has been going on for so long a time. A defence which rests solely on precedents, however numerous, cannot be a rational argument for denying Scotland self-government now.

5. *Arguments against Scottish self-government*

So far I have sought merely to get the situation into perspective and to blow away some of the mists of ignorance and prejudice by which it is enshrouded. We cannot simply take it for granted that if the Scots want self-government, this is a demand so obviously wanton that they must justify it to a shocked world before any kind of argument is required.

If we are to deny to the Scottish people rights freely accorded to all others, it is obvious that the arguments required must be very strong; and it is astonishing, even in this muddled world, to find how weak so many of them are.

Too often, for example, we are told that water has flowed under the bridges or that we must not try to put back the clock or alternatively that the time is not ripe. We are entitled to something more weighty than platitudes about the flow of water or speculations about the more recondite characteristics of the temporal process.

R 257

Sometimes the arguments used are almost unbelievably irrelevant. Even Scottish candidates for Parliament, when asked why they oppose Home Rule for Scotland, have been known to reply that they don't believe in divorce or that they don't want to go back to the 'black houses' of the Highlands. If presumably intelligent men can think such irrelevancies a sufficient answer, this suggests that there can be no sufficient answer at all.

On a slightly higher level is the contention – favoured by some ex-Secretaries of State for Scotland – that the Scots would become more and more parochial and inward-looking if they were allowed to manage their own affairs. This concern for the spiritual welfare of the Scottish people is touching, but what makes men fiercely parochial is having their parish affairs mismanaged from outside. What has to be explained is why self-government should have an effect on the Scottish people precisely opposite to the effect it has on others.

If we are looking for more serious arguments, we can find them best in a book entitled '*Thoughts on the Union between England and Scotland.*' This is a learned and persuasive work, as might be expected from the names of its authors – A. V. Dicey and R. S. Rait. It assumes from the outset that the Union is 'a triumph of legislative wisdom'; and in the light of this question-begging assumption it runs through some parts of Scottish history, and especially the periods preceding and following the Treaty of Union. It makes every effort to be fair: it recognises, for example, that the restoration of Church Patronage – really of lay patronage – in 1712 was a violation of the Treaty and did great harm in Scotland; it admits that the language of the Treaty may have deliberately been made ambiguous so that it seemed to exclude all appeals to English courts from any causes tried in Scotland, but left a loop-hole for arguing that there could still be appeals to the English House of Lords; and it maintains that the union with Scotland was the 'unshakable foundation' of British power and liberty, without which there could never have been a British – or rather an English – Empire. Even in such cases it takes the English point of view and seeks to tone down the Scottish side of any argument. In other matters its bland assumptions produce strange arguments and lead to queer conclusions based on shaky evidence.

For example, by what looks like a gross breach of the Treaty of Union, Scottish members of Parliament, before they could take their seats, were compelled to receive the Sacrament according to the rites of the Church of England. This our learned authors defend partly by obscuring the difference between entry into what was now supposed to be a British Parliament and admission to purely English offices of profit at a time when such an imposition might seem less unreasonable than it does to-day. They even stress as a weighty consideration that the English clergy would probably have been offended if no Anglican test had been imposed on Scottish members of Parliament; and they argue seriously that a religious Scotsman of that period may possibly have preferred that the Sacramental forms imposed on him should be those prescribed by the Church of England, and not those prescribed by the Church of Scotland. To support so improbable a conclusion the only evidence they adduce is a rhetorical defence of the Test Act delivered as late as 1791 by 'Jupiter' Carlyle, a rumbustious Scottish divine not remarkable either for indifference to worldly interests or for reluctance to scandalise his clerical brethren. Soon afterwards the obnoxious Test was quietly abandoned.

It would be interesting to examine more examples in detail, but there is no space for this here. In any case the book is concerned mainly with past history rather than with present problems. Because it was published in 1920, it can take no account of the invasion of English administrators into Scottish affairs throughout the last half century. Even so, it is probably the best and most sympathetic, if too complacent, statement of the English case. As such it may be commended to all students of these problems.

At this stage it is not possible to review – still less refute – all the arguments that have been used, or might be used, against Scotland's claim for self-government. The most that can be done is to call attention to some typical lines of argument hitherto overlooked or under-estimated. These arguments may be classified as political, administrative, and economic.

6. *Political arguments*

One argument is common to both Conservative and Labour politicians, and it seems to form the basis for the policy adopted by the Labour party since it came to enjoy real power. It is this. If Scotland were given self-government, her representation and influence in the British Parliament would have to be proportionately reduced. She has therefore to make a painful choice. Surely it is better that she should contribute her wisdom and energy to the United Kingdom and to the wide world than that she should concentrate all her forces on managing parochial affairs within her own narrow borders.

The choice would certainly be painful, but why should it be necessary? It would be reasonable enough to say that Scottish members should be excluded from voting on purely English affairs or – still better – that the English should have a regional parliament or parliaments of their own. But Scotsmen, if they had some real control over their own affairs, would have no less interest than before in legislation affecting the United Kingdom as a whole – including such questions as defence and foreign policy and tariffs, to mention only the most obvious. To say that Scotland must lose her voice on all these matters in proportion to the amount of self-government she enjoys would be manifestly unfair. It is extraordinary, even under the present party system, that intelligent Scotsmen should let themselves be so bemused as to accept such a stipulation without questioning its justice.

Ideally what is wanted is some sort of federal system, and in a federal system no one dreams of such stipulations. Its members do not lose the right of representation in the central legislature; and their influence is increased, rather than diminished – as in Canada and Australia and the United States and Germany – when they have their own representative bodies for managing their own affairs and meeting their own special needs.

England may not want a federal system for herself; but this is no reason why Scotland (and Wales) should be denied such federal rights as have been advocated here. No one would suggest that Londoners should have less representation in

Parliament because London has something like a local parliament of her own. The present system may suit England very well, but it does not suit her partners.

A purist may argue that it is anomalous and illogical to allow federal rights to some parts of a country unless a federal system is extended to the country as a whole. This verbal argument comes curiously from those Englishmen who vaunt their indifference to logic and their willingness to accept anomalies so long as these can work in practice. Anomalies are willingly accepted for the Isle of Man, the Channel Islands, and Northern Ireland. Why should it be only for Scotland (and Wales) that they must be rejected without consideration? Have we not here only another example of the unexamined assumption that whatever suits the English majority must be imposed on other parts of the country, no matter how different the desires and needs and interests of these may be?

If we are to accept the principle that every step in self-government must mean less representation in the central Parliament, the logical conclusion for Scotland would be to seek complete independence.

7. Administrative arguments

It is sometimes argued that self-government for Scotland should be rejected because it would mean a further proliferation of bureaucracy with all its extravagance and waste.

It is difficult to take such a contention seriously at a time when bureaucracy is encouraged to proliferate everywhere else with an almost tropical luxuriance. It is also hard to believe that any method of administration could be more wasteful and extravagant than the present ramshackle and top-heavy system, which no one could have invented deliberately (unless perhaps in order to bamboozle Scotsmen into imagining that they control their own affairs). Whatever may be the view of centralised officials anxious to smooth their tasks and add to their empire, a coherent system of administration in Edinburgh would probably require fewer men and less money: it would certainly be able to avoid the heart-breaking frustrations and delays and misunderstandings which do so much spiritual as well as economic harm. Scotsmen are not notorious for extravagance and waste – qualities which can be found more easily elsewhere. They have been able in the past to do great things with few men and little money, and we need not assume that they have been entirely corrupted by the existing distresses. There would be some temporary administrative inconvenience in making the change, but this would be a small price to pay.

The argument would not be convincing even if we were to accept the dubious premise that there would be a further proliferation of bureaucracy. Control would at least be less remote than it is; but the fundamental point is that the bureaucrats dealing with Scottish affairs would be exposed to democratic criticism and control as they can never be in a Westminster Parliament. In any case the fundamental claims of Scotland are not to be decided on the ground that their satisfaction would require a few more bureaucrats or a few less.

8. *Economic arguments*

The field of economic argument offers special difficulties: it is too vast and varied for a brief review. Almost every topic already discussed – notably that of administration – has its economic aspects. Unsatisfactory though it may be, we shall have to content ourselves with some very general considerations. Details may be filled in from earlier chapters.

One difficulty, as we have seen, is that we are not supplied, and are not likely to be supplied, with accurate figures about the economic traffic between Scotland and England – not even as regards public taxation and expenditure. The obscurity surrounding these matters forms, as we have argued, an ideal smoke-screen under which the wealth of Scotland can, to a greater or less extent, be drained away to the South without anybody being the wiser. Nevertheless we cannot sweep aside economic arguments for self-government simply on the ground that we lack the necessary information. There are quite enough known facts on which our case may rest. Indeed, especially in these days when governments seek to control the entire economy, the centre of government is bound to attract wealth away from the 'regions', unless the 'regions' are themselves given some real power. In their new-found zeal for the 'regions', even English economists occasionally find themselves driven by the logic of the situation towards an ideal of regional parliaments with power to raise taxes and control their own revenue. At this point they are apt to shy away hurriedly on the ground that – as I heard one of them say – 'if this happened, the Welsh might want to secede!' Here, as in other cases, political prejudice may interfere with economic thinking; and everywhere we come up against the political assumption that economic co-operation depends on domination by the central government.

Another way of arguing against self-government is to introduce such a disordered mass of economic detail that we are unable to see the wood for the trees. 'You might gain sixpence here, but you would lose another sixpence there'. The fate of Scotland cannot be allowed to rest on the principle of 'Bang went saxpence'.

We need not spend time on the more ludicrous types of economic argument with which we are so often favoured. It is not true that if we had self-government, we should all have to go back and live in the old 'black houses' of the Highlands. It is not true that we should have to set up a customs barrier at the Border; nor would it be the end of the world if we did. It is not true that we should have to cut off trade with England and other countries – that we should no longer be able to drink French wine out of Swedish glasses; and so on *ad absurdum*.

If we are looking for arguments within the bounds of common sense, these must presumably be very general, or else must be concerned with the special economic needs of Scotland and England.

The very general types of argument are not altogether promising.

It might be argued, for example, that the bigger the unit, the more efficiently it can be run. This view, highly favoured by London centralisers, may actually hold in some cases; but it does not hold in all cases, and it is sadly contrary to Scottish experience – perhaps even contrary to the experience of outlying English provinces. Once more it seems to assume that efficiency must depend on domination from a centre, not in free co-operation of the parts. There is little reason for accepting such a principle, and still less for allowing it to over-ride all other relevant considerations.

A more simple-minded, if less convincing, version of the same type of argument, is that a system will work more efficiently if its parts are all alike. I mention this only because it seems to lie behind the English passion for assimilation when they decide the affairs of Scotland in the interests of what they are pleased to call 'the whole'. The plants native to Scotland are always being encouraged, or compelled, sometimes after a little perfunctory praise, to be trained up an English wall. But the principle here is in the main false. A plant may develop better if it is allowed to grow in its own natural way; and a garden may be all the richer because of the diversity of its parts.

If we turn to arguments based on the special economic needs of Scotland and England, we are back at the type of argument already outlined more generally in section 3. We are trying to find something so exceptional in the character of Scotland or of England that it can over-ride principles accepted everywhere else.

If the argument means that because of her special poverty or special situation, Scotland is not what is called 'viable' and cannot get on without England and England's help, this obviously requires a vast amount of elucidation. Here we have a topic on which it is difficult not to be satirical. In the year 1966 poverty did not prevent two tiny islands in the Caribbean – St. Kitts and Nevis – from being cheerfully granted, not only immediate Home Rule, but also the right to declare their independence at any time that they might wish to do so. It is true that they have one advantage over Scotland – they are very much farther away from England; but it is not easy to believe that political justice should depend entirely on geographical location. It is also true that unless Scotland could trade with the rest of the world (including England), she would be in a difficult position; but there is nothing very exceptional about that. Nor can we take it for granted that without continual subsidies from England Scotland would totter to her doom – this may be the reverse of the truth. As to 'help' in general, we can hardly assume that Scotland would be less prosperous and less contented if she could decide for herself where her roads and railways and steamers should run, which ports and airports should be developed, where her new factories should be located, and so on. Under the present system such things have in the last resort to be settled, in horrifying detail, by some unknown London officials who are primarily concerned with English interests and need never have seen the regions they control. This is the kind of 'help' we could well do without. It is one of the main sources of the present discontents.

Throughout this book I have tried – I hope with at least partial success – to criticise the English, not as such, but only in their treatment of Scotland; yet all this talk about Scotland's need of 'help' is almost bound to raise the question whether the English are competent to provide it.

British governments since the Second World War – to go no further back – have tottered from crisis to crisis and left the whole country on the verge of bankruptcy. They seem not to have learned even the most elementary precepts of the nursery – 'Don't bite off more than you can chew' and 'Don't count your chickens before they are hatched'. It is not easy to believe that politicians and administrators who make such a hash of matters in which they are really interested are able, as it were in their spare time, to solve the problems of Scotland with their superior wisdom. But here perhaps I yield to prejudice; and this must be avoided at all costs.

The economic argument against self-government in Scotland might be more convincing if we reversed it and suggested that England cannot do without Scotland and Scotland's help. We may even suspect, however unworthily, that this is the real ground for English inflexibility on the subject.

This argument is not so unplausible as may seem at first sight, although we are not given the information necessary to prove how much England is enriched by her control over Scotland. Here we may give one example, where we do have the facts. We often hear complaints of the heavy burden laid on the British economy by the £80,000,000 a year that must be paid annually, and paid in foreign currency, for the upkeep of the British Army of the Rhine. We hear less often that the revenue from the duty on Scotch Whisky amounts, in round figures, to £100,000,000 a year, and that the same precious fluid earns also £100,000,000 a year in foreign currency. This is a contribution which British governments would be reluctant to lose, though there may be some danger of their killing the goose that lays the golden eggs. Their merciless imposition of ever heavier duties is already verging on a diminution of returns. What is worse, it encourages foreign governments to impose similar duties on imported whisky and so to reduce the amount of foreign currency that it can earn.

Such an example proves nothing by itself, but it does suggest possible lines of enquiry. The claim of the Scottish National Party is that by herself Scotland would have no problem about the balance of payments. This is partly born out by the fact that even in the present difficulties Scottish exports increase more rapidly than those from the rest of the United Kingdom.

The contention that England cannot do without the Scottish contribution to the British economy cannot be set aside without enquiry; and if there is any truth in it, it would have further implications. It might suggest, for example, that so competent a partner should have his wishes seriously considered and should be granted some autonomy in managing his own side of the business.

It must be insisted again that all these economic arguments, however important they are, cannot by themselves properly determine the issue of Scottish self-government. The question is not ultimately whether Scotland would gain or lose a little in material wealth. What is at stake is the whole character and tradition of Scotland, and in particular the freedom which has been her ideal through so many centuries.

One last point. It may have been observed that some of the arguments considered might seem more appropriate if they were directed against claims for Scotland's complete independence rather than against the modest proposals put forward here. This raises questions which deserve at least some consideration.

9. *Independence*

What Scotland wants and needs is genuine, and not bogus autonomy. If hope of this is continually deferred, if interference from London becomes ever more extensive and more arbitrary, and if as a result Scotland appears to be going down hill and to be losing her national identity and her national pride, it is not surprising that some Scotsmen should begin to talk about independence. What is surprising is that this talk is so limited.

The high hopes raised by the signing of the Covenant in 1949 were smothered by well-tried methods of procrastination with the help of a Royal Commission. Since then London interference in Scottish affairs has steadily and insidiously increased: even the Scottish system of education is being knocked about to fit in with the latest innovations from the South. It is hardly surprising if the demand for independence has become stronger in Scotland, as also in Wales, and has won increasing support in Parliamentary elections.

This is the only kind of argument that English politicians cannot entirely ignore; but they try to sweep it aside as a 'protest' vote – generally against the Party to which they do not themselves belong. They are strangely reluctant to open their eyes to the truth and to see that it is a protest against both the main political Parties and against the London misgovernment which they practise and defend. The first reaction to the success of National Parties is to dismiss their policies, not merely as folly, but as 'criminal' folly. But abuse is not a substitute for argument. If there has been any criminal folly, it has been displayed by successive British Governments which have closed their ears to the most just and moderate claims.

The case argued throughout this book is that the ideal solution would be to have a complete federal system like that of the U.S.A., where the separate States have equality in the Senate as well as full representation in Congress. If this is impossible, as so many think, the next best solution would be to set up subordinate national parliaments with real, and not illusory, control over their own affairs. If this too is resolutely ruled out, what is left open to Scotsmen and Welshmen except to seek for independence? If reasonable Englishmen would only begin to try to understand the situation, it would be far better for everybody concerned.

There is a heavy burden of proof on those who assert that no matter what Scotland may desire, she is not entitled to the independence freely acknowledged as the common right of all other nations in the world. The burden is all the greater since Scotland entered freely into the Union with England and may reasonably claim that she has a further, and very special, right to leave it in equal freedom – a right certainly not weakened because the predominant partner has so often ignored the conditions of the Union. The Scots, like other reasonable men, may not insist on exercising all their acknowledged rights; but the brash denial of these rights might easily produce a different attitude. The topic of rights is one which reasonable Englishmen would do well to avoid. Their concern should rather be to remove the grievances from which Scotland suffers and to meet the demands which have been put forward with such moderation.

Again, it would be unconvincing to argue that whatever be the theoretical rights of Scotland, she is in practice incapable of independence. Scotsmen are not unacquainted with what happens in comparable sister countries in Europe, and especially in Scandinavia. They can see how well these countries manage their own affairs, how competent and progressive and trig they are, and how they grow richer rather than poorer even without the natural advantages which Scotland enjoys. They may even ask themselves how many Norwegians – whose standard of living has recently become higher than that of Britain – would wish to go back to their former dependence on Stockholm. It must carry little conviction to assert that Scotsmen alone could never manage their own country without some benevolent stranger breathing down their necks and supervising their every movement.

It is sometimes argued that an independent Scotland would have less influence on world affairs. This too is hardly plausible. At present she has no such influence – not even in matters that concern her deeply, such as the three-mile limit for territorial waters, where a tiny independent country like Iceland is able to defend her own interests. No one could argue seriously that Eire has less influence in world affairs than she had before she broke away.

It may seem more plausible to say that an independent Scotland could not defend herself against external enemies. This argument might have had some weight in the past, but to-day it applies to Scotland no more than it does to all independent European countries. We are all in the same boat, and – if I may mix the metaphor – our safety depends on the American nuclear umbrella. Furthermore there is no reason whatever to suppose that an independent Scotland within the Commonwealth would be unable or unwilling to enter into the closest possible co-operation with England in all matters concerned with defence. It might even be hoped that the independence of Scotland could be a first step towards a genuine British federation or confederation, or at least a close defensive alliance, which Ireland too might be willing to join on a footing of equality.

Perhaps the strongest argument for independence is that without a change of heart in England modest measures of self-government, even if they were permitted, could never cure the ills from which Scotland suffers. The central government would still be too strong, and English nationalism is so deeply engrained that the interests of Scotland would always be sacrificed to the real or imaginary interests of England. The sad facts of history lend only too much support to this contention; and even to-day the habit of deriding all Scottish claims without any attempt to understand them is enough to make some Scotsmen despair of any solution short of independence. Is it too much to hope that our English brothers might at long last develop a truly British patriotism which would regard Britain as something more than an England possessed of a few recalcitrant provinces not yet completely assimilated? England has long enjoyed the most loyal partnership any nation has ever had. If she still regards Scotland with suspicion and distrust, is it not time that we should kiss and part?

Our discussion of Scotland's right to independence is obviously incomplete, but it was necessary in order to get the situation into perspective. It may help to show how moderate and reasonable are the claims I have put forward for a generous measure of self-government and to dispose of the belief that they are manifestly crazy. It may also serve to remind us that there can be many degrees of self-government between a subordinate parliament on the Ulster model and the full-blown independence of Ireland.

10. A final plea

Throughout this chapter, and throughout this book, I have sought to present the claim of Scotland as essentially an appeal to right and reason. In so doing, I hope I have not seemed to set forth Scottish patriotism as if it were something remote and academic. Genuine patriotism is more like being in love: it has its roots deep in the hearts of men. Yet even a man in love is not precluded from giving rational answers to amiable or officious busybodies who seek to place obstacles in his way.

It is sometimes imagined that those who seek self-government for Scotland must hate the English as individuals. This is a profound mistake. Even if the greatest of modern Scottish poets has listed Anglophobia as his recreation, there may be in this an undercurrent of dry humour; and in any case there is no accounting for the ways of genius. If I have given any impression of sharing such a view I have failed in my object. From many long-standing personal friendships I know the best kind of Englishmen to be among the wisest and most just of men as well as the most charming. What I should like them to do is to direct their wisdom and justice to the plight of Scotland. She is in greater danger now than she was at Bannockburn because she has fewer means of defence.

If in the course of this plea for Scotland I have fallen into errors of details, I regret it; but in matters so complex and so changing some error is inevitable. I have tried to give a picture of the Scottish case as a whole, and this picture I believe to be substantially correct.

If I have shown bias and unfairness and occasional irritation, this too I regret; but it is hard not to feel some emotion as one examines the raw deal given to Scotland in the past and in the present; and for any one accustomed to civilised discussion it is difficult not to become irritated when her claim is dismissed offhand with a minimum of thought and an insufferable air of superiority. I could even forgive myself a little unfairness if it would help to sting some of our English brothers out of a complacent lack of interest which is the source of half our troubles. As to bias, it would require a very great deal of Scottish bias to counterbalance the amount of bias on the other side.

I have not attempted to put forward a detailed plan for a parliamentary and administrative system suited to modern conditions in Scotland, but for this I make no apology. Such plans have been drawn up, and readers may be referred for one example to the Memorandum of Evidence submitted by the Scottish Covenant Association to the Royal Commission on Scottish Affairs and published separately by the Hanover Press in March, 1953, under the title *The Case for Scottish Devolution*. My own aim has been only to describe, however roughly, the present problem and to outline the principles necessary for its solution. It is this problem that requires first of all to be understood. Once it is agreed that Scotland, if she so desires, should have a legislature for her own affairs, the time would come to discuss detailed proposals, and these would have to be made acceptable to a British government determined that English interests, real or supposed, would be given at least their just weight. Any kind of Scottish parliament, provided it had some real power, would to my mind be better than none; for in it the voice of Scotland could no longer be muffled and smothered, and it would be impossible to maintain that nobody knew what Scotland really wanted. This by itself would be an immense gain. No sensible man can suppose that all the ills of Scotland would immediately be cured, but at least she would have the possibility of taking an initiative denied to her at present, and the effects of this in every walk of life might be far-reaching indeed. What is so devastating is the feeling that she is at the mercy of events wholly beyond her control and is unable to develop naturally in her own distinctive way.

The claims of Scotland, so often dismissed as irrational, are fundamentally an appeal to reason and to common sense or

271

common justice. Sometimes it may seem that this is why they receive so little attention. It almost looks as if British governments will yield only to violence, or at least to non-violent disobedience to the law: Ireland and Ulster and the suffragettes and Cyprus and India are cases in point. Amid all the Scottish discontents there have been extraordinarily few outbreaks of this kind – the defacing of some pillar boxes, the 'lifting' of a Scottish stone from Westminster Abbey, a couple of misguided Scottish students imprisoned, not because they did anything destructive, but because they were found in possession of explosives alleged to have been supplied by the police. The bogey of a Scottish Republican Army comparable to the I.R.A. never had any basis in fact. Intemperate language may have been used by some agitators, but the Scots are a law-abiding race and could not even under great provocation take to the shooting which won Ireland her freedom. They still retain a pathetic belief that the voice of reason may be listened to even in the United Kingdom. Is it too much to ask that our English brothers should be wise and generous enough to understand?

Perhaps I may be allowed to end by adopting as my own the words of a private letter sent to me by one of the wisest men in Scotland – Sir Thomas Taylor, Principal of Aberdeen University – shortly before his untimely death.

'Personally I am so sick of the mess that is being made of my native country that I should be glad of anything that would arouse contention and even passion, rather than that things should be allowed to slide.'

INDEX

INDEX

275